MATHEMATICS QUESTIONS AT 11+ (YEAR 6)

Book B:
Algebra (pre-algebra), Shape, Space and Measures, Handling Data

compiled by
David E Hanson

www.galorepark.co.uk

Published by ISEB Publications, an imprint of Galore Park Publishing
19/21 Sayers Lane, Tenterden, Kent TN30 6BW
www.galorepark.co.uk

Text copyright © David E Hanson 2006

The right of David E Hanson to be identified as the author of this Work has been asserted by him in accordance with sections 77 and 78 of the Copyright, Designs and Patents Act 1988.

Printed and bound in the UK by Charlesworth Press, Wakefield

ISBN: 978 1 907047 89 3

All rights reserved. No part of this publication may be sold, reproduced, stored in a retrieval system, or transmitted, in any form or by any means, electronic, mechanical, photocopying, recording, or otherwise, without either the prior written permission of the copyright owner or a licence permitting restricted copying issued by the Copyright Licensing Agency, Saffron House, 6–10 Kirby Street London EC1N 8TS.

First published 2006, reprinted 2013

Details of other ISEB publications and examination papers, and Galore Park publications are available at www.galorepark.co.uk

CONTENTS OF BOOKS A AND B

The list of contents is based upon *The National Numeracy Strategy: Framework for teaching mathematics from reception to Year 6*, DfEE, March 1999. A few changes to the original DfEE order and wording have been made and the sections have been given numbers and letters for convenience.

BOOK A

STRAND 1: NUMBERS AND THE NUMBER SYSTEM

A **Properties of numbers:** understanding properties of numbers and number sequences, including negative numbers

B **Place value; ordering:** understanding place value; ordering numbers; reading and writing numbers

C **Estimation and approximation:** estimating and rounding

D **Fractions, decimals, percentages; ratio:** understanding fractions, decimals, percentages, and their equivalence; ratio and proportion

STRAND 2: CALCULATIONS

A **Number operations:** understanding number operations; relationships between operations

B **Mental strategies:** developing mental calculation strategies, including deriving new facts from known facts

C **Written methods:** using written calculation (pencil and paper) methods

D **Calculator methods:** using a calculator

E **Checking results:** checking that results of calculations are reasonable

STRAND 3: SOLVING PROBLEMS

A **Decision making; strategies:** deciding which operation, which method (mental, mental with jottings, pencil and paper, calculator), which equipment

B **Reasoning about numbers or shapes:** working out numbers or shapes; number puzzles; making general statements

C **'Real life' mathematics:** solving problems involving numbers in context; 'real life', money, measures

BOOK B

STRAND 4: ALGEBRA (PRE-ALGEBRA)

A **Equations and formulae:** forming simple equations; expressing relationships; solving simple equations; using inverses; finding equivalent forms; factorising numbers; understanding the commutative, associative and distributive laws

B **Sequences and functions:** identifying number patterns

C **Graphs:** drawing graphs; developing ideas of continuity

STRAND 5: SHAPE, SPACE AND MEASURES

A **Measures:** using measures, including choosing units and reading scales; measurement of length, mass, capacity, perimeter, area, time

B **Shape:** knowing the properties of 2-D and 3-D shapes, including symmetry

C **Space:** understanding position, including co-ordinates; understanding direction, angle; movement

STRAND 6: HANDLING DATA

A **Data handling:** collecting, presenting and interpreting data

B **Probability:** understanding basic ideas of probability

INTRODUCTION

THE CURRICULUM AND THE EXAMINATION SYLLABUS

The mathematics curriculum and the examination syllabus are subject to relatively minor changes or emphases from time to time, whereas the body of mathematical skills and knowledge which teachers consider valuable seems to remain fairly constant.

For completeness, and to allow greater flexibility in the use of this material, some questions included here may be outside the syllabus currently examined, even though they are likely to be within the capability of the majority of pupils in most schools. It is left to teachers to select questions which they consider appropriate and, in any case, it is assumed that teachers will wish to differentiate according to pupil abilities. Capable pupils may benefit from 'stretching' the current examination syllabus.

The material is mostly at National Curriculum Level 4, with some of Level 5 but, for completeness, questions cover ideas met in all years up to and including Year 6.

The contents pages outline the way in which questions have been grouped. This closely follows the latest official publications by the DfEE. The strands have been numbered and the subdivisions of the strands have been lettered, for easier reference. It should be noted that these numbers and letters are not official.

THE QUESTIONS

The majority of the questions come from the 11+ Common Entrance papers (January 1990 to January 1999) and, for these questions, the paper and original question number are generally indicated. The original mark distribution has been retained in all but a very few cases when some adjustment seemed sensible in the light of experience. A number of new questions have been written in order to provide extra practice. These have been given appropriate mark allocations for consistency. Some grading in difficulty has been undertaken. Inevitably some original questions involve several skills and these have either been split or have been placed wherever seemed most appropriate. Some re-wording and redrawing has been undertaken for clarity and consistency.

USING THIS BOOK

The book has been designed for use by pupils, under the guidance of a teacher or parent, as a resource for practice of basic skills and recall of knowledge.

Revision notes and worked examples have generally not been included, since such material is available in existing publications. Answers to the questions are not included in this publication since it is anticipated that teachers will wish to work the questions for themselves before setting pupils to work. A separate, comprehensive answer book is available.

CALCULATORS

It is assumed that calculators will not be used in answering the questions in this book. Questions involving calculators concentrate on interpreting the display.

STRAND 4: ALGEBRA (PRE-ALGEBRA)

A **Equations and formulae:** forming simple equations; expressing relationships; solving simple equations; using inverses; finding equivalent forms; factorising numbers; understanding the commutative, associative and distributive laws

1. A simple equation expresses a fact.

    Imagine that each ◯ is a bead.

    ◯◯◯◯◯ and ◯◯◯ is the same as ◯◯◯◯◯◯◯◯

    We can represent this by the equation 5 + 3 = 8

    (i) Represent the following by an equation:

    ◯◯ and ◯◯◯◯◯◯◯ is the same as ◯◯◯◯◯◯◯◯◯

    Answer: .... (2)

    (ii) Represent the following by an equation:

    ◯◯◯◯ and ◯◯◯◯◯ is the same as ◯◯◯◯◯◯◯◯◯

    Answer: .... (2)

    (iii) Draw beads to show a situation which could be represented by the equation

    $$5 + 7 = 12$$

    Answer: .... (2)

    (iv) Draw beads to show a situation which could be represented by the equation

    $$6 + 4 = 10$$

    Answer: .... (2)

2. Taking ●●● from ●●●●●●● leaves ●●●●

We can represent this by the equation 7 − 3 = 4

(i) Represent the following by an equation:

Taking ●●●● from ●●●●●● leaves ●●

Answer: .... (2)

(ii) Represent the following by an equation:

Taking ●●● from ●●●●●●●● leaves ●●●●●

Answer: .... (2)

(iii) Represent the following by an equation:

Taking ●●●●●●● from ●●●●●●●● leaves ●

Answer: .... (2)

(iv) Draw beads to show a situation which could be represented by the equation

9 − 6 = 3

Answer: .... (2)

(v) Draw beads to show a situation which could be represented by the equation

10 − 3 = 7

Answer: .... (2)

(vi) Draw beads to show a situation which could be represented by the equation

16 − 9 = 7

Answer: .... (2)

3. Here we have 3 groups of 4 beads:

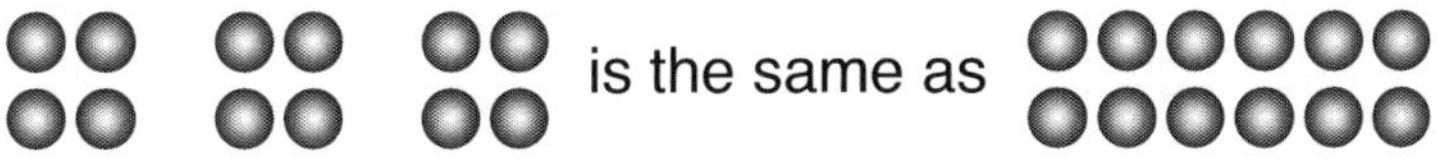

   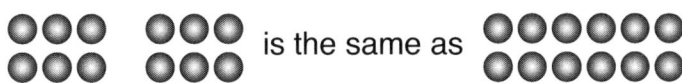

   This can be represented by the equation 3 × 4 = 12

   (i) Represent the following by an equation:

   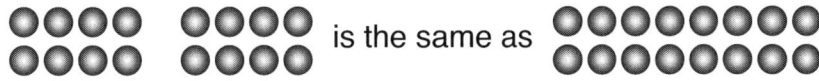

   Answer: .... (2)

   (ii) Represent the following by an equation:

   00000000 00000000 is the same as 00000000 00000000

   Answer: .... (2)

   (iii) Represent the following by an equation:

   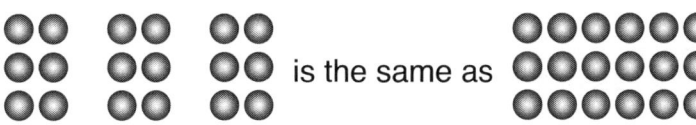

   Answer: .... (2)

   (iv) Draw beads to show a situation which could be represented by the equation

   5 × 2 = 10

   Answer: .... (2)

   (v) Draw beads to show a situation which could be represented by the equation

   5 × 3 = 15

   Answer: .... (2)

4. Imagine sharing 12 beads between 3 people.

   ●●●●●● shared between 3 gives ●● ●● ●●
   ●●●●●●   ●● ●● ●●

   This can be represented by the equation 12 ÷ 3 = 4
   Each person gets 4 beads.

   (i) Represent the following by an equation:

   ●●●● shared between 4 gives ● ● ● ●
   ●●●●   ● ● ● ●

   Answer: .... (2)

   (ii) Represent the following by an equation:

   ●●●●●● split into 2 groups gives ●●● ●●●
   ●●●●●●   ●●● ●●●

   Answer: .... (2)

   (iii) Draw beads to show a situation which could be represented by the equation

   $$14 \div 2 = 7$$

   Answer: .... (2)

   (iv) Draw beads to show a situation which could be represented by the equation

   $$15 \div 3 = 5$$

   Answer: .... (2)

5. Here are four simple equations which use the same numbers: 8, 12 and 20

$$8 + 12 = 20$$
$$12 + 8 = 20$$
addition facts

$$20 - 12 = 8$$
$$20 - 8 = 12$$
subtraction facts

(i) Complete these four simple equations which use the numbers 3, 15 and 18

$$3 + 15 = \ldots$$
$$15 + \ldots = 18$$

$$18 - 15 = \ldots$$
$$\ldots - 3 = 15$$

(2)

(ii) In the same way, write four simple equations which use the numbers 4, 7 and 11

$$4 + \ldots = \ldots$$
$$\ldots + \ldots = \ldots$$

$$\ldots - \ldots = \ldots$$
$$\ldots - \ldots = \ldots$$

(2)

6. Write two simple equations which use the numbers 5, 9 and 14

Answer: .... (1)

 (1)

7. Write two simple equations which use the numbers 13, 7 and 6

Answer: .... (1)

.... (1)

8. Here are some simple equations which use the same numbers: 12, 3 and 4

$$3 \times 4 = 12$$
$$4 \times 3 = 12$$

multiplication facts

$$12 \div 4 = 3$$
$$12 \div 3 = 4$$

division facts

(i) Complete these four simple equations which use the numbers 6, 7 and 42

$$6 \times 7 = \ldots$$
$$7 \times \ldots = 42$$

$$42 \div 6 = \ldots$$
$$42 \div \ldots = 6$$

(2)

(ii) Write four simple equations which use the numbers 7, 9 and 63

$$\ldots \times \ldots = \ldots$$
$$\ldots \times \ldots = \ldots$$

$$\ldots \div \ldots = \ldots$$
$$\ldots \div \ldots = \ldots$$

(4)

9. (i) Write two simple equations which use the numbers 5, 9 and 14

Answer: .... and .... (2)

(ii) Write two simple equations which use the numbers 4, 9 and 36

Answer: .... and .... (2)

10. (i) The price of one *Choco* bar is ten pence.

The cost, in pence, of three *Choco* bars is given by the equation
cost = 3 × 10
The cost of any number of *Choco* bars is
cost = number × 10
Write an equation for the cost of five *Choco* bars.

Answer: .... (1)

(ii) We do not know the cost of a *Goo* bar.
We can write an equation for the cost of three *Goo* bars.
cost = 3 × ?

Where '?' is the price of one *Goo* bar,

(a) write an equation for the cost of six *Goo* bars

Answer: .... (1)

(b) write an equation for the cost of any number of *Goo* bars.

Answer: .... (2)

(iii) The word equation
cost = number × price
is a little wordy!
Suggest how this could be shortened.

Answer: ....

.... (2)

11. (i)

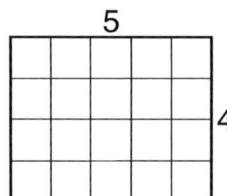

The area, in squares, of this rectangle can be found by multiplying the length by the width.

area = 5 × 4

Write a word equation for finding the area of any rectangle.

Answer: .... (2)

(ii)

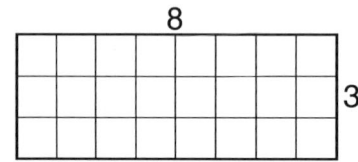

The perimeter, in units, of this rectangle can be found by writing

perimeter = 8 + 3 + 8 + 3

which is the same as

perimeter = 2 × (8 + 3)

Write a word equation for finding the perimeter of any rectangle.

Answer: .... (2)

12.

Write a word equation for the perimeter of an equilateral triangle of side length ℓ.

Answer: .... (2)

13. In this word equation there are three **variables**: cost, number and price.

$$\text{cost} = \text{number} \times \text{price}$$

This type of equation is often called a **formula**.

If we know all but one of the variables, we can solve the equation to find the unknown variable.

Choco bars cost ten pence each.

Peter bought *Choco* bars costing a total of 80 pence.

(i) Solve the equation

$$80 = \text{number} \times 10$$

Answer: number = ... (1)

7 *Chompy* bars cost a total of £1.40

(ii) Solve the equation

$$140 = 7 \times \text{price}$$

to find the cost of one *Chompy* bar.

Answer: price = ... pence (1)

14. 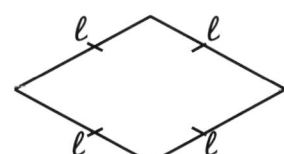 The perimeter of this rhombus is 24 cm.

$$\text{perimeter} = 4 \times \text{side length}$$

so $24 = 4 \times \ell$

Solve this equation to find the length of the side of the rhombus.

Answer: ℓ = ... cm (2)

15. Write in the missing numbers.

(i) 7 + 6 = ……… (1)

(ii) ……… + 8 = 17 (1)

(iii) 13 − 5 = ……… (1)

(iv) ……… − 7 = 15 (1)

16. Write in the missing numbers.

(i) 3 × 8 = ……… (1)

(ii) 7 × ……… = 56 (1)

(iii) 72 ÷ 9 = ……… (1)

(iv) 36 ÷ ……… = 9 (1)

17. Write in the missing numbers.

(i) 3 + 9 = ……… + 5 (1)

(ii) 21 − 4 = 7 + ……… (1)

(iii) 24 ÷ 4 = 2 × ……… (1)

(iv) ……… ÷ 3 = 3 + 4 (1)

18. Write in the missing number.

$$23 + 12 = \boxed{} \times 5$$ (2)

January 99 Q3

19. Find the mystery number. The missing number in the clues is the same each time. $\boxed{?}$ stands for the number.

A square with sides of $\boxed{?}$ units has a perimeter of 20 units.

$$9 \times \boxed{?} = 45$$

Answer: .... is the mystery number. (4)

January 90 Q15

20. Find the numbers represented by the symbols in these equations.

(i) $5 + \blacktriangle = 12$

Answer: $\blacktriangle$ = ... (1)

(ii) $\bullet - 8 = 12$

Answer: $\bullet$ = ... (1)

(iii) $3 \times \blacksquare = 21$

Answer: $\blacksquare$ = ... (1)

(iv) $2 \times \heartsuit - 5 = 3$

Answer: $\heartsuit$ = ... (2)

ALGEBRA A

11

An **unknown** number (a 'mystery' number) can be represented by ☐ or ? or ▲ or any symbol.

We find it convenient to represent an unknown number by a letter.

21. Jane thinks of a number and calls it *j* (for Jane's number).

    When she adds 5 to her number, she gets 12

    We can represent this by the equation

    $$j + 5 = 12$$

    Solve this equation to find Jane's number.

    Answer: *j* = ... (1)

22. Solve these equations to find the unknown numbers represented by letters.

    (i) $6 + x = 11$

    Answer: *x* = ... (1)

    (ii) $y - 7 = 8$

    Answer: *y* = ... (1)

    (iii) $a + 4 = 6$

    Answer: *a* = ... (1)

    (iv) $2 \times b = 10$

    Answer: *b* = ... (1)

A — ALGEBRA

23. Flora had a box of 40 chocolates.

    She cannot remember how many she has eaten and calls this unknown number f.

    She counts the chocolates left in the box. There are 19

    (i) Write an equation in terms of f for this.

    Answer: .... (2)

    (ii) Solve the equation to find how many chocolates Flora has eaten.

    Answer: $f =$ .... (1)

24. Rory does not know how many marbles he had in his pocket at the start of the day, so he calls this number r.

    He knows that he has won 13 more than he has lost.

    He now has 32 marbles.

    (i) Write an equation in terms of r.

    Answer: .... (2)

    (ii) Solve the equation to find how many marbles Rory had at the start of the day.

    Answer: $r =$ .... (1)

25. Anna has made a machine which multiplies every number she puts in (input number) by 5

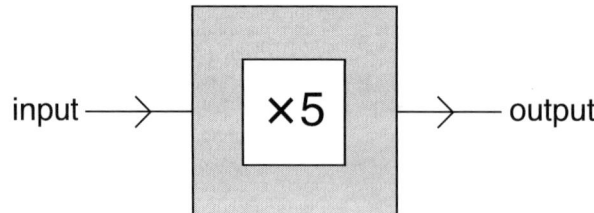

(i) What will be the output if Anna puts 4 into the machine?

Answer: .... (1)

(ii) If 45 comes out, which number did Anna put in?

Answer: .... (2)

26. Basil has made a machine which subtracts 3 from every input number.

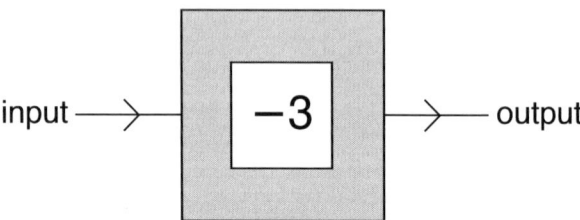

(i) What will be the output if Basil puts 4 into the machine?

Answer: .... (1)

(ii) What will be the output if Basil puts 2 into the machine?

Answer: .... (2)

(iii) If 7 comes out, which number did Basil put in?

Answer: .... (1)

27.

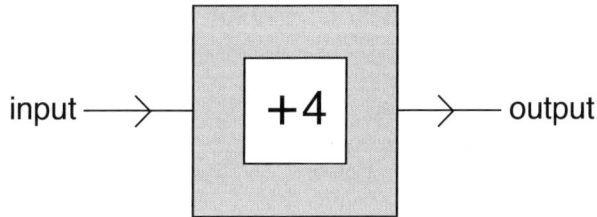

Write the missing inputs and outputs for this machine.

1 ⟶ 5

3 ⟶ ....

.... ⟶ 4

(2)

28. Jenny has made a more complicated machine.

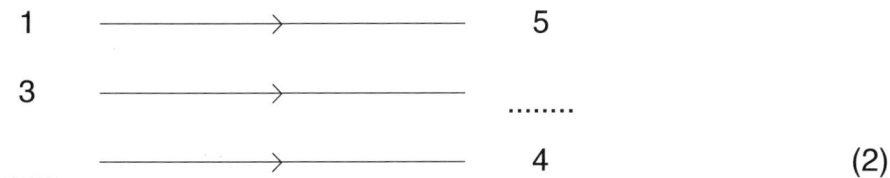

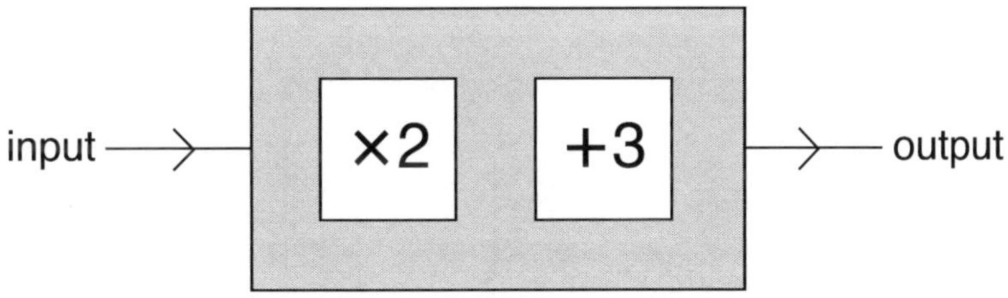

Her machine multiplies an input number by 2 and then adds 3
Write the missing inputs and outputs for this machine.

1 ⟶ 5

2 ⟶ ....

5 ⟶ ....

.... ⟶ 21

(3)

29. Paul has made a machine which subtracts 2 from an input number and then multiplies by 3

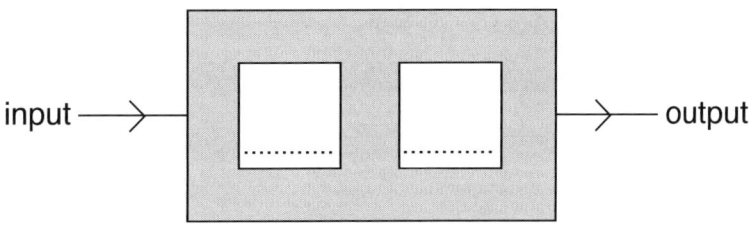

Label Paul's machine.

(2)

30. One of the labels has fallen off Sally's machine.

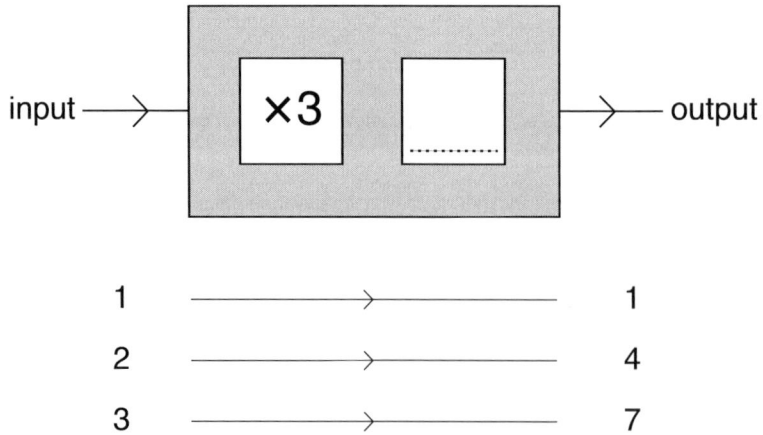

1	→	1
2	→	4
3	→	7

Write the missing label. (2)

31. Both the labels have fallen off Brenda's machine!

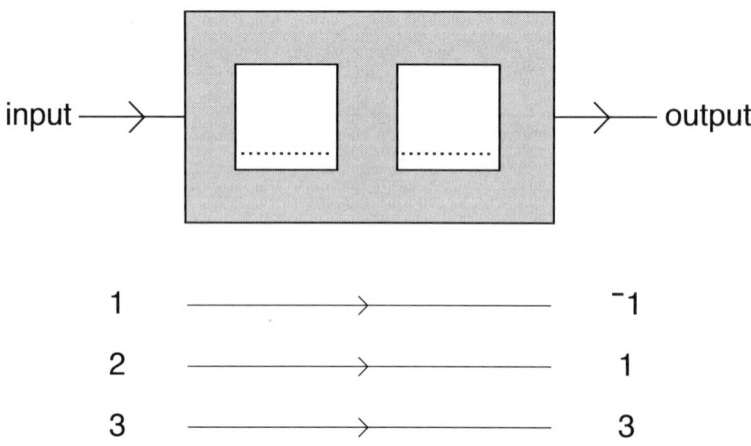

1	→	⁻1
2	→	1
3	→	3

Label the machine. (3)

32. Basil has made two machines which appear to do the same thing!

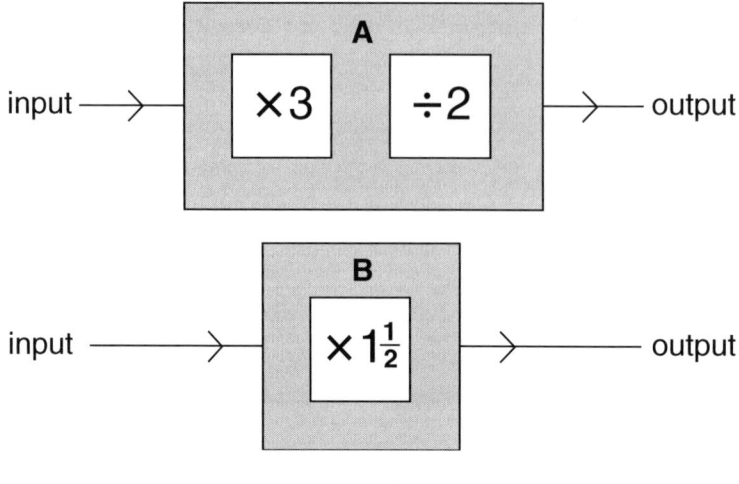

Explain why machine **B** gives the same output as machine **A**.

Answer: ....

.... (2)

33. Jane has drawn a flowchart to represent her function machine.

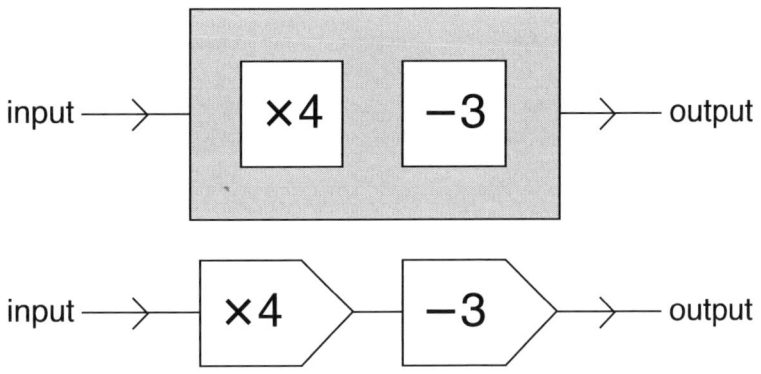

(i) If the input is 5, what will be the output?

Answer: .... (1)

(ii) What will be the input if the output is 37?

Answer: .... (1)

(iii) Which input will give an output of 7?

Answer: .... (2)

(iv) What will be the output if the input is zero?

Answer: .... (1)

34. This function machine multiplies by 5 then adds 2
    Fill in the missing inputs and outputs.

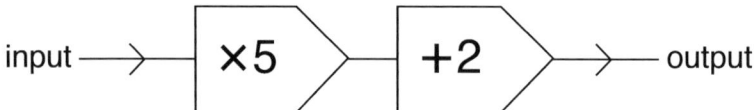

6	→	32	
....	→	....	(1)
3	→	....	(1)
0	→	....	(1)
....	→	7	(2)
....	→	22	(2)

January 96 Q6

A ALGEBRA

35. This calculating machine divides by 3 then adds 5
    Fill in the missing outputs and inputs.

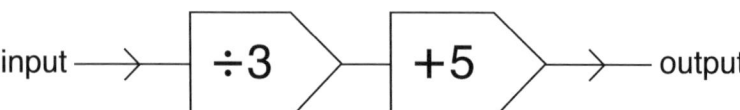

9	→	8	
3	→	....	(1)
....	→	14	(2)
....	→	5	(2)

November 96 Q7

36. Put numbers in the boxes to complete the following.

(i)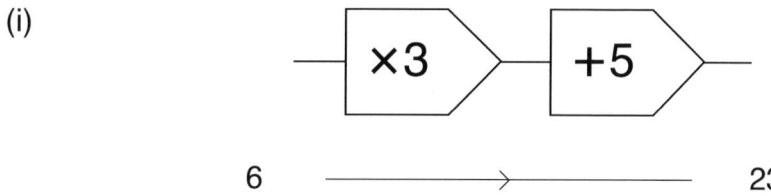

6	→	23
0	→	....
4	→	....

(2)

(ii)

16	→	11
....	→	9
....	→	4

(2)

January 95 Q16

37. Write the missing numbers for this calculating machine.

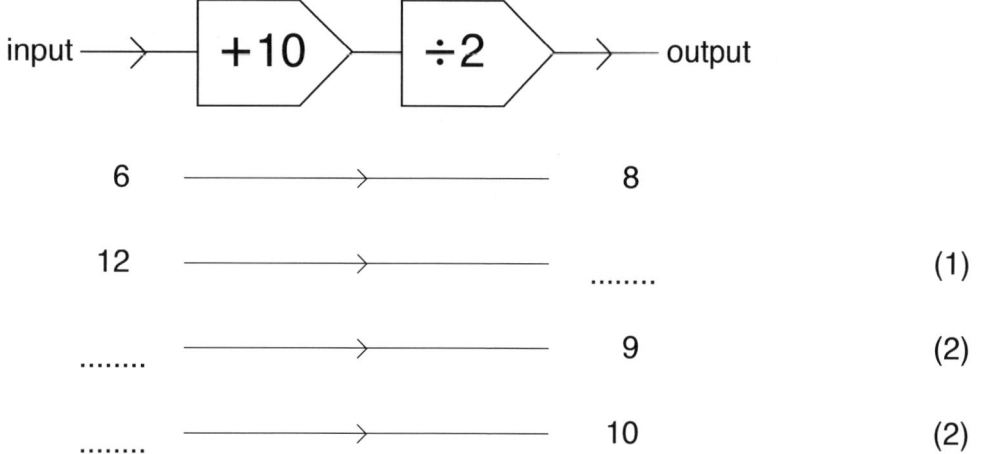

6	→	8
12	→	....	(1)
....	→	9	(2)
....	→	10	(2)

January 99 Q6

ALGEBRA A

19

38. A function machine doubles a number and then subtracts 3
    Complete the missing outputs.

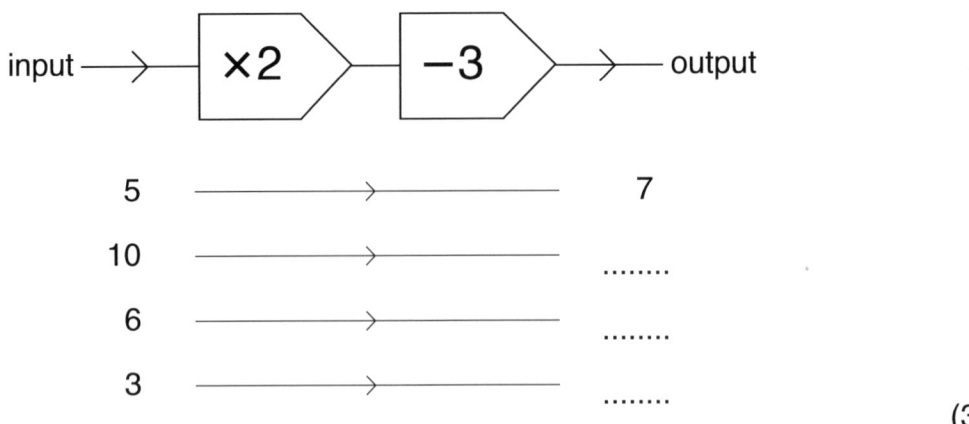

(3)

Specimen 94 Q15(i)

39. This function machine adds 4 then multiplies by 3

    (i) Fill in the missing inputs and outputs.

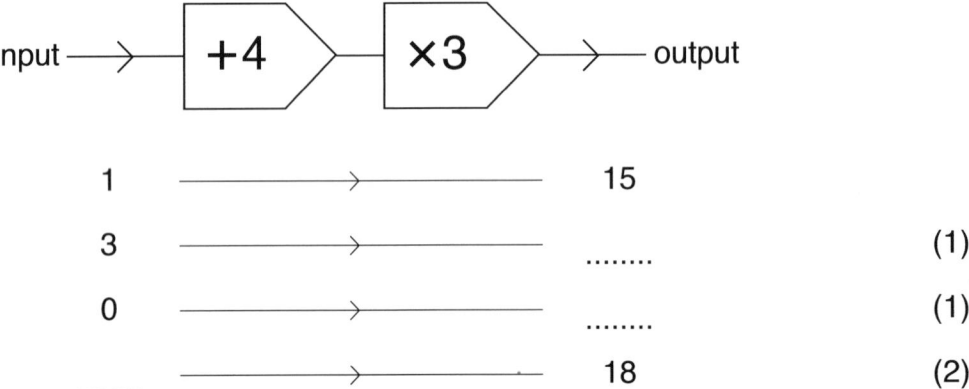

(1)
(1)
(2)

The inputs and outputs of another function machine are shown below.

(ii) Fill in the boxes which would make this machine work correctly.

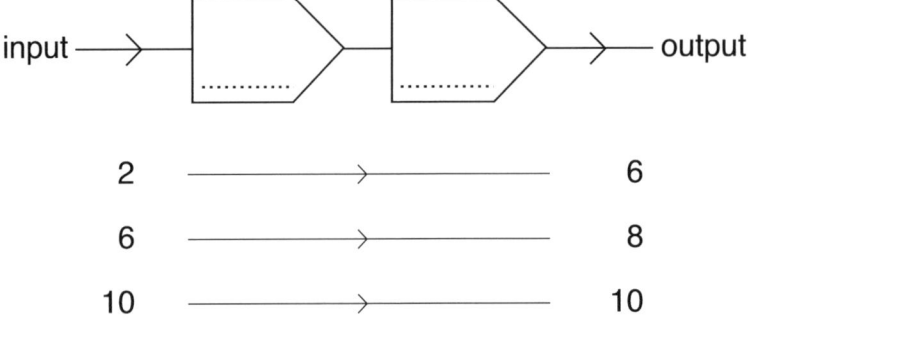

(3)

November 97 Q18

40. Clare has drawn a reversed flowchart which will help her to find an input number.

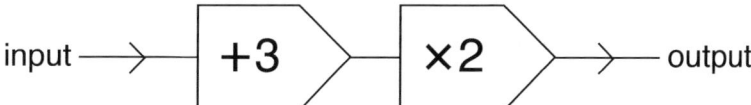

reversed

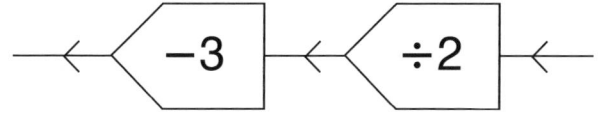

Use Clare's idea to find the input when the output was 20

Answer: .... (2)

Reversed flowcharts can be helpful in solving 'think of a number' problems.

41. I thought of a number, added 5 and divided by 3

    The result was 6

    Complete the flowchart to find the number I first thought of.

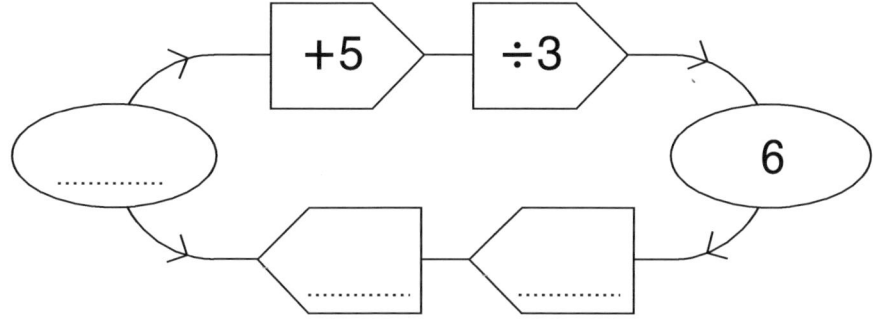

(3)

Specimen 94 Q15(ii)

42. Brenda thought of a number, doubled it and took away 2

    The result was 16

    What was Brenda's number?

Answer: .... (2)

January 93 Q8

43. Sally thought of a number and added 4
    She got the same result when she doubled her number.

    (i) What was the number Sally thought of?

    Answer: .... (2)

    John thought of a number, doubled it and then added 5
    His result was 33

    (ii) What was the number John thought of?

    Answer: .... (3)

    January 97 Q12

44. I think of a number, double it and then subtract 5
    The result is 9
    What is the number I thought of?

    Answer: .... (3)

    November 94 Q8

45. Alison thought of a number, doubled it and added 4
    The result was 30
    What was Alison's number?

    Answer: .... (3)

    November 93 Q9

46. I think of a number and subtract 2

   (i) If the result is 23, what is the number?

   Answer: .... (1)

   I think of a number, double it and then add 3

   (ii) If the result is 27, what is the number?

   Answer: .... (2)

   I think of a number, halve it and then add 3

   (iii) If the result is 27, what is the number?

   Answer: .... (2)

   November 98 Q9

47. (i) Jane thinks of a number, halves it and then subtracts 4
   Her result is 1
   What is her number?

   Answer: .... (2)

   (ii) Fill in the missing numbers.

   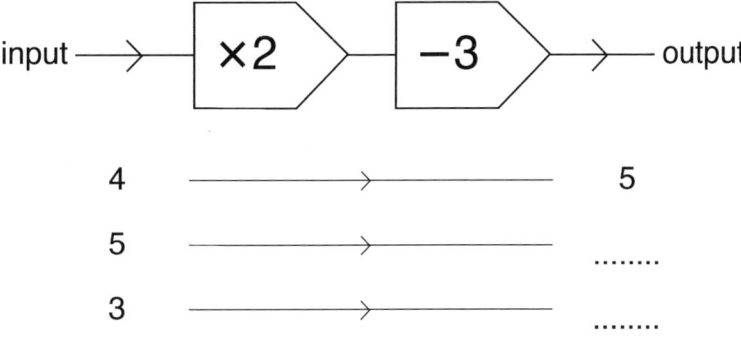

   (2)

   November 95 Q7

48. This function machine subtracts 3 from every input number.

The inverse machine (which does the opposite) will add 3 to every input number.

Here is Bella's machine:

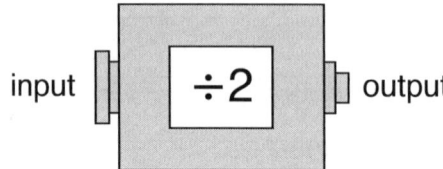

(i) Write, in words, what the inverse machine will do.

Answer: .... (2)

(ii) Fill in the details on the function machine labels.

(a) $+5$ is the inverse of ☐ (1)

(b) ☐ is the inverse of $\times 4$ (1)

49. This flowchart divides the input number by 2 and then by 3

input —— $\div 2$ —— $\div 3$ —— output

(i) Find three input numbers which give whole number outputs.

Answer: .... (3)

(ii) What can you say about the three numbers you found in part (i)?

Answer: ....

.... (2)

50. We could replace the machine

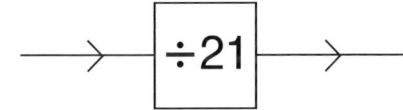

by the two machines

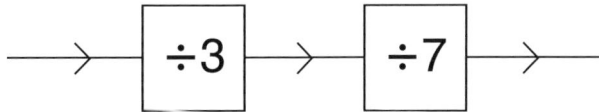

Use this fact to divide 252 by 21

Answer: .... (2)

51. John and Janet have each thought of a positive whole number.

    The sum of their numbers is 7

    List all the possible combinations of numbers.

    Answer: John   Janet

    ....

    ....

    ....

    ....

    ....

    .... (3)

52. Kane and Kerry have each thought of a positive whole number.

    The sum of their numbers is 10

    The product of their numbers is 24

    What are the two numbers?

    Answer: .... (2)

53. Lola has thought of two numbers.

    Their product is 48

    The difference between them is 8

    What is their sum?

    Answer: .... (3)

54. Share 50p between George and Mary so that Mary has 10p more than George.

Answer: Mary has .... p

George has .... p   (3)

January 90 Q3

55. Mary is four years older than Ben.

If their ages add up to 20, how old is Mary?

Answer: .... years   (2)

November 92 Q10

56. Bill and Ben have each thought of a positive whole number less than nine.

The sum of their numbers is 9

On this diagram, two possibilities are shown by the crosses:

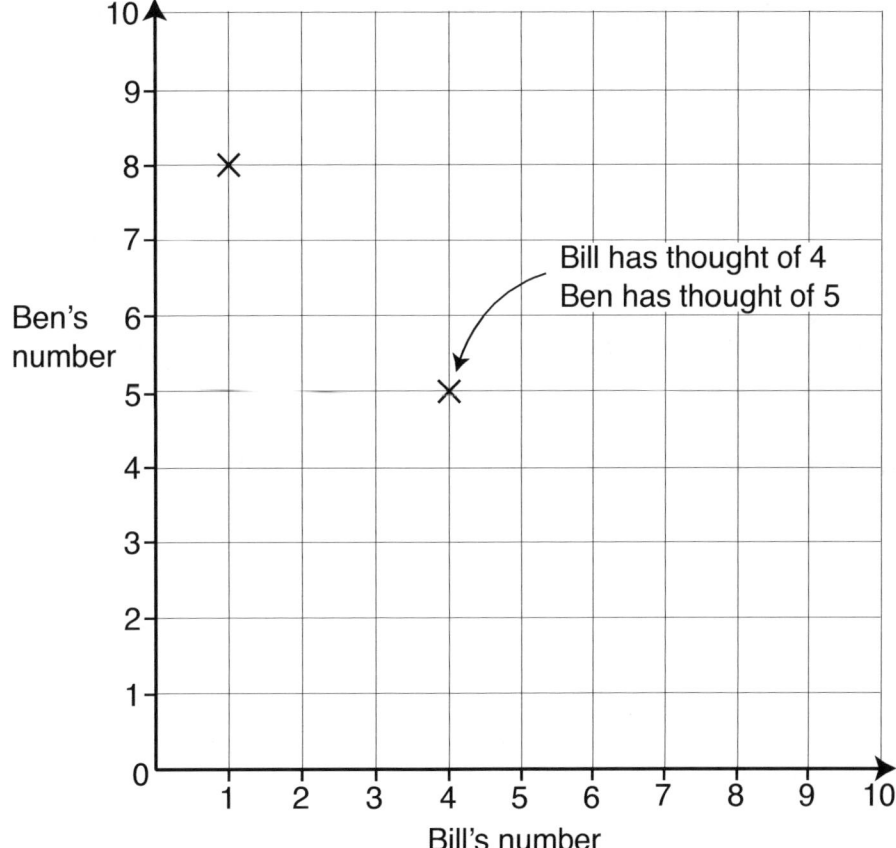

Complete the diagram to show all the other possibilities.   (4)

27

57. When travelling in outer space, Mike lands on a strange planet.

    The creatures he sees are called Tripets, which have three legs, and Quadpets which have four legs.

    Tripet   Quadpet

    When he peeps out from his hiding place he can see only the creatures' legs. He sees 15 legs.

    He works out that he could be looking at either one Tripet and three Quadpets or five Tripets.

    (i) If he sees 20 legs, how many of each creature could he be looking at?

    Answer: ....

    or: .... (3)

    (ii) If he sees 24 legs, how many of each creature could he be looking at?

    Answer: ....

    or: ....

    or: .... (4)

January 98 Q12

B Sequences and functions: identifying number patterns

(Note: more material can be found in Book A: 1A pages 2–15)

1. Sarah has arranged nine beads in a pattern.

   Continue the pattern for the next eight beads. (2)

2. Complete this repeating pattern.

   1 2 .... 1 2 2 1 .... 2 .... (2)

3. Write the next two numbers in each of these sequences.

   (i)   1 , 3 , 5 , 7 , 9 , ... , ... (1)

   (ii) 1 , 4 , 7 , 10 , 13 , ... , ... (2)

   (iii) 20 , 18 , 16 , 14 , 12 , ... , ... (2)

   (iv) $\frac{1}{2}$, 1 , $1\frac{1}{2}$, 2 , $2\frac{1}{2}$, ... , ... (2)

4. Write the next two numbers in this sequence.

   1 , 4 , 3 , 6 , 5 , ... , ... (2)

5. (i) Complete the list of outputs for this function machine.

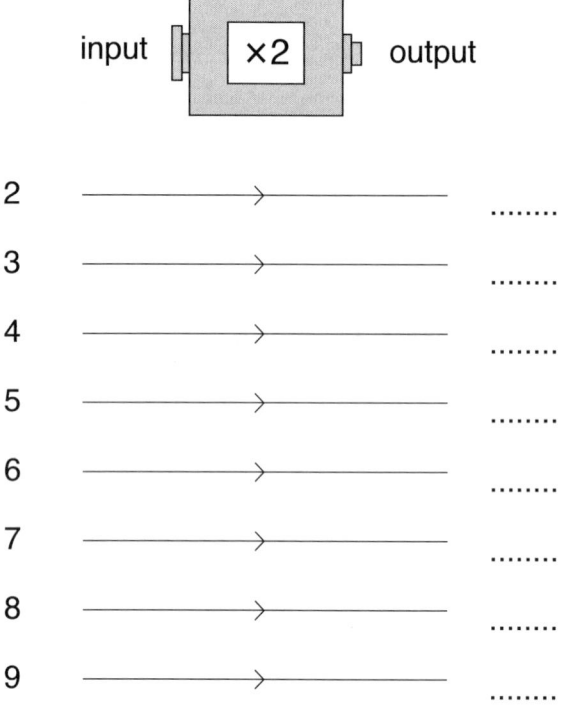

2 ⟶ ....

3 ⟶ ....

4 ⟶ ....

5 ⟶ ....

6 ⟶ ....

7 ⟶ ....

8 ⟶ ....

9 ⟶ ....

(2)

(ii) Complete this statement.

For the ×2 machine, the outputs are all numbers in the .... times multiplication table. (1)

B ALGEBRA

6. (i) Label this machine which produces numbers in the 7 times multiplication table.

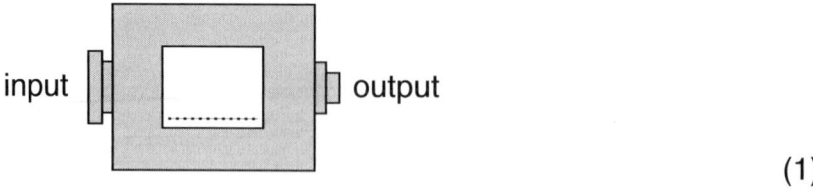

(1)

(ii) Choose two input numbers between 4 and 12 and complete these details for the machine.

input ⟶ output

.... ⟶ ....

.... ⟶ ....

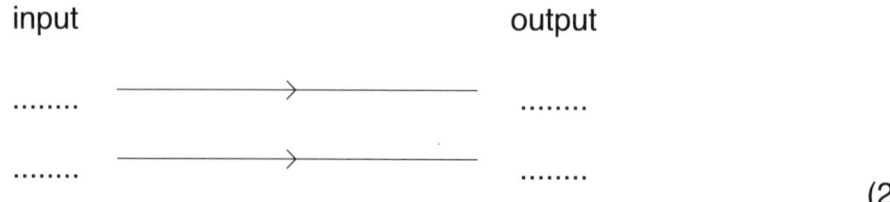

(2)

7. Which machine will produce these pairs of input and output numbers?

input	output
2	6
3	9
4	12

Answer: .... (2)

8. Which multiplication function machine will produce all these outputs?

      10   20   35   40   70   85

Answer: .... (2)

9. Here is an unusual arrangement of counting numbers up to 95:

	1	2	3	4	5	6	7	8	9	10	11
12	13	14	15	16	17	18	19	20	21	22	23
24	25	26	27	28	29	30	31	32	33	34	35
36	37	38	39	40	41	42	43	44	45	46	47
48	49	50	51	52	53	54	55	56	57	58	59
60	61	62	63	64	65	66	67	68	69	70	71
72	73	74	75	76	77	78	79	80	81	82	83
84	85	86	87	88	89	90	91	92	93	94	95

(i) Circle all the numbers which would be produced by a ×3 machine. (3)

(ii) Shade all the numbers which would be produced by a ×8 machine. (3)

ALGEBRA B

10. Here is an arrangement of counting numbers up to 55:

0	1	2	3	4	5	6	7
8	9	10	11	12	13	14	15
16	17	18	19	20	21	22	23
24	25	26	27	28	29	30	31
32	33	34	35	36	37	38	39
40	41	42	43	44	45	46	47
48	49	50	51	52	53	54	55

(i) Circle all the numbers which would be produced by a ×4 machine. (3)

(ii) Shade all the numbers which would be produced by a ×7 machine. (3)

11. These four multiplication function machines are all showing the same output.

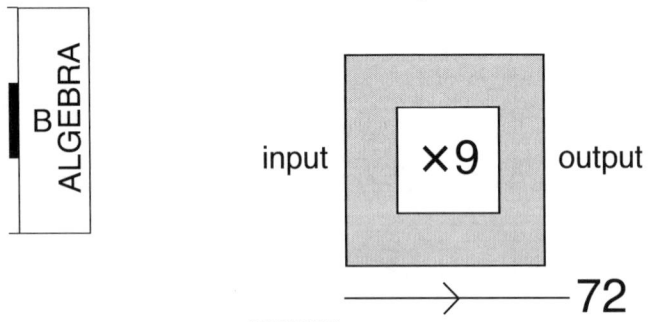

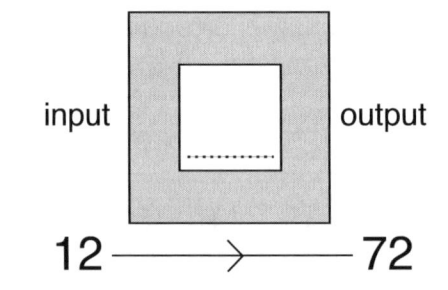

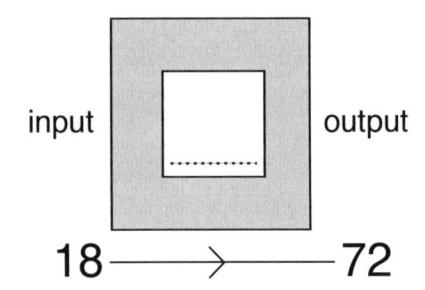

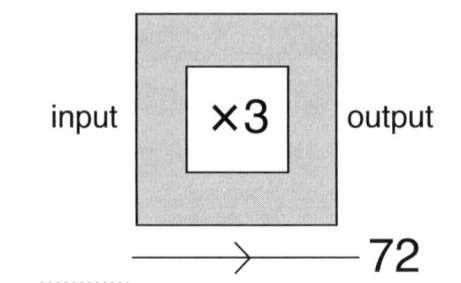

input ×9 output
.... → 72

input ☐ output
12 → 72

input ☐ output
18 → 72

input ×3 output
.... → 72

Write the missing input numbers and labels. (4)

C **Graphs:** drawing graphs; developing ideas of continuity

1. (i) Complete the table of outputs for this function machine.

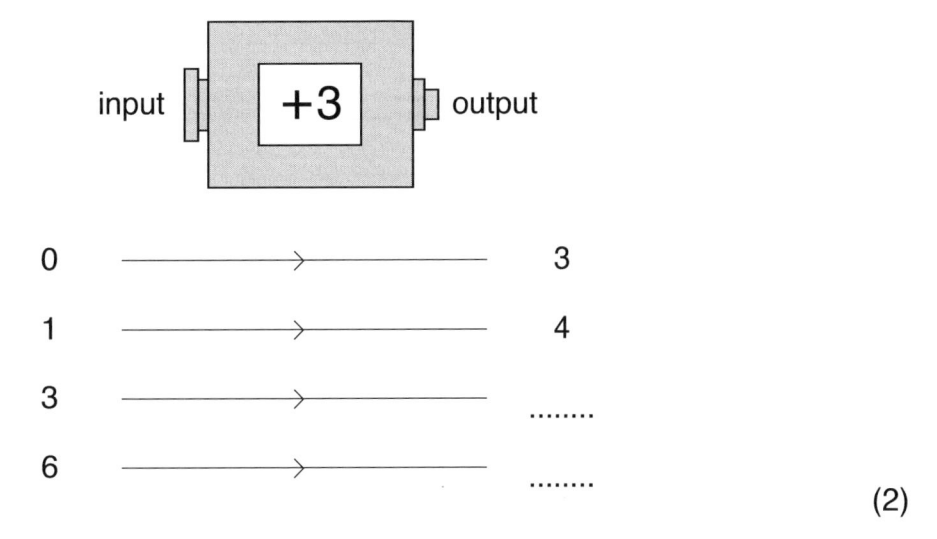

    input +3 output

    0 ⟶ 3
    1 ⟶ 4
    3 ⟶ ....
    6 ⟶ ....

    (2)

   (ii) Plot points representing the pairs of input and output numbers on this grid.

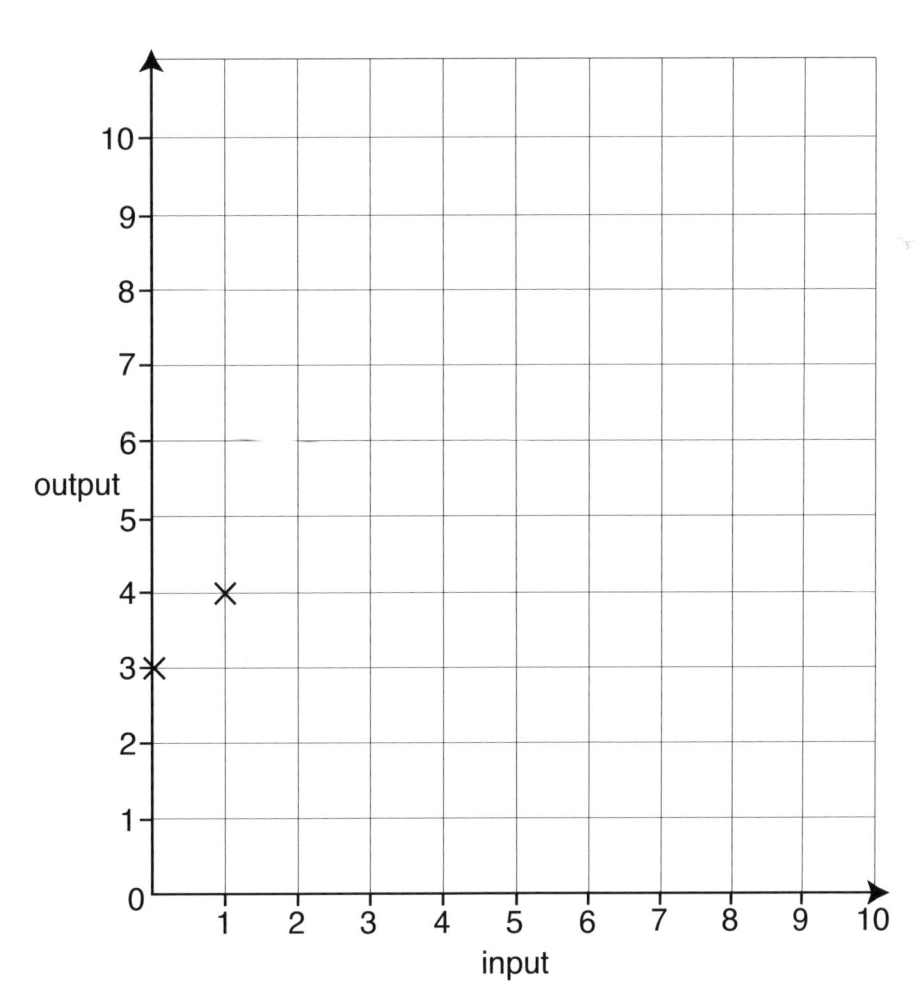

   (2)

2. (i) Complete the table of outputs for this function machine.

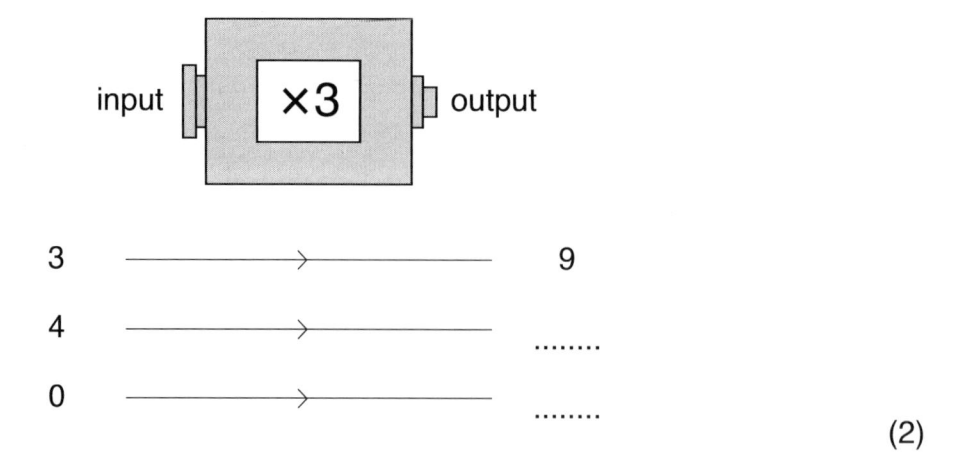

input → ×3 → output

3 ⟶ 9

4 ⟶ ....

0 ⟶ ....

(2)

(ii) Plot points representing the pairs of input and output numbers on this grid.

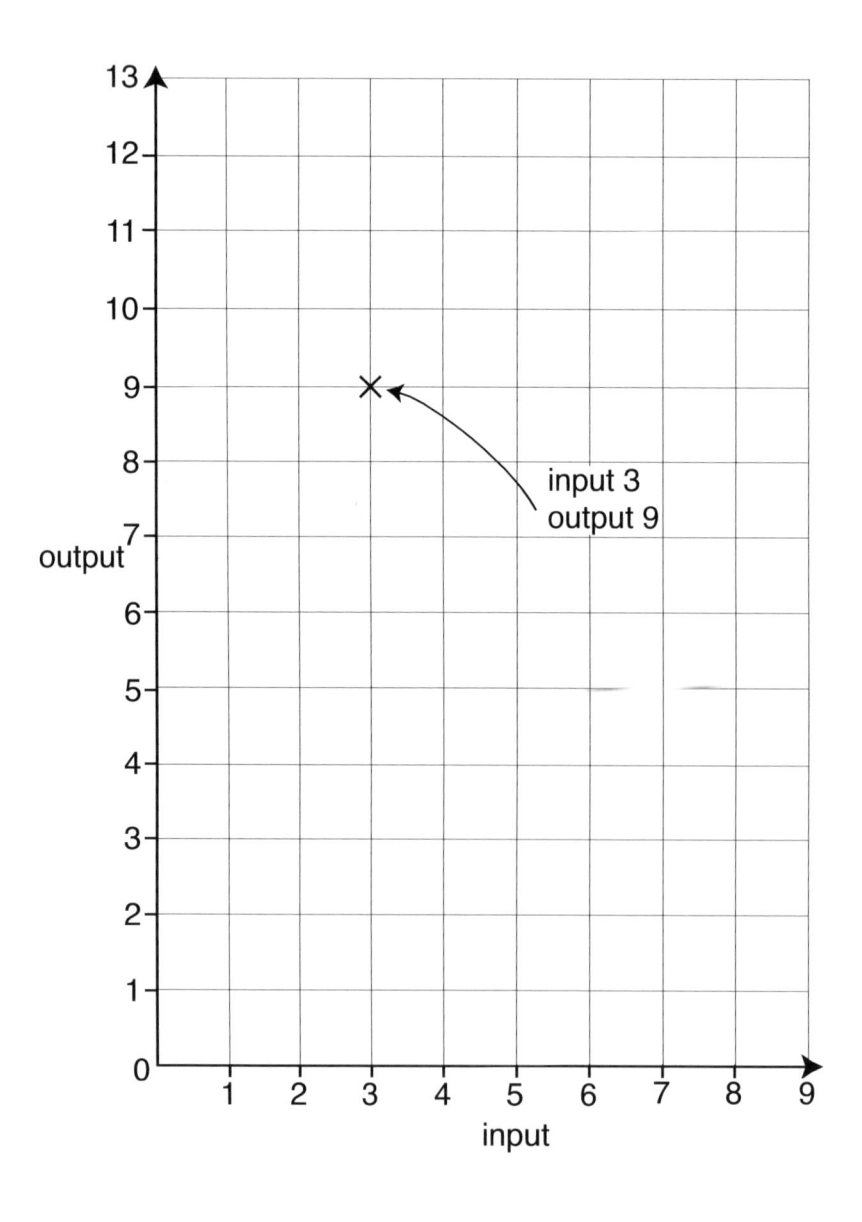

× input 3 output 9

(2)

(iii) Draw a straight line passing through the three points. (2)
This line is the **graph** of the function.

(iv) Read from your graph

(a) the output from an input of 2

Answer: .... (1)

(b) the input which gives an output of 3

Answer: .... (1)

(c) the output from an input of $2\frac{1}{2}$

Answer: .... (1)

3. On this grid is drawn the graph of a function.

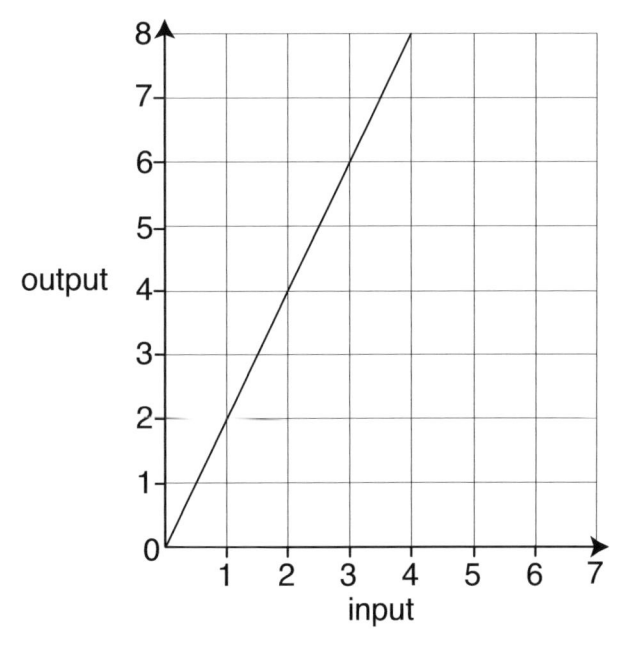

Label the function machine.

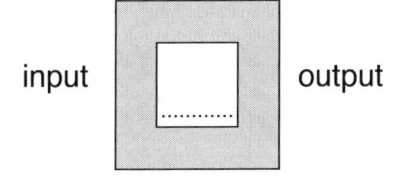

input [☐] output

(2)

4. A function machine has produced the input / output pairs of numbers plotted on this grid.

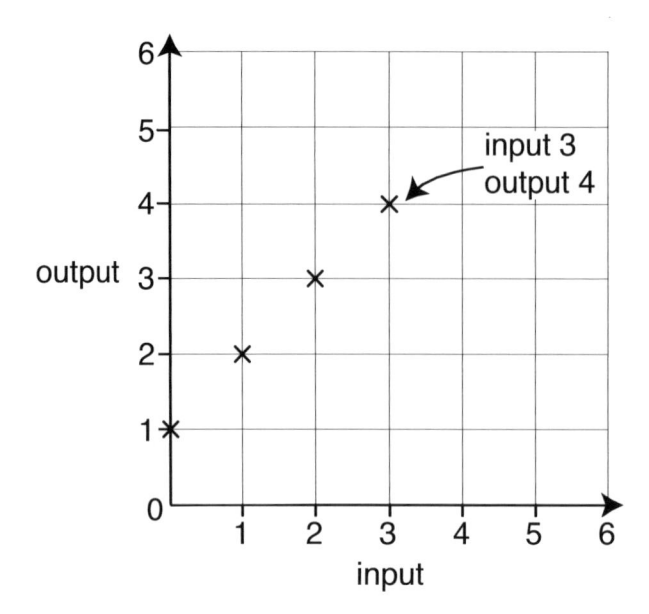

(i) What would be the output for input 5?

Answer: .... (1)

(ii) What would be the input for output 6?

Answer: .... (1)

(iii) Complete this word equation which describes the function.

Answer: output = ... (2)

(iv) Draw the graph of the function. (1)

5. A function can be described by this word equation.

output = 4 × input

(i) Label the function machine.

(1)

(ii) Choose three suitable input numbers and find the output numbers.

input		output
....	⟶	....
....	⟶	....
....	⟶	....

(3)

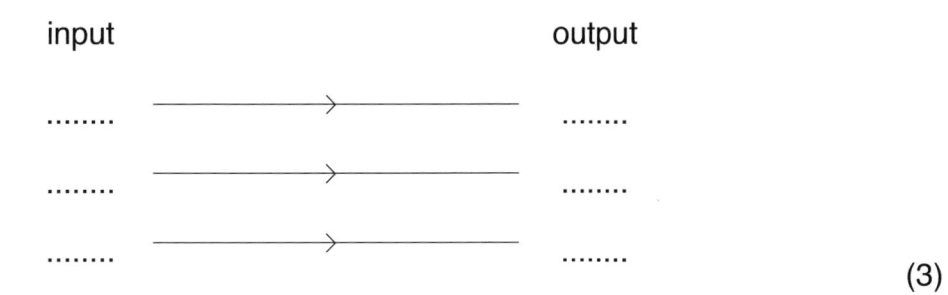

6. This drawing shows a function machine.

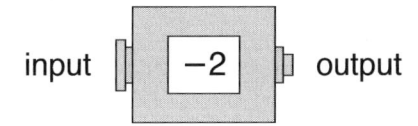

input ▭ −2 ▭ output

(i) Write a word equation for this function.

Answer: output = ... (2)

(ii) Choose three suitable input numbers and find the output numbers.

input		output
....	⟶	....
....	⟶	....
....	⟶	....

(3)

(iii) Plot the points representing the input / output pairs of numbers and draw the graph of the function.

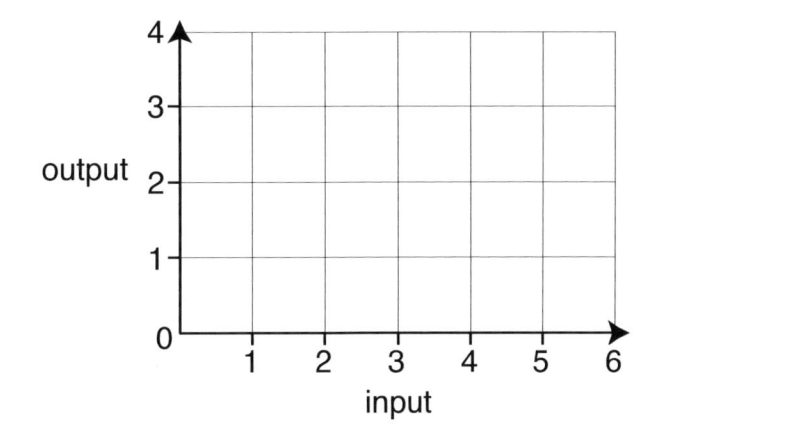

(3)

7. (i) Complete the table of outputs for this function machine.

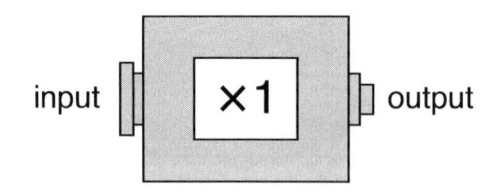

input → ×1 → output

4 ⟶ ....

2 ⟶ ....

0 ⟶ ....

(2)

(ii) Draw the graph of the function.

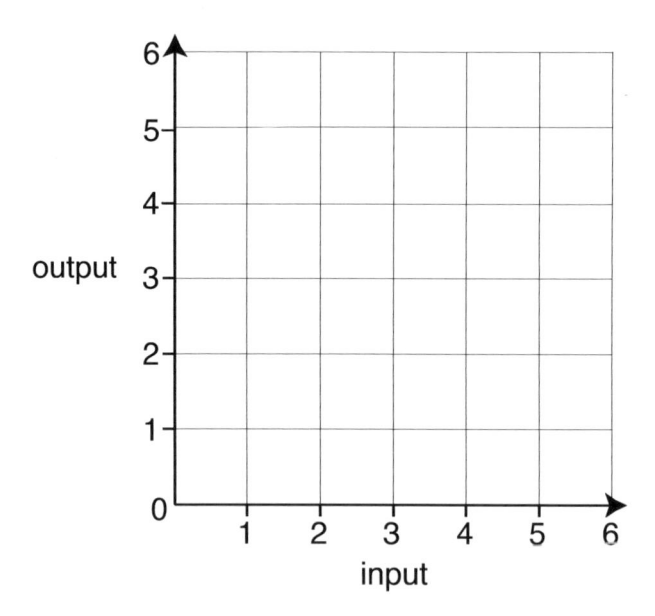

(3)

(iii) Complete this word equation for the function.

Answer: output = ... (2)

(iv) What would be the output for input 12?

Answer: .... (1)

(v) What would be the input for output ⁻1?

Answer: .... (2)

8. The points marked on this grid represent the input / output numbers for a function.

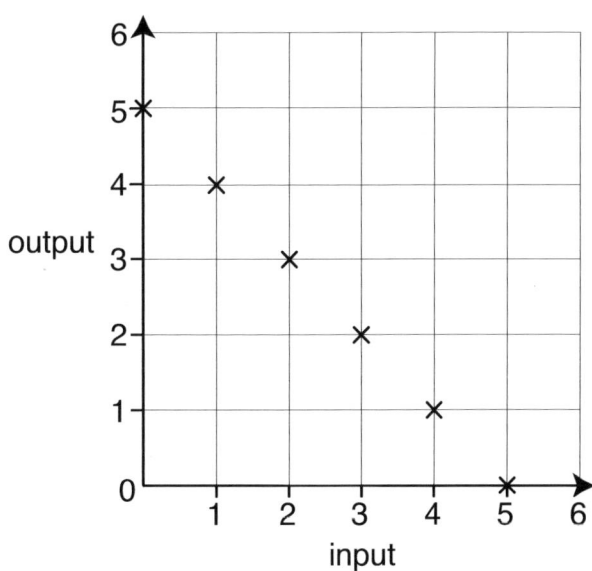

(i) Complete the table of numbers below for three of the points.

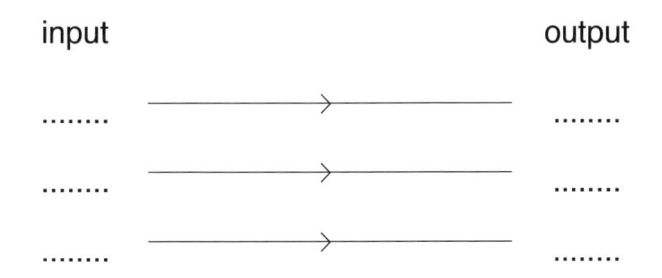

input		output
....	⟶	....
....	⟶	....
....	⟶	....

(3)

(ii) What do you notice about the sum of the input and output numbers?

Answer: ....

.... (2)

(iii) Complete this word equation for the function.

Answer: output = ... minus input (1)

9. Bertie has made this machine:

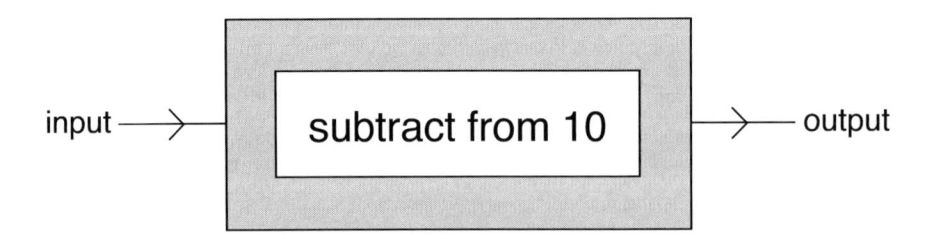

input → | subtract from 10 | → output

(i) Complete this table of input and output numbers.

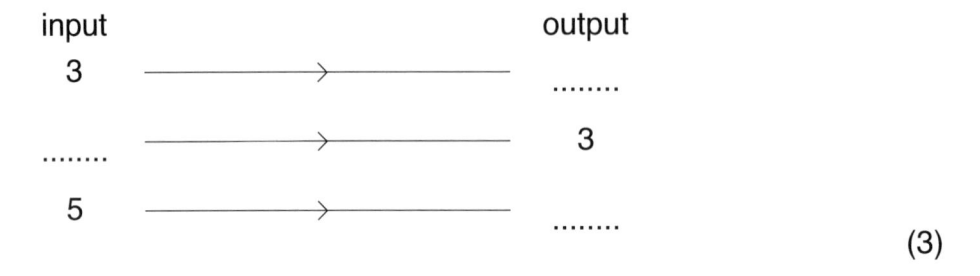

input		output
3	→	....
....	→	3
5	→	....

(3)

(ii) Draw the graph of the function.

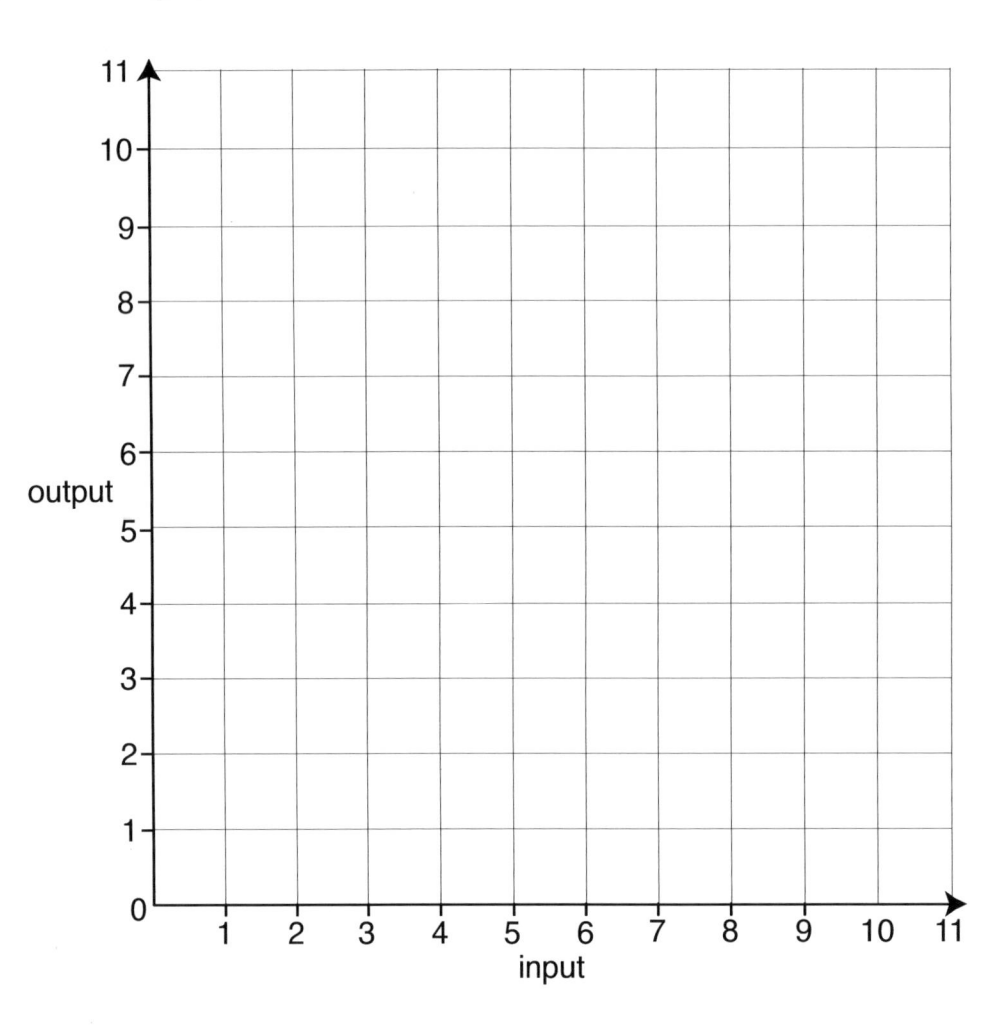

(3)

10. *Melty* ice creams cost £1.50 each. A shop uses the graph below to find the total cost when a customer buys more than one ice cream.

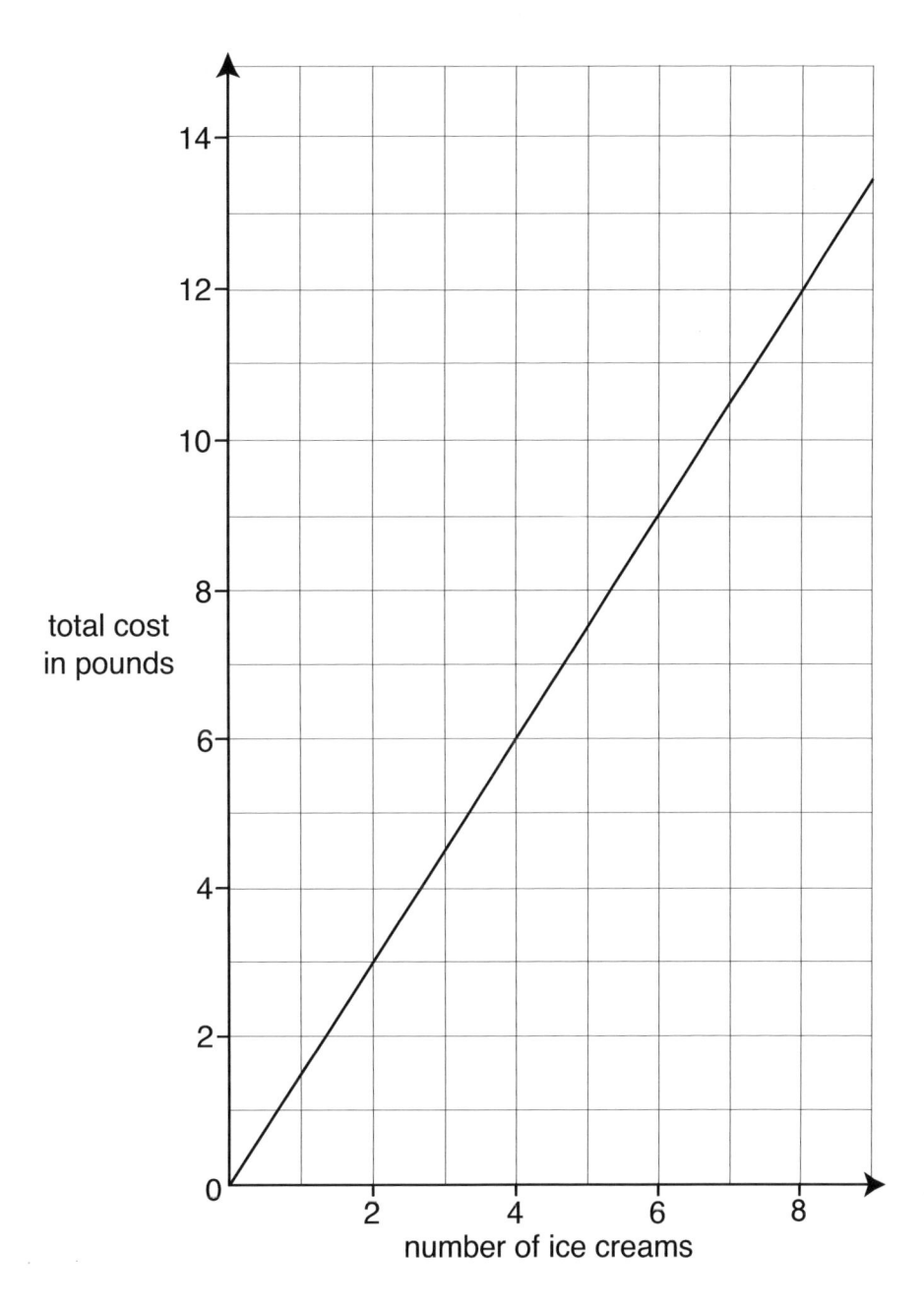

Use the graph to find

(i) the cost of seven ice creams

Answer: .... (2)

(ii) how many ice creams could be bought for £9.00

Answer: .... (2)

11. Ellie has made some cards to sell on a charity stall.

    She sells them for four pence each.

    (i) What will she charge altogether for a customer who buys

    (a) 5 cards

    Answer: .... pence (1)

    (b) 50 cards?

    Answer: .... pence (1)

    John suggests that Ellie can use a function machine to help work out what to charge each customer.

    number of cards (input) → ×4 → total charge in pence (output)

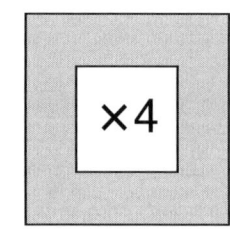

    Mrs Smith bought 12 cards.

    (ii) What was she charged?

    Answer: .... pence (2)

    Mr Brown was charged 96 pence.

    (iii) How many cards did he buy?

    Answer: .... (2)

    (iv) Use your answers to part (i) to help you to draw a graph on the page opposite.

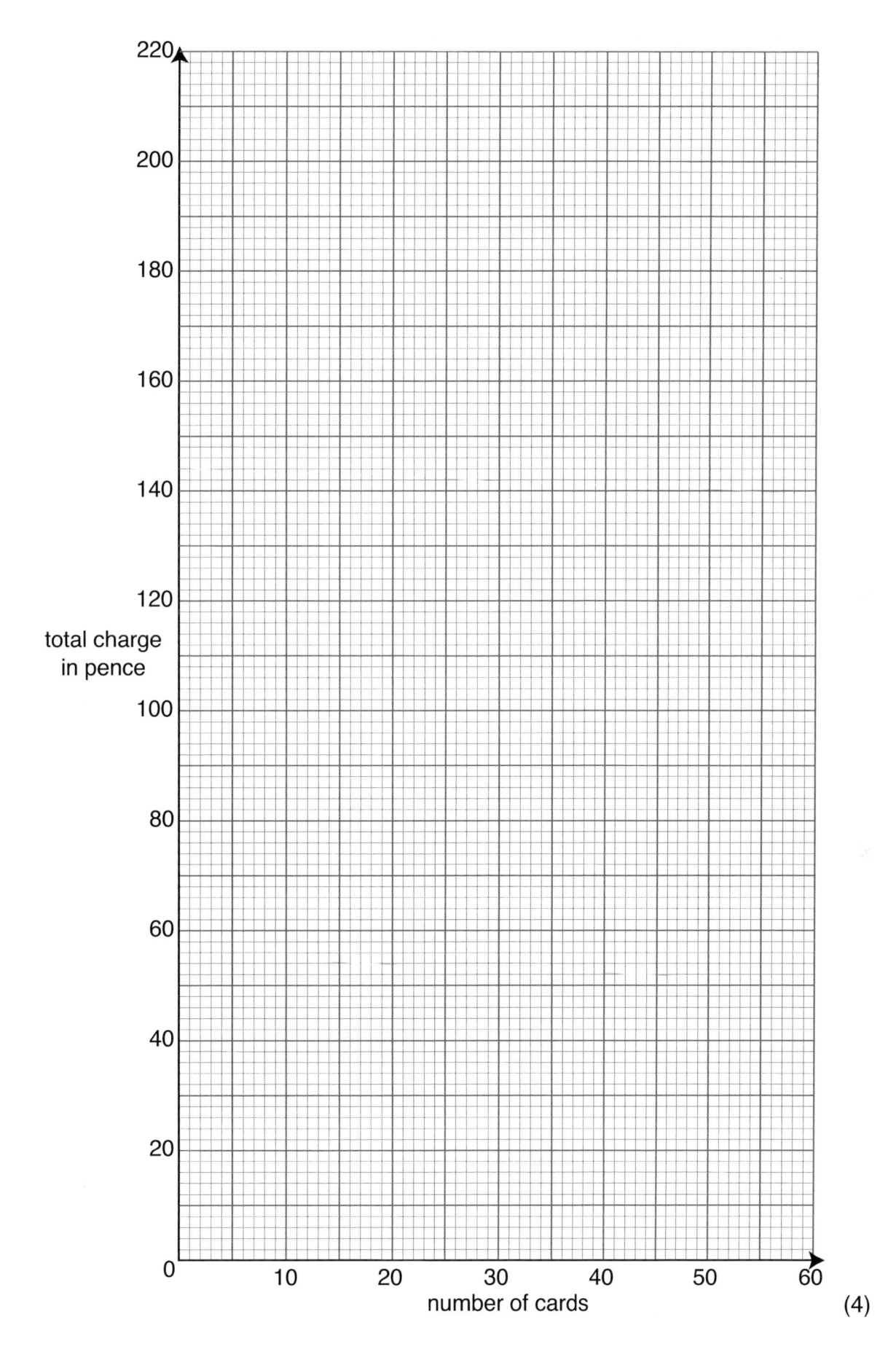

total charge in pence (y-axis, 0 to 220)
number of cards (x-axis, 0 to 60)

(4)

12. The ship *Patricia* travels at a steady speed of 20 miles per hour.

    (i) Complete the table below for the distance the ship travels in eight hours.

time taken, in hours	1	2	3	4	5	6	7	8
distance travelled, in miles	20							

    (3)

    (ii) Using the table and the grid shown below, draw a line graph to show this information.

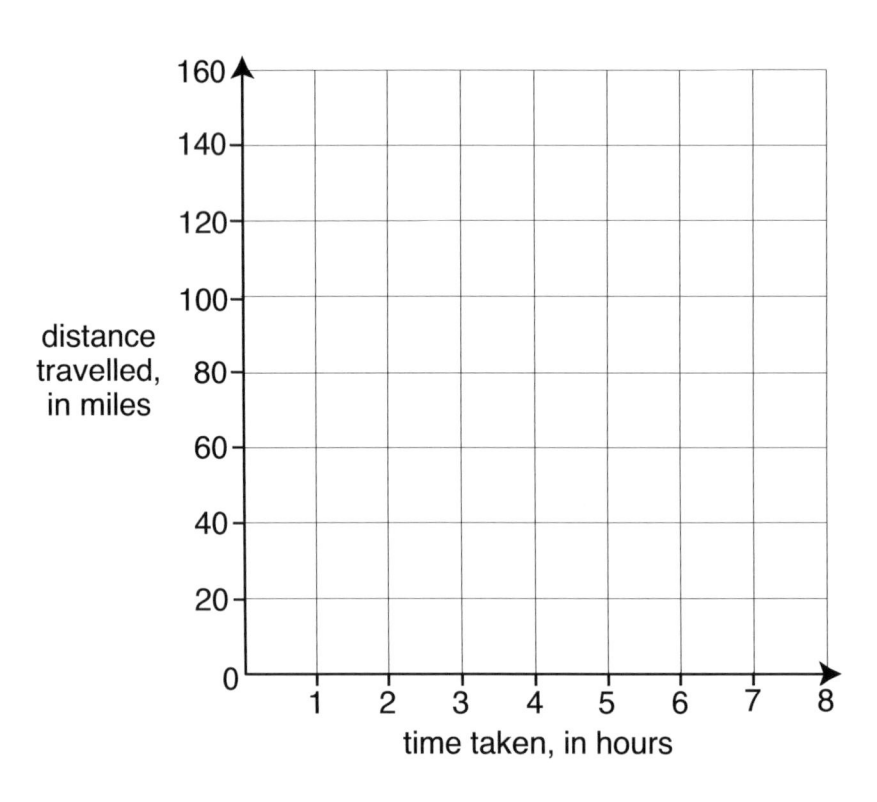

    (4)

    (iii) Read from your graph how many miles the ship *Patricia* travels in seven and a half hours.

    Mark clearly on the graph where you have taken your reading.

    Answer: .... miles (2)

November 96 Q15

13. Below is a graph used to convert pounds (£) to francs.

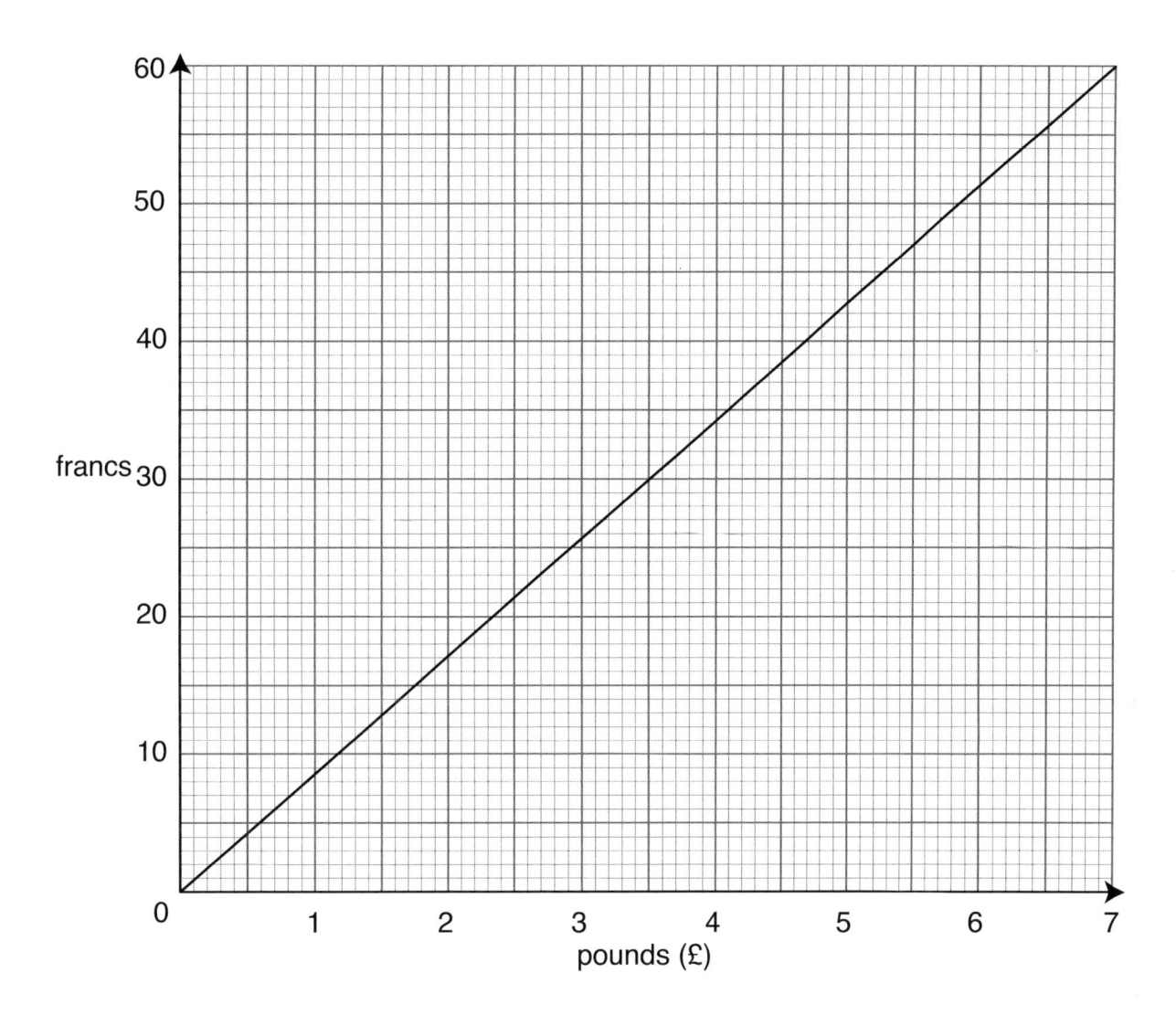

Use the graph to convert

(i) £4 to francs

Answer: .... francs (2)

(ii) 55 francs to pounds (£).

Answer: £ .... (2)

November 98 Q6

14. Tamsin has made a machine which converts dollars into pesetas.

number of dollars (input) → ×60 → number of pesetas (output)

(i) Complete this word equation:

Answer: number of pesetas = ... number of dollars (2)

(ii) How many pesetas are equivalent to

(a) 1 dollar

Answer: .... (1)

(b) 5 dollars?

Answer: .... (1)

(iii) Using your answers to part (ii) draw a graph on the grid below.

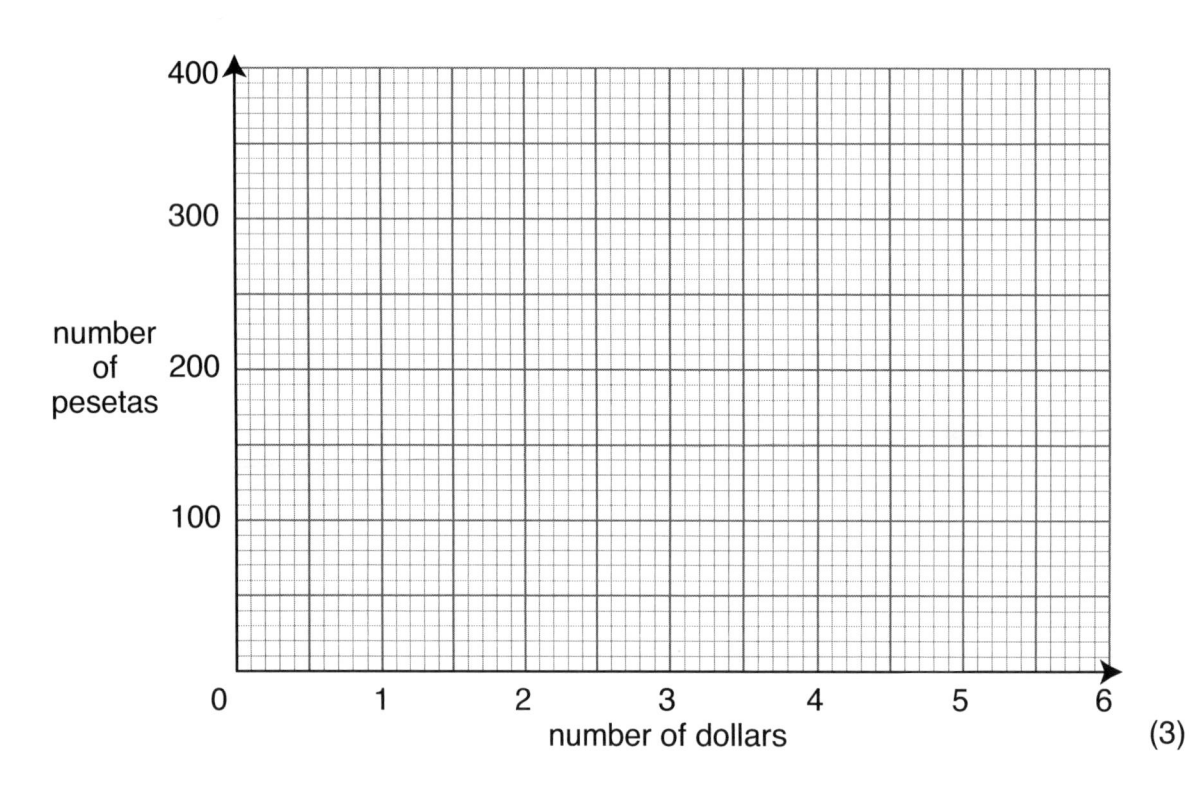

(3)

(iv) Show clearly on the grid how you would find how many dollars are equivalent to 260 pesetas.

Answer: .... dollars (2)

STRAND 5: SHAPE, SPACE AND MEASURES

A **Measures:** using measures, including choosing units and reading scales; measurement of length, mass, capacity, perimeter, area, time

1. **Without measuring**, by comparing lengths, list these strips in order of increasing length.

   A
   B
   C
   D
   E

   Answer: .... (2)

2. Compare (do not measure) the lengths of these pencils. List the pencils in order of increasing length.

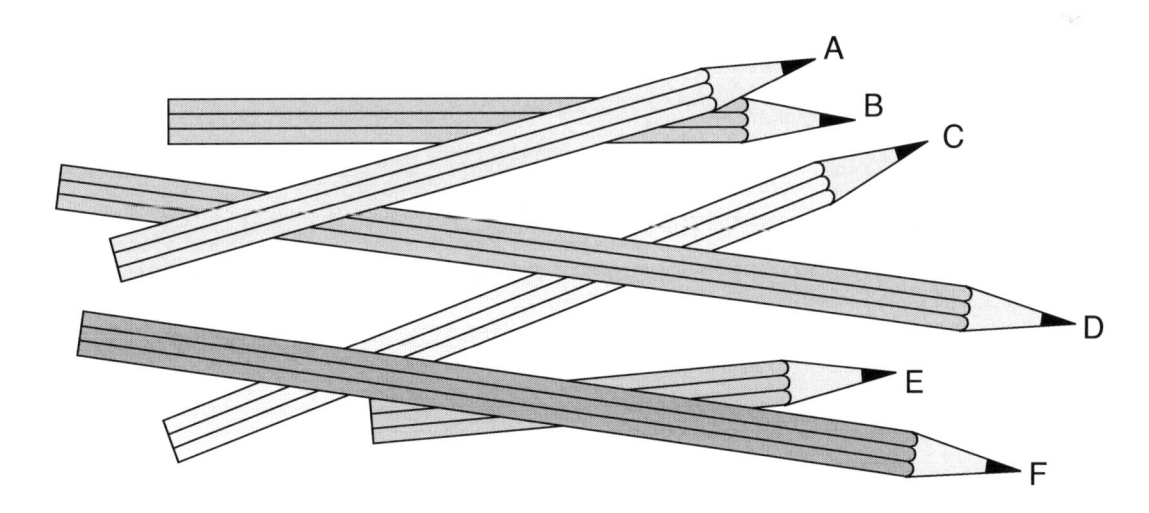

   Answer: .... (3)

3. Harry has a small spoon, a large spoon, a cup, a pot and a bucket.
   The drawing shows the small spoon.

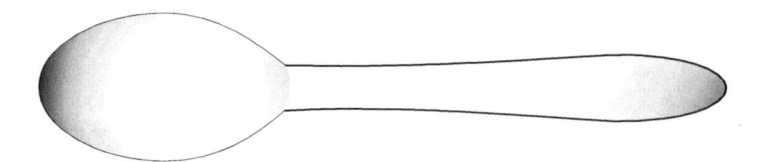

   He finds that it takes five small spoonfuls to fill the large spoon.

   It takes 14 large spoonfuls to fill the cup, 12 cupfuls to fill the pot and 5 potfuls to fill the bucket.

   (i) How many small spoonfuls would be needed to fill the cup?

   Answer: .... (1)

   (ii) How many cupfuls would it take to fill the bucket?

   Answer: .... (1)

   (iii) Harry finds a jug which needs 106 small spoonfuls.

   How could he fill the jug most quickly using his non-standard measures?
   (He can't just put the jug under the tap!)

   Answer: ....
   ....
   .... (3)

4. Choose from these units of length:

   mm   cm   m   km

   Which unit would you use to write the measurement of

   (i) the thickness of an exercise book   Answer: .... (1)

   (ii) the distance between two towns   Answer: .... (1)

   (iii) the length of a school corridor?   Answer: .... (1)

5. Choose from these units of mass:

   mg   g   kg   tonne

   Which unit would you use to write the measurement of

   (i) the mass of a sheet of paper   Answer: .... (1)

   (ii) the mass of a large dog   Answer: .... (1)

   (iii) the mass of an ocean liner?   Answer: .... (1)

6. Choose from these units of area:

   mm^2 cm^2 m^2 km^2 ha(hectare)

   Which unit would you use to write the measurement of

   (i) the area of your hand   Answer: .... (1)

   (ii) the area of a large field   Answer: .... (1)

   (iii) the area of a fly's wing   Answer: .... (1)

   (iv) the area of the floor of your classroom?   Answer: .... (1)

7. Choose from this list of units to make these answers sensible.
   You may use a unit more than once.

milli-metre	centi-metre	metre	kilo-metre	gramme	kilo-gramme	millilitre	litre	minute	hour
mm	cm	m	km	g	kg	mℓ	ℓ	min	h

   (i) On my bicycle I ride 2 km in 15 ……………………… .

   (ii) A train going for 2 hours could travel 220 ……………………… .

   (iii) My pencil measures 12.4 ……………………… .

   (iv) My uncle's height is 1.86 ……………………… .

   (v) The thickness of my skipping rope is 7 ……………………… .

   (vi) A brick has a mass of 1860 ……………………… .

   (vii) A drawing pin has a mass of 0.9 ……………………… .

   (viii) A wine bottle holds 750 ……………………… .

   (8)

   January 95 Q9

8. Here is a list of measures:

   kilometres   metres   centimetres   millimetres

   litres   millilitres   kilograms   grams

   Which one of them would you be most likely to use for each of the measurements below?

   (*Answer the short way, for example kg for kilograms.*)

   (i) the length of a pencil   Answer: …………………

   (ii) the mass of a girl   Answer: …………………

   (iii) the distance between two towns Answer: …………………

   (iv) the capacity of a bucket   Answer: …………………

   (v) the thickness of a piece of cardboard Answer: …………………

   (vi) the mass of a pen   Answer: …………………

   (6)

   November 97 Q11

9. (i) For each of the following, choose the most sensible answer.

   (a) The height of a door of a room could be

       20 cm   2 m   20 m   Answer: .... (1)

   (b) The mass of an apple could be

       1.2 g   12 g   120 g   Answer: .... (1)

   (c) The volume of coffee in a full mug could be

       25 mℓ   250 mℓ   2.5 litres   Answer: .... (1)

   (ii) Estimate your own height, giving your answer in centimetres.

                            Answer: .... cm (1)

   November 94 Q4

10. Underline the answer which you think is **best** in each case.

   (i) The area of your hand is about

       10 cm^2 100 cm^2 500 cm^2 20 cm^2 (1)

   (ii) The capacity of a bucket is about

       200 mℓ   2 ℓ   20 ℓ   200 ℓ   (1)

11. (i) 0.7 metres = ... cm   (1)

   (ii) 1250 mℓ = ... litres   (1)

   Specimen 94 Q5

12. (i) 600 mℓ = ... litres   (ii) 0.8 cm = ... mm   (2)

   (iii) 3.5 kg = ... g   (iv) 125 cm = ... m   (4)

   January 90 Q13

13. Complete this statement:

   .... m is the same as 102 cm or .... mm.

   (2)

14. The recipe for a fruit cake is as follows:

        250 g butter
        250 g sugar
        350 g flour
        550 g mixed fruit
        5 eggs each of mass 50 g

(i) What is the total mass, in kg, of the ingredients?

Answer: .... kg (4)

(ii) If the cake loses one tenth of its mass in the baking, what does it weigh after it is baked?

Answer: .... kg (3)

November 91 Q12

15. The masses of some packets of sweets are:

Jane's	450 g
Fred's	$\frac{1}{2}$ kg
Mary's	0.55 kg
Charlie's	505 g

(i) Who has the heaviest packet of sweets?

Answer: .... (2)

(ii) How many more grams has Charlie than Fred?

Answer: .... g (2)

January 96 Q17

16. John says his kitten weighs 1.17 kg. Ruth says her kitten weighs 1060 g. What is the total mass of their kittens

(i) in kilograms   Answer: .... kg (2)

(ii) in grams?   Answer: .... g (1)

January 95 Q2

52

17. In a science lesson, a class made some cars which were driven by rubber bands.

    The list below shows the pupils in the class and the distances travelled by their cars.

Julia	Ben	David	Anna	Sarah	Henry	Mary
106 cm	1.5 m	1.75 m	1.25 m	176 cm	1.6 m	175 cm

    (i) Whose car travelled furthest?

    Answer: .... (1)

    (ii) Whose cars travelled the same distance?

    Answer: .... and .... (2)

    (iii) How many centimetres did Henry's car travel?

    Answer: .... cm (2)

    November 92 Q17

18. Measure the length of this pen

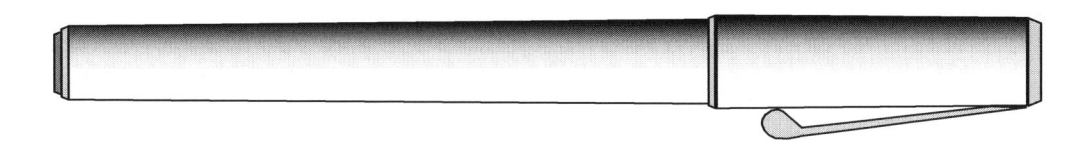

    (i) in millimetres

    Answer: .... mm (1)

    (ii) in centimetres.

    Answer: .... cm (1)

    November 96 Q1

19. Lengths of 45 cm and 32 cm were cut from a 1 m piece of string. How many cm were left?

    Answer: .... cm (3)

    November 91 Q10

20. A piece of wood is 225 centimetres long.

   (i) How many metres is this?

   Answer: .... m   (1)

   Mr Jones wants to fit four shelves, each of this length.

   (ii) What is the total length of wood, in metres, that he will need?

   Answer: .... m   (2)

   January 98 Q3

21. Helen's pencil case is 20.8 cm long.
    John's is 280 mm long.

   (i) Whose pencil case is longer?   Answer: ....   (1)

   (ii) How much longer is it?
        Write your answer in millimetres.

   Answer: .... mm   (2)

   November 93 Q2

22. Ali's height is 1.48 m.
    Kerry is five cm taller.

    How tall is Kerry (i) in centimetres   Answer: .... cm   (2)

    (ii) in metres?   Answer: .... m   (1)

    November 97 Q3

23. The length of a kitchen worktop is 183 cm.
    Write this measurement in

    (i) millimetres

    Answer: .... mm   (1)

    (ii) metres.

    Answer: .... m   (1)

    January 99 Q2

24. Write the following quantities as litres.

    (The first part has been done for you.)

    (i) 1 litre and 500 ml   (ii) 1 litre and 5 ml

    (iii) 4 litres and 50 ml   (iv) 950 ml

    (i) ....1.5 litres.... (ii) .... (iii) .... (iv) .... (6)

    January 91 Q17

25. How many five ml spoonfuls can you get from one litre of liquid?

    Answer: .... spoonfuls (2)

    January 92 Q9

26. A one-litre bottle of ginger beer is shared equally among eight friends.
    How much does each have?

    Answer: .... ml (2)

    January 91 Q3

27. Which of the following measures are the same?

    (i) 1 litre   (ii) 0.3 litre   (iii) 300 ml   (iv) 30 ml   (v) 3 litres

    Answer: .... and .... (2)

    January 92 Q17

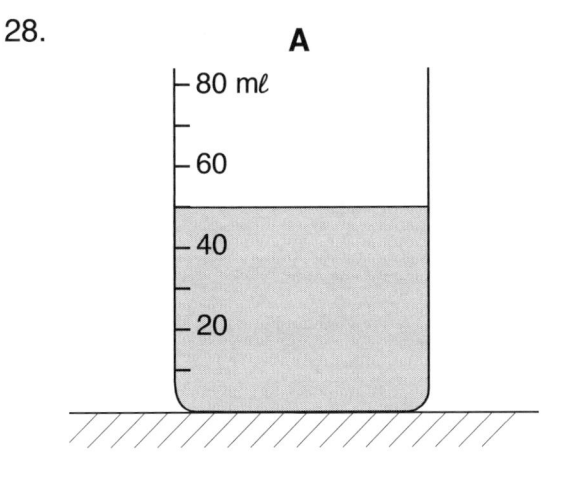

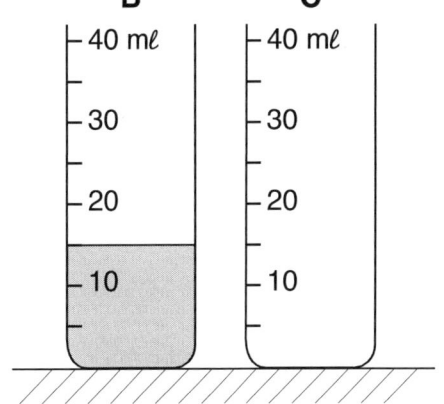

28.

    All the water in measuring cylinder **A** is poured into the cylinders **B** and **C**.
    Draw the water in cylinder **C**. (2)

29. 20 children attend a party.

They are each given a glass of lemonade.

A glass holds 250 mℓ.

(i) How many millilitres of lemonade will be needed?

Answer: .... mℓ (2)

A bottle of lemonade holds two litres.

(ii) How many bottles will be needed?

Answer: .... (2)

January 99 Q10

30. Mrs Neal has a new 125 mℓ bottle of *Petalsafe*.

She uses two measures of *Petalsafe* each time she sprays her roses.

Each measure holds eight mℓ.

(i) What volume of liquid is left in the bottle after Mrs Neal has sprayed her roses once?

Answer: .... mℓ (2)

(ii) How many times is Mrs Neal able to spray her roses using this one bottle?

Answer: .... (2)

(iii) (a) If she bought ten bottles, how many millilitres would she have?

Answer: .... millilitres (2)

(b) Write this in litres.

Answer: .... litres (1)

February 94 Q8

31. In a craft lesson, the pupils are making bridges out of pieces of wood.

    Angela uses three pieces, each 15 cm long.

    George uses five pieces, each 98 mm long.

    Henry uses six pieces, each 0.13 m long.

    Judy uses four pieces, each 11.5 cm long.

    (i) How many centimetres of wood does each child use?

    Answer: Angela .... cm (1)

    George .... cm (2)

    Henry .... cm (2)

    Judy .... cm (2)

    (ii) What is the total length of wood, in metres, used by all four pupils?

    Answer: .... m (2)

    (iii) How many centimetres of wood will be left over from a 5 m length?

    Answer: .... cm (2)

    November 93 Q16

32. Jane's book weighs $\frac{1}{2}$ kg and Mary's weighs 380 g.

    How much heavier is Jane's book than Mary's?

    Answer: .... g (2)

    February 94 Q6

33. Jim's bag weighs 4.610 kg.
    Mary's is 750 g lighter.
    What is the mass of Mary's bag?

    Answer: .... kg   (2)

    Specimen 94 Q3

34. A piece of wood is one metre long.
    A piece 32 cm long is sawn off.

    (i) What length is left?

    Answer: .... cm   (1)

    (ii) Write your answer to part (i) in millimetres.

    Answer: .... mm   (1)

    (iii) Write your answer to part (i) in metres.

    Answer: .... m   (1)

    November 94 Q1

35. A book has a mass of 456 grams.

    (i) What would be the total mass, in grams, of six of these books?

    Answer: .... g   (2)

    (ii) Write your answer to the nearest kilogram.

    Answer: .... kg   (1)

    January 97 Q2

36. Some sweets are weighed.
    They are then put in a jar and weighed again.

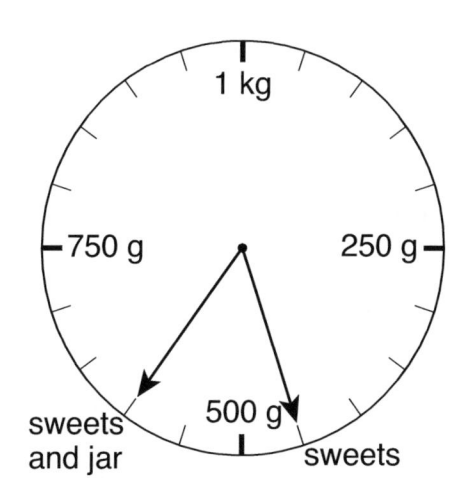

    (i) What is the mass of the sweets and the jar?

    Answer: .... g (2)

    (ii) What is the mass of the sweets?

    Answer: .... g (2)

    (iii) What is the mass of the jar?

    Answer: .... g (2)

    Specimen 94 Q7

37. John's bag weighs 1 kg 700 g.
    Mary's bag weighs 900 g.
    How much do they weigh together?

    Answer: .... kg .... g (2)

    November 95 Q2

38. Two pounds worth of 2p coins has a mass of 725 g.

   (i) How many 2p coins are worth £2?

   Answer: .... (1)

   (ii) What is the mass of one 2p coin?

   Answer: .... g (2)

   February 94 Q10

39. This is a life-size drawing of Lorna's goldfish as it was two years ago.
    It has since grown in length by seven mm.
    How long is it now? Answer in centimetres.

   Answer: .... cm (2)

40. The mass of one parcel is $\frac{1}{2}$ kg.
    The mass of a second parcel 436 g more.

   (i) What is the mass of the second parcel?

   Answer: .... g (2)

   (ii) What is the mean mass of the two parcels?

   Answer: .... g (2)

   January 99 Q7

41. These measuring beakers are empty.

Beaker **A** has a scale reading up to one litre.

Beaker **B** has a scale reading up to 500 millilitres.

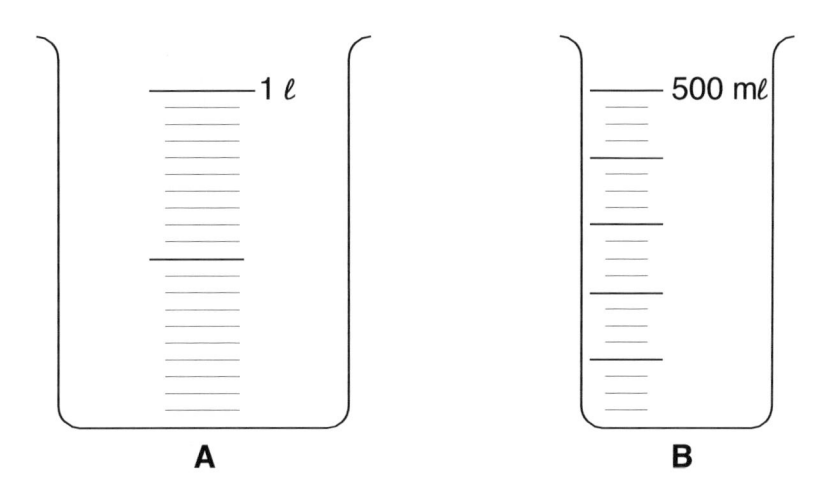

How many millilitres does one small division on each scale stand for?

(i) beaker **A**

Answer: .... mℓ (2)

(ii) beaker **B**

Answer: .... mℓ (2)

350 mℓ of water is poured into each beaker.

(iii) Draw a line on each beaker to show the water level. (2)

November 97 Q17

42. (i) Write down the measurements shown by the arrows on the pictures below.

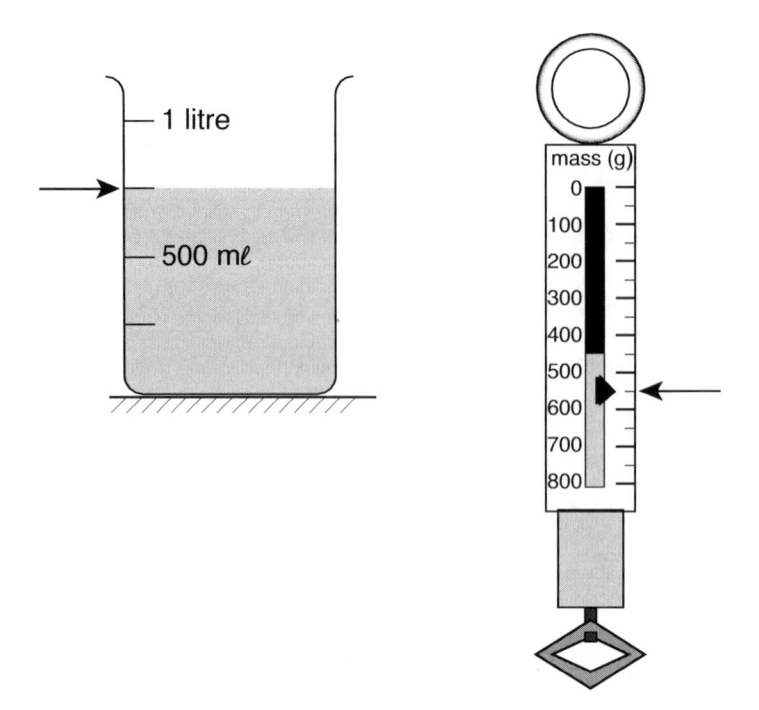

(a) .... mℓ   (b) .... g   (4)

(ii) Place an arrow in position to show 0.75 kg on the spring balance. (2)

(iii) Underline the best estimate of the mass of the following:

(a) a tennis ball	**550 g**	**55 g**	**5.5 g**
(b) a litre carton of milk	**2000 g**	**1000 g**	**200 g**

(2)

January 93 Q12

43. Part of an enlarged cm ruler is drawn below.

Write down the measurements in cm which are indicated by the arrows, starting with the smallest measurement.

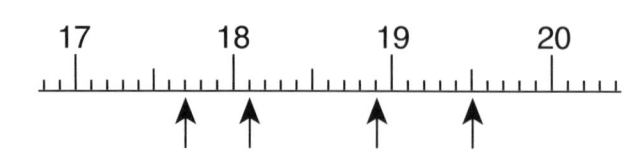

Answer: .... cm .... cm .... cm .... cm   (4)

January 91 Q15

44. Here are parts of the faces of two different weighing scales.

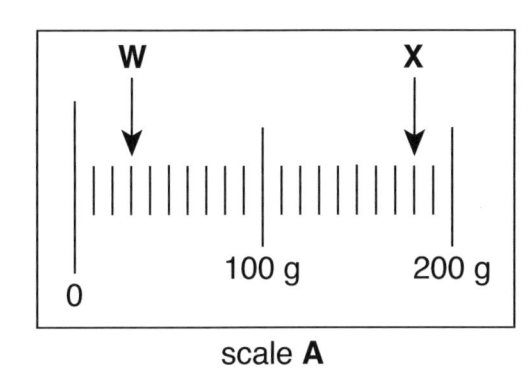

scale **A**

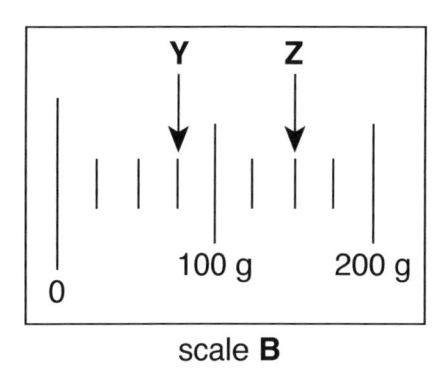

scale **B**

(i) Complete these statements.

Each little division on scale **A** shows .... grams. (2)

Arrow **W** shows a mass of .... grams. (1)

Arrow **X** shows a mass of .... grams. (1)

(ii) Draw an arrow on scale **A** to show a mass of 50 grams. (2)

(iii) Complete these statements.

Each little division on scale **B** shows .... grams. (2)

Arrow **Y** shows a mass of .... grams. (1)

Arrow **Z** shows a mass of .... grams. (1)

(iv) Draw an arrow on scale **B** to show a mass of 50 grams. (2)

November 96 Q13

45. What are the readings on these scales?

(i)

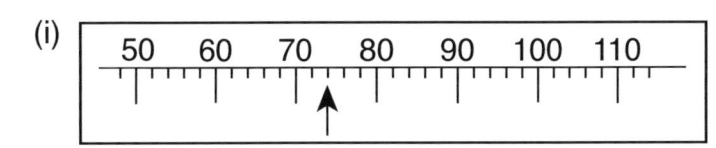

Answer: .... (2)

(ii)

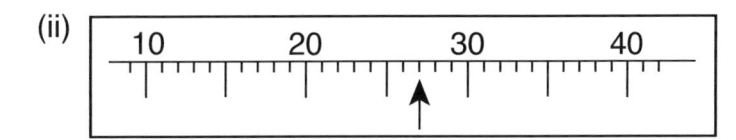

Answer: .... (2)

63

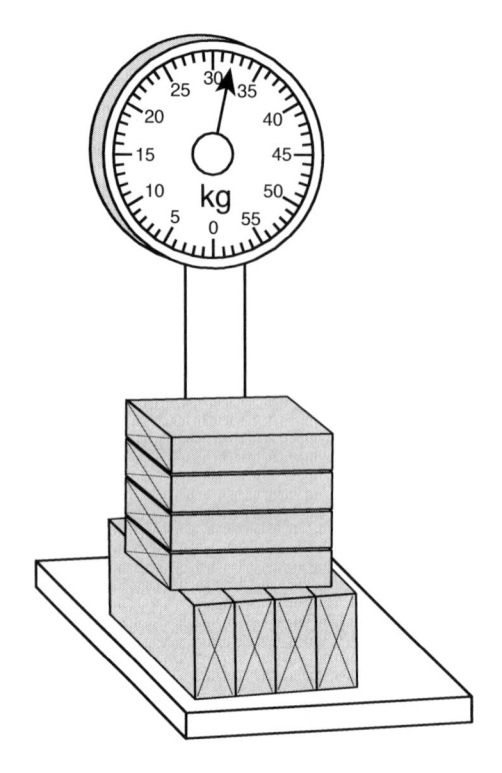

46. The diagram shows eight identical parcels on scales.

(i) What is the mass shown on the scales?

Answer: .... kg   (1)

(ii) What is the mass of each parcel?

Answer: .... kg   (2)

As a special offer, the parcels can go free if the total mass is **less** than 21 kg.

(iii) How many parcels must be removed so that there is no charge?

Answer: ....   (2)

47. Here are the midday temperatures for each day of one week:

day	Sun	Mon	Tue	Wed	Thu	Fri	Sat
temperature, in °C	15	19	18	19	17	16	15

(i) What was the maximum midday temperature?

Answer: .... °C (1)

(ii) What was the minimum midday temperature?

Answer: ....°C (1)

(iii) What was the mean midday temperature?

Answer: .... °C (2)

(iv) On the thermometer, mark a scale which could be used to measure these temperatures.

0 °C   20 °C

(2)

(v) On the thermometer, continue the shading to show the median midday temperature.

(2)

January 98 Q9

48. On one particular day, the temperature in Rome was 9 °C and in Edinburgh it was ⁻2 °C.

    How many degrees colder was it in Edinburgh?

    Answer: .... degrees   (2)

    January 97 Q8

49. One night in January the lowest temperature was ⁻5 °C.

    The next day it rose by three degrees.

    What was the temperature the next day?

    Answer: .... °C   (2)

    January 95 Q3

50. At midday the temperature was 5 °C.

    At midnight it was ⁻3 °C.

    How many degrees did the temperature fall?

    Answer: .... degrees   (2)

    November 91 Q6

51. One night last winter the temperature was ⁻4 °C.

    By lunchtime the following day the temperature had risen ten degrees.

    What was the new temperature?

    Answer: .... °C   (2)

    November 94 Q3

52. (i) Which temperature is recorded on this thermometer scale?

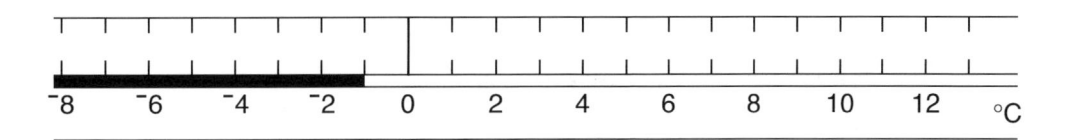

Answer: .... °C (1)

(ii) On this thermometer scale, clearly mark a temperature of ⁻4 °C

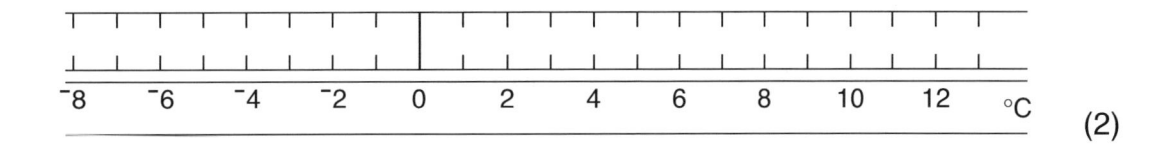

(2)

53. At midday the temperature was 11 °C.

At midnight it had fallen to ⁻2 °C.

By how many degrees had the temperature fallen?

Answer: .... degrees (2)

November 93 Q8

54. A maximum and minimum thermometer records the highest and lowest temperatures reached until it is reset.

Hannah's thermometer records the following temperatures in a 24-hour period:

maximum   7 °C
minimum   ⁻3 °C

What was the range of temperatures during that period?

Answer: .... degrees (2)

55. Inside Mary's greenhouse the temperature is eight degrees warmer than it is outside.

The temperature inside is 13 degrees Celsius (13 °C).

What is the temperature outside?

Answer: .... °C (1)

56. This thermometer shows the temperature at midday one day.

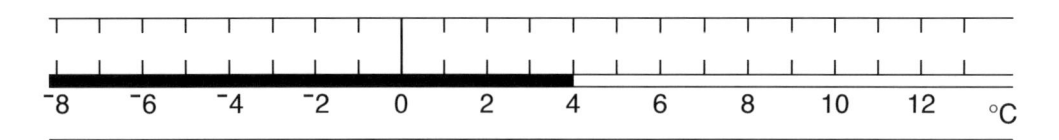

   (i) What was the temperature?

   Answer: .... °C (1)

   Five hours later the temperature had fallen by seven degrees.

   (ii) On this thermometer, draw in the mercury column to show the new temperature.

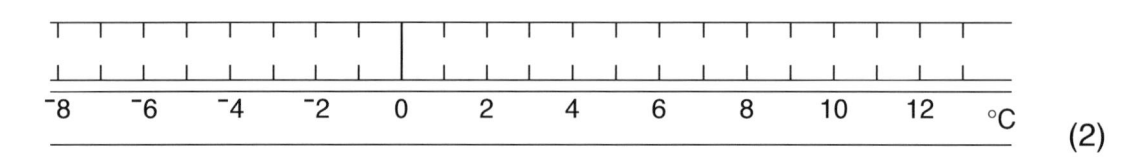

   (2)

57. In a weather news broadcast, the following temperatures were shown:

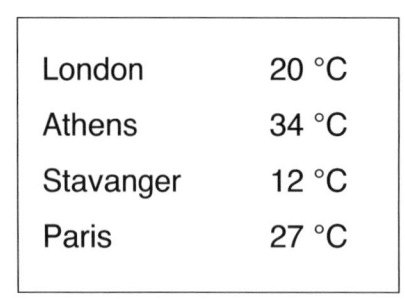

London	20 °C
Athens	34 °C
Stavanger	12 °C
Paris	27 °C

   (i) How many degrees warmer was it in Athens than in Stavanger?

   Answer: .... degrees (1)

   (ii) How many degrees cooler was it in Paris than in Athens?

   Answer: .... degrees (1)

58. (i) What is the perimeter of this rectangle?

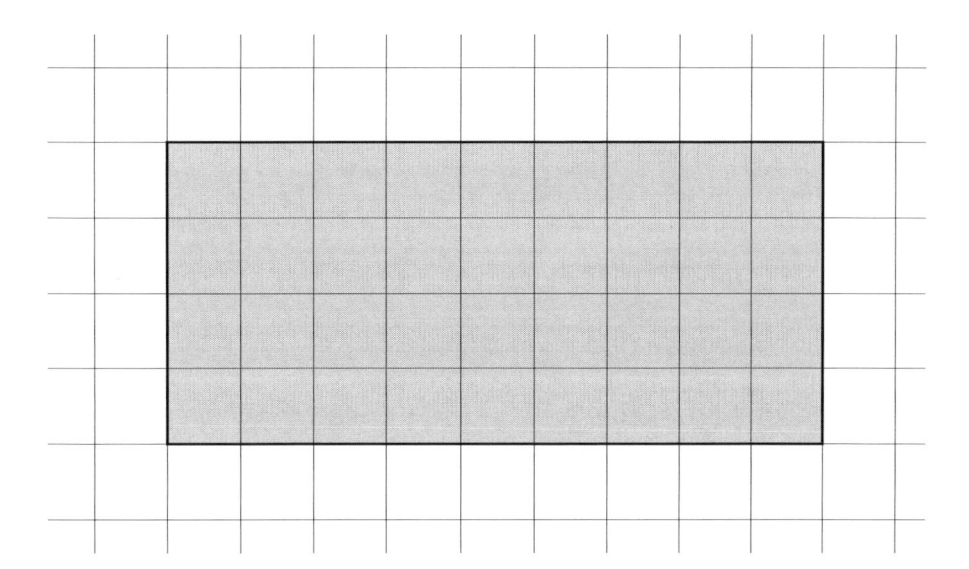

Answer: .... cm (2)

(ii) What is the area of the rectangle?

Answer: .... cm² (2)

The square below has the same area as the rectangle.

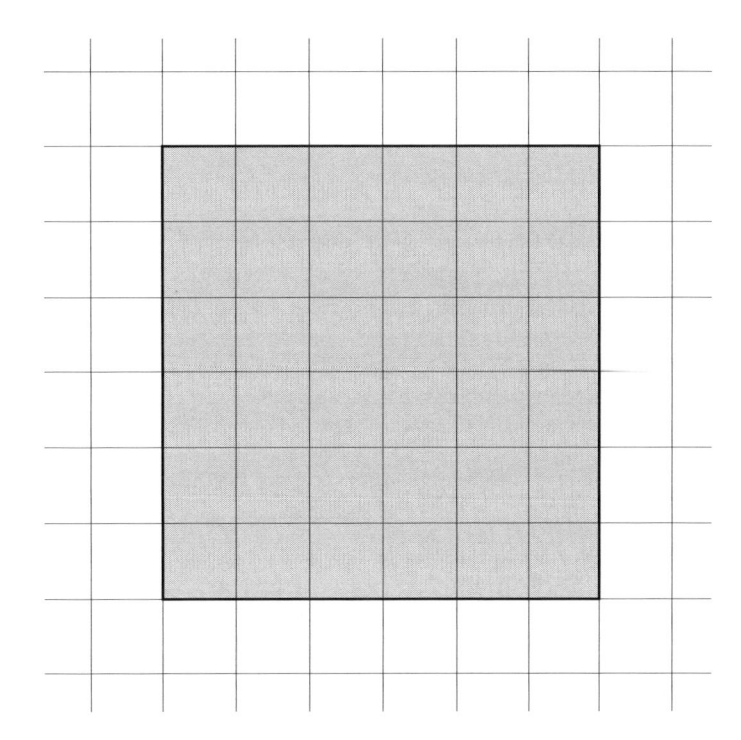

(iii) What is the perimeter of the square?

Answer: .... cm (1)

59. The shape below has a perimeter of 12 cm and area of 5 cm².

Draw a shape on the dotted paper which has

(i) perimeter 12 cm, area 9 cm²

(ii) perimeter 12 cm, area 8 cm².

(6)

January 93 Q15

60. Sketch two different rectangles whose perimeters are each 32 cm.
Label the lengths of each side clearly.

(6)

November 90 Q20

61. What is the perimeter of a square with sides of 20 cm?

Answer: .... cm   (2)

January 92 Q2

62. A square has a perimeter of 32 cm. What is its area?

Answer: .... cm²   (3)

November 91 Q8

63. What is the perimeter of a square lawn with sides of 18 m?

Answer: .... m   (2)

January 91 Q10

64. (i) Work out the total area of each of these courts.

  (The drawings are not drawn to the same scale.)

  tennis: 24 m × 11 m

  netball: 30 m × 15 m

  volleyball: 18 m × 9 m

Answer: tennis .... m²   netball .... m²   volleyball .... m²   (6)

(ii) If one side of a badminton court is 6 m and the surface area is 78 m², what is the length of the other side?

Answer: .... m   (2)

January 91 Q19

65. Here is the plan of a lawn for a garden of a new house:

    (*The measurements are in metres.*)

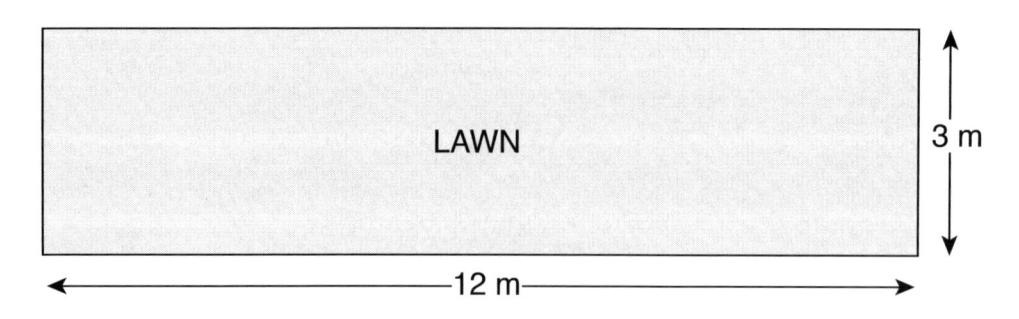

    (i) What is the perimeter of the rectangular lawn?

    Answer: .... m   (2)

    (ii) What is the area of the lawn?

    Answer: .... m²   (2)

    (iii) Another lawn, with the same area, is square.
    What is the length of each side of this lawn?

    Answer: .... m   (2)

    January 93 Q11

66. A farmer is renewing the fencing round a rectangular field 35 metres long and 29 metres wide.

    The field has one gateway three metres wide.

    What length of fencing will he require?

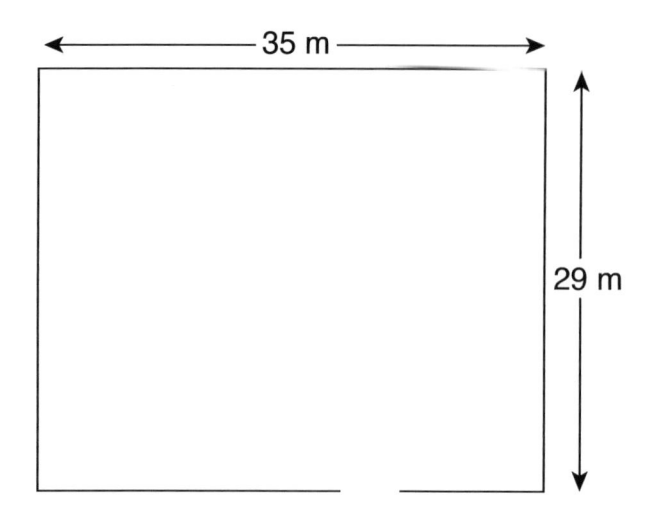

    Answer: .... m   (4)

    February 94 Q9

67. (i) This diagram represents an L-shaped room.

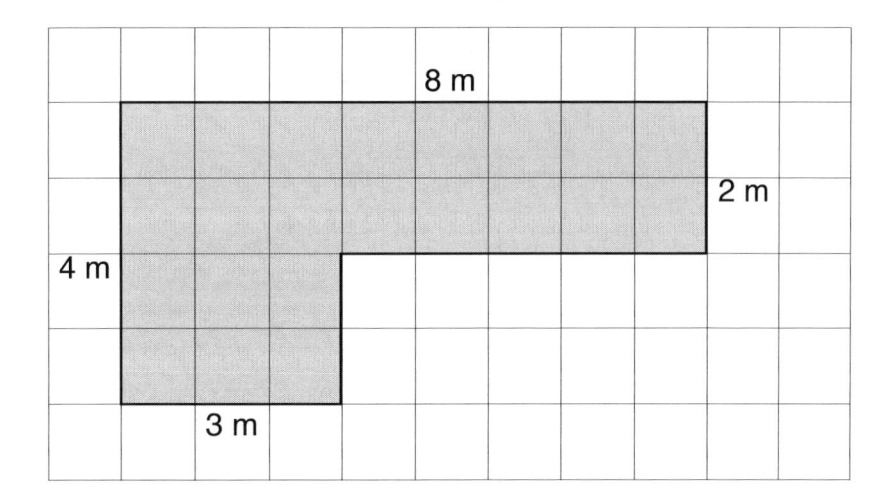

(a) Calculate the perimeter of the room.

Answer: .... m   (2)

(b) Calculate the area of the room.

Answer: .... m²   (3)

(ii) The length of a rectangle is 2 cm more than its width.
Calculate the perimeter of the rectangle when the width is 8 cm.

Answer: .... cm   (3)

(iii) John uses a piece of string to measure the perimeter of shapes.
It fits exactly round a rectangle 10 cm by 8 cm.
He then fits it exactly round a square.
How long is one side of the square?

Answer: .... cm   (3)

November 98 Q7

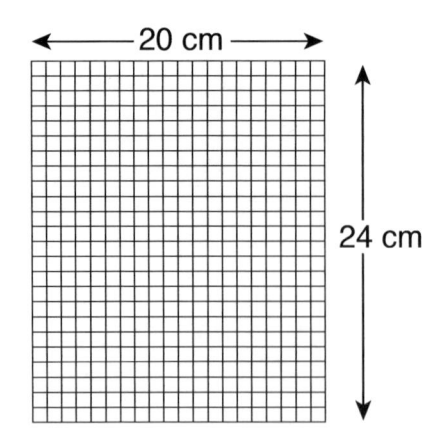

68. The front of Peter's maths textbook is drawn below.

    (i) What is the area of the front cover?

    Answer: .... cm² (2)

    The front of his maths notebook is drawn below.

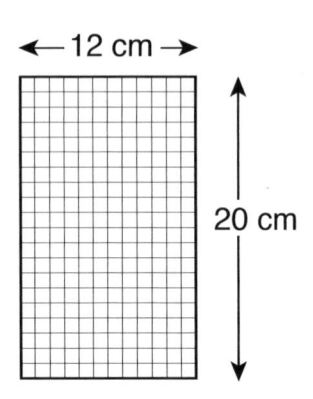

    (ii) What is the area of the front cover of this book?

    Answer: .... cm² (2)

    (iii) What do you notice about the areas of the front covers of these two books?

    Answer: ....

    ....

    .... (2)

January 95 Q17

69. An artist paints a picture on a canvas.

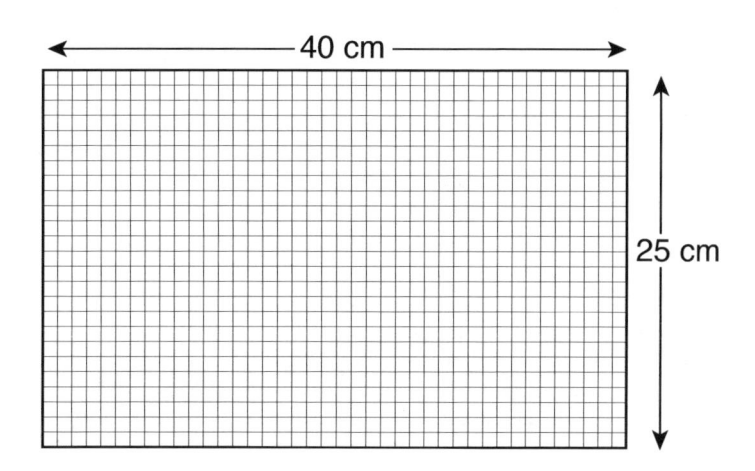

    It measures 25 cm by 40 cm.

    (i) What is the area of the picture?

    Answer: .... cm² (2)

    The picture is then framed.

    The final measurements of the framed picture are shown on the diagram.

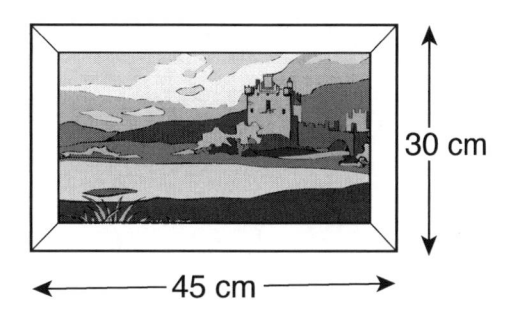

    (ii) What is the perimeter of the framed picture?

    Answer: .... cm (2)

    (iii) Write this measurement in metres.

    Answer: .... m (1)

    (iv) If I buy this length of wood at £2.30 per metre, how much will it cost for the wood to frame the picture?

    Answer: £ .... (3)

November 94 Q11

70. The plan shows a field.

    It is drawn to a scale of 1 cm to 2000 cm.

    [Rectangle ABCD shown, with A top-left, B top-right, C bottom-right, D bottom-left]

    (i) What does 1 cm represent on the plan?
    Give your answer in metres.

    Answer: .... m   (1)

    (ii) Measure the lengths of *AB* and *BC* on the plan.

    Answer: *AB* = ...   cm

    BC = ... cm
    (2)

    (iii) What lengths, in metres, do these represent?

    Answer: *AB* = ...   m

    BC = ... m
    (2)

    (iv) What is the area of the field in square metres?

    Answer: .... m²   (2)

71. A rectangular piece of paper is cut into two equal triangles.
    What is the area of one of these triangles?

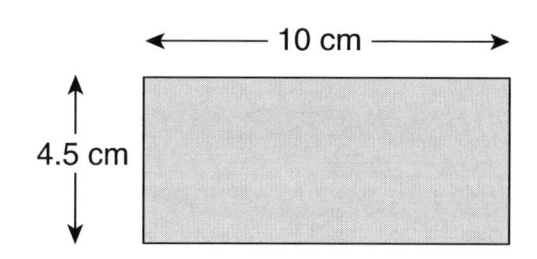

    ←——— 10 cm ———→
    ↕ 4.5 cm

    Answer: .... cm² (3)

    February 94 Q7

72. (i) What is the perimeter of a square flooring tile the sides of which are 300 mm?

    Answer: .... mm (3)

    (ii) The kitchen floor is rectangular.
    Two sides are each of length 5 metres.
    The area of the floor is 16.5 m².
    What length is each of the other two sides?

    Answer: .... m (4)

    January 90 Q14

73.

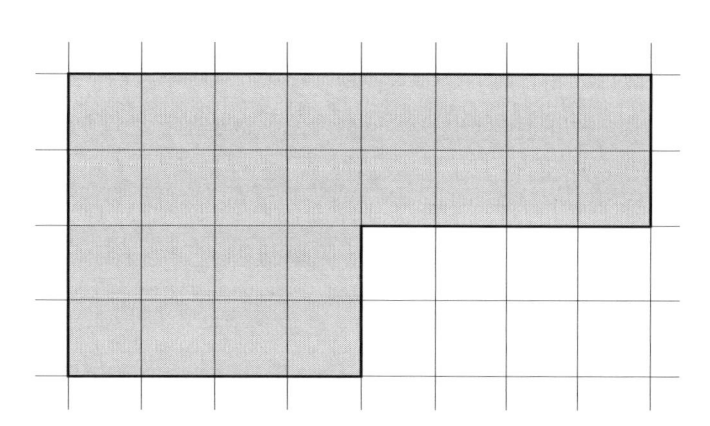

    (i) What is the perimeter of this shape?

    Answer: .... cm (2)

    (ii) What is the area of the shape?

    Answer: .... cm² (2)

77

74. Here is a plan of a classroom:

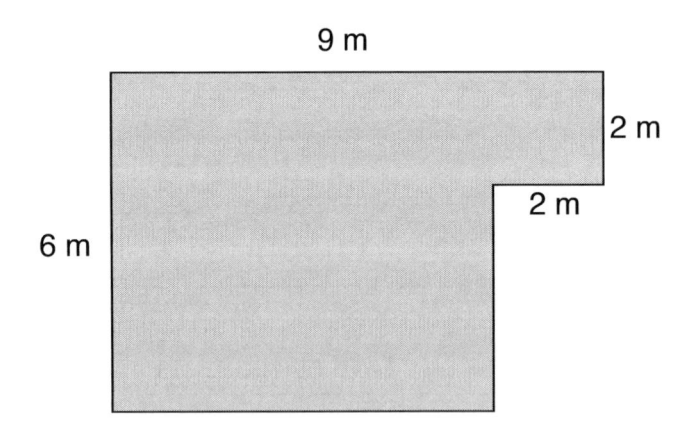

9 m
2 m
2 m
6 m

The whole floor is to be covered in carpet.

(i) What is the area of the floor?

Answer: .... m² (3)

The school orders 54 square metres of carpet.

(ii) What will be the cost of this carpet if the price is £9 per square metre?

Answer: £ .... (2)

Fixing strip is put round the edge of the floor before the carpet is laid.

(iii) What length of strip is needed?

Answer: .... m (3)

November 92 Q18

75. These drawings show cuboids made of centimetre cubes.

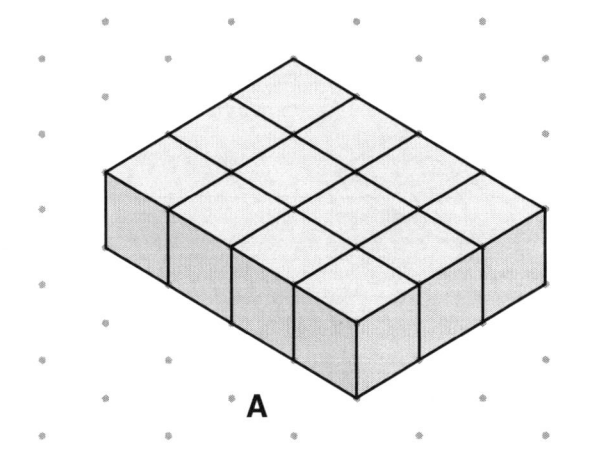

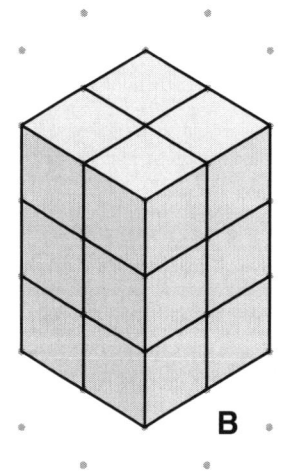

How many cubes are needed to build these cuboids?

Answer: **A** .... cubes   (1)

Answer: **B** .... cubes   (2)

76.

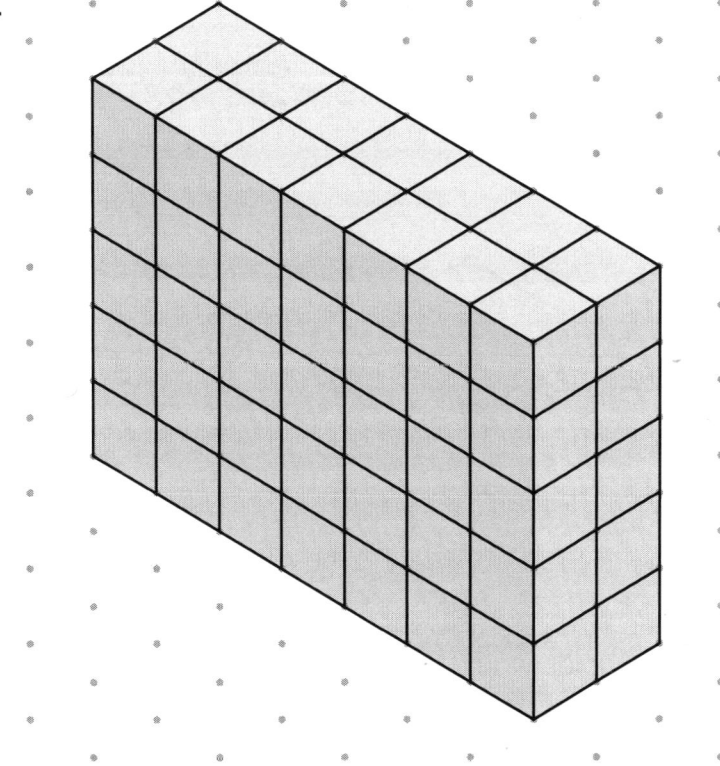

How many small cubes have been used to make this cuboid?

Answer: .... cubes   (2)

77. This cuboid is made of centimetre cubes:

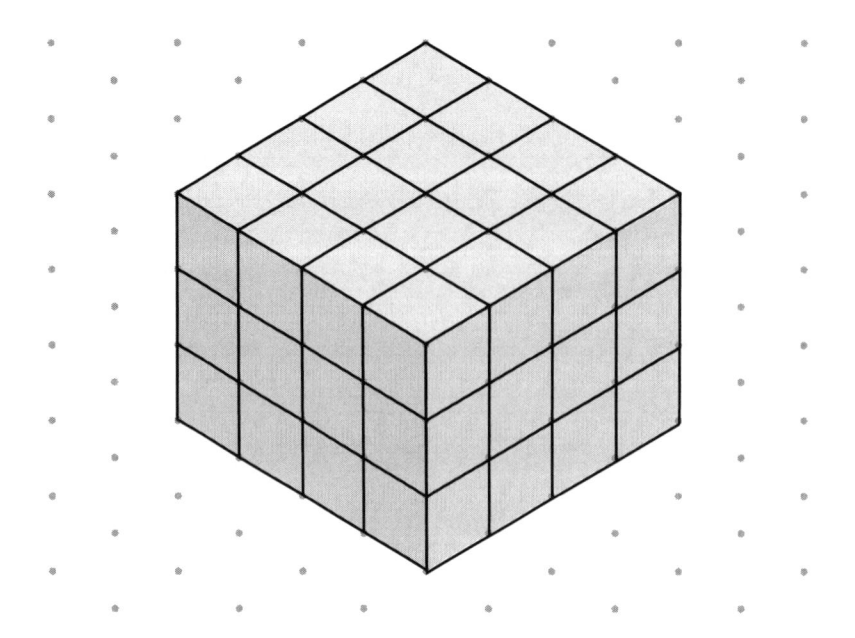

(i) What is the volume of the cuboid?

Answer: .... cm³ (3)

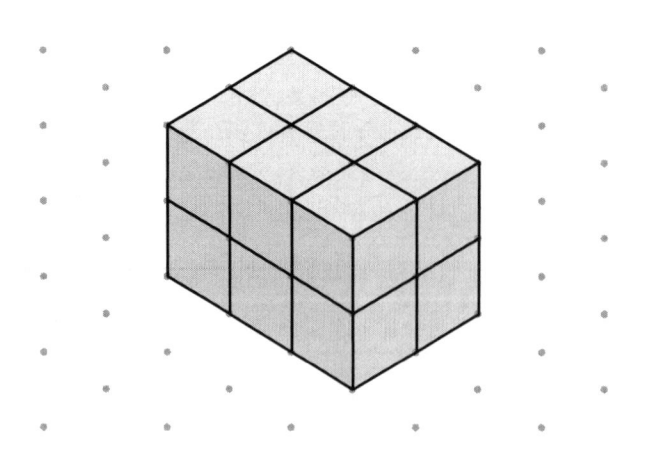

(ii) How many of these smaller cuboids would be required to build the larger one?

Answer: .... cuboids (2)

(iii) On the grid draw another cuboid with the same volume as the smaller one.

(3)

November 95 Q17

78. How many centimetre cubes will fit into a box measuring 10 cm by 7 cm by 6 cm?

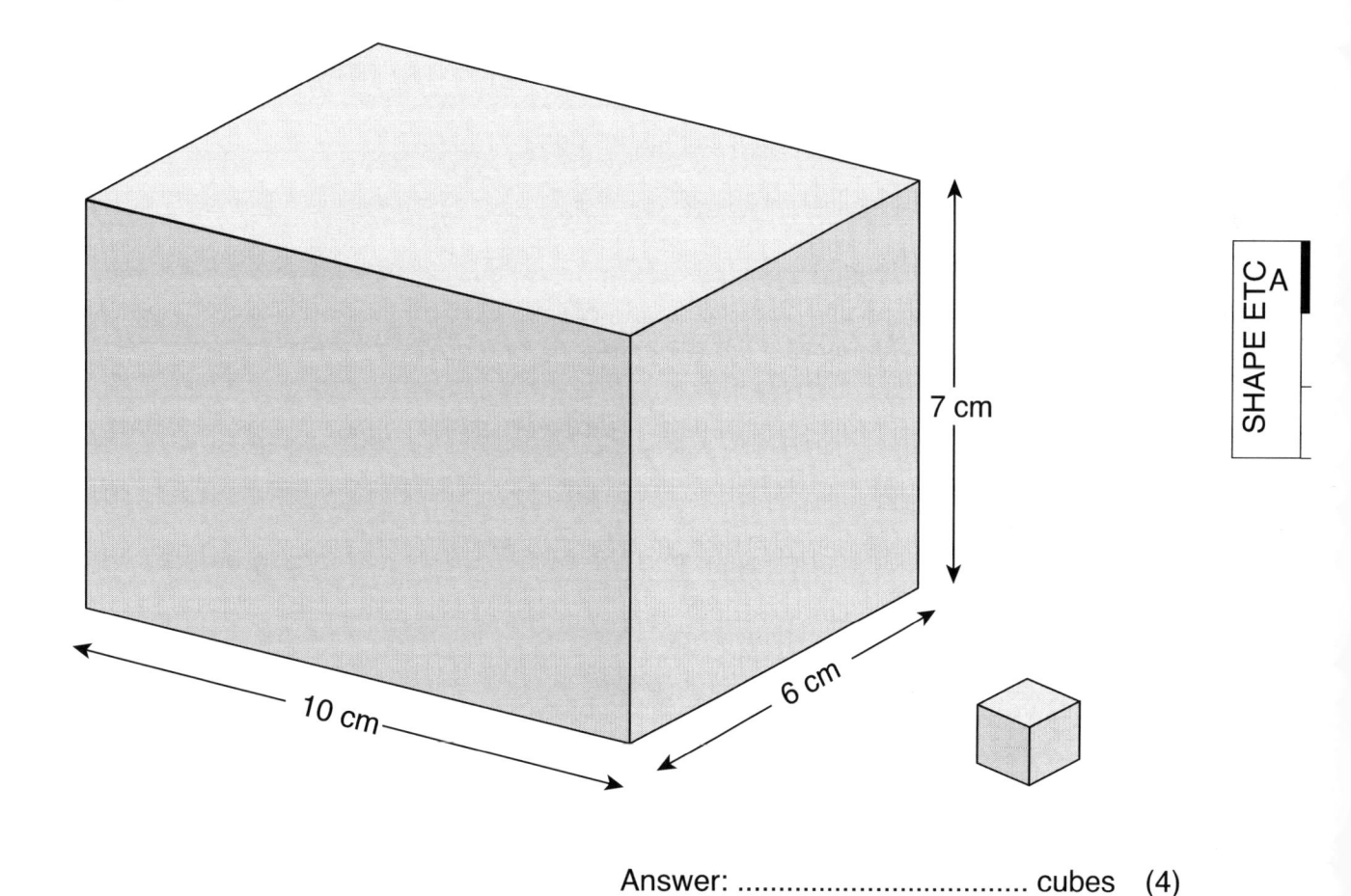

Answer: .... cubes (4)

January 93 Q8

79.

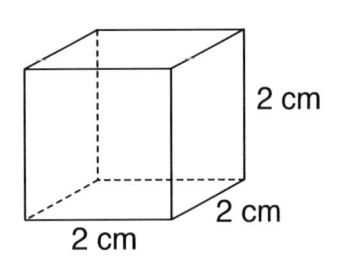

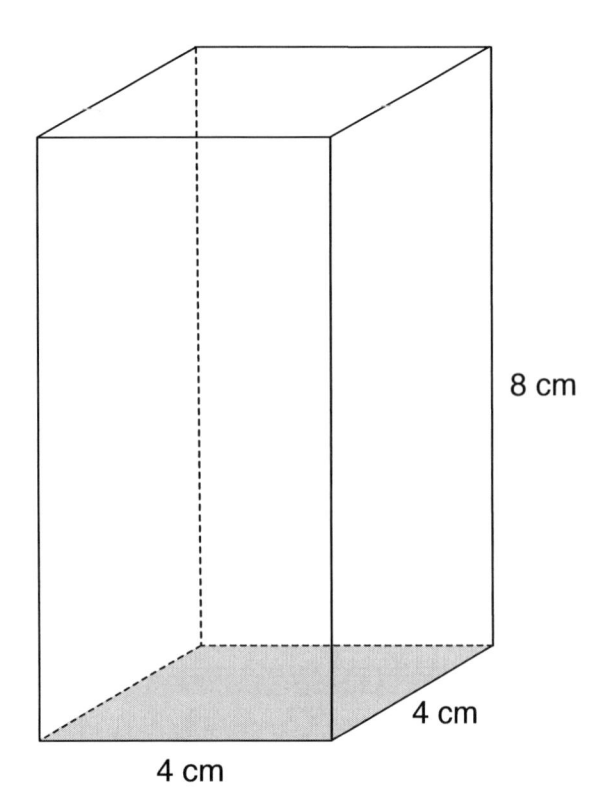

(i) How many small cubes will be needed to cover the shaded base of the large box?

Answer: .... (2)

(ii) How many of these cubes will fill the box?

Answer: .... (2)

November 98 Q8

80. (i) What is the volume of a cube with edges of 6 cm?

Answer: .... cm³ (2)

Eight of these cubes, each with an edge of 1 cm, are to be packed in a box.

One such box is 1 cm × 1 cm × 8 cm.

(ii) Give the dimensions of other possible boxes which will hold only eight cubes.

Answer: .... (4)

January 92 Q17(b),(c)

81. (i) Arrange the letters of these solids in order of **increasing** volume.

A

B

C

D

Answer: .... (3)

(ii) How many small cubes would be needed to make **all** the solids **A**, **B**, **C** and **D**?

Answer: .... (2)

82. This drawing shows the clock when Katie arrives at school.

(i) What is the time?

Answer: .... am (2)

(ii) What is this when written as a 24-hour time?

Answer: .... (1)

Assembly starts at 08:45

(iii) How long is there before assembly starts?

Answer: .... minutes (2)

83. John's analogue watch shows this time.

Show the same time on Jane's digital watch.

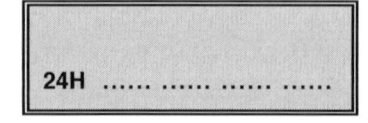

24H ....

(2)

84. Write 7:29 pm as a time on the 24-hour clock.

Answer: .... (1)

November 90 Q6

85. Mary watched *Noel's House Party*, which started at 18:05 and ended at 18:55

    (i) How long did it last?

    Answer: .... minutes   (1)

    She recorded this on a new three-hour video tape.

    (ii) How many minutes were on this tape?

    Answer: .... minutes   (1)

    (iii) What fraction of the tape did she use?

    Answer: ....   (1)

    November 94 Q7

86. Mark left home at 08:35 and arrived at school at 09:08
    How long did it take him to walk to school?

    Answer: .... minutes   (2)

    February 94 Q5

87. How long is Robert's journey to school if he leaves home at 07:55 and arrives at school at 08:20?

    Answer: .... minutes   (2)

    January 90 Q10

88. Jane leaves home at 4:35 pm and walks to her friend's house.
    If she arrives at 5:07 pm how long does the walk take her?

    Answer: .... minutes   (2)

    November 90 Q18

85

89. This picture shows the school clock.
    It is three minutes slow.

    The bell goes at 15:05
    How long is there until the bell?

    Answer: .... minutes (2)

90. This is the school timetable:
    Each lesson lasts for 35 minutes.
    Assembly and break each last for 20 minutes.

	starts	ends
assembly	....	09:15
lesson 1	09:15	09:50
lesson 2	09:50	....
break	....	....
lesson 3	....	....
lesson 4	....	....

    (5)

    (i) Complete the school timetable.

    Angela's class has Art for lessons 1 and 2
    (ii) How long does she spend at Art?

    Answer: .... minutes (2)

    Jane leaves home at 08:10
    She arrives at school at 08:45
    (iii) How long does her journey take?

    Answer: .... minutes (1)

November 92 Q12

91. Here is John's Monday morning timetable:

09:00 to 09:15	Assembly
09:15 to 09:50	Maths
09:50 to	Maths
.... to	Break
.... to	English
.... to	English
.... to	History
.... to 13:35	Lunch break

Each lesson lasts 35 minutes, break is 15 minutes and lunch break lasts 1 hour and 10 minutes.

(i) Complete the timetable. (6)

During the afternoon there are three 35-minute lessons.

(ii) At what time does John finish school?

Answer: .... (3)

November 95 Q12

92. Sam has to catch a bus to go to Kim's house which is in Cliffview.

    Here is part of the bus timetable:

Kirkton	07:35	08:10	08:45
Cowgate	07:50	08:25	09:00
Berryford	08:05	08:40	09:15
Cliffview	08:15	08:50	09:25

    Sam has to go from Kirkton to Cliffview.
    All the buses take the same time for the journey.

    (i) How long does Sam's bus journey take?

    Answer: .... minutes   (2)

    Kim would like Sam to arrive in Cliffview just before 9 o'clock.

    (ii) At what time will Sam's bus arrive at his destination?

    Answer: .... (1)

    (iii) At what time does Sam's bus leave Kirkton?

    Answer: .... (1)

    Sam goes home on a bus from Cliffview to Kirkton.
    This bus takes the same time for the journey as the morning bus.
    Sam leaves Cliffview at 16:45

    (iv) At what time should he get to Kirkton?

    Answer: .... (2)

November 96 Q17

93. Use these Sunday television timetables to answer the questions below.

CHANNEL A

6.30 ITN News 6.35 LWT News
6.40 Highway The team makes second visit to Chelmsford.
7.15 The Two of Us* Nicholas Lyndhurst and Janet Dibley star in a newly-weds sitcom.
7.45 Denis Norden's 21 Years of Laughter Clips show dozens of funny turns in this personal selection from LWT's comedy archives (R).
8.45 ITN News, Weather 9.00 LWT Weather
9.05 Agatha Christie's Poirot* After the last two excursions into the world of spies and terrorists, where he looked a little out of place, Poirot returns to the high society territory that suits him best. When some amusing tittle-tattle about diamonds belonging to Lady Yardley and the film star Marie Marvelle turns into something more serious, it is Poirot (David Suchet) who proves to be the girls' best friend. Last in the series.
10.05 The Craig Ferguson Show This features the Glaswegian motormouth comedian in his own show.

CHANNEL B

6.25 News and Weather
6.40 Songs of Praise* This week's programme is from the Welsh border town of Abergavenny, which is celebrating its 900th anniversary.
7.15 Don't Wait Up* Tony Britton and Nigel Havers star as the father and son medics; Tom seeks ways of boosting his NHS salary, while his father toadies for a knighthood.
7.45 Bergerac* John Nettles, Terence Alexander and Gary Bond star in another episode. Jim spends a day at the races studying the form of a gang of counterfeiters, only to become involved with the seedier side of showbiz.
8.40 Mastermind Magnus Magnusson poses questions on Arthur Ransome, the geography of continental USA, Thomas Gainsborough, and the life and operas of Verdi.
9.10 That's Life!
9.55 News and Weather

(i) Which channel has a News and Weather report before 7 o'clock?

Answer: .... (1)

(ii) How many minutes does *Bergerac* last?

Answer: .... minutes (2)

(iii) How long is the programme about a visit to Chelmsford?

Answer: .... minutes (2)

(iv) Before going out, you set a three-hour video tape to record from the beginning of *Don't Wait Up* (Channel B) to the end of *That's Life!*.

How many minutes of the tape will be left?

Answer: .... minutes (3)

January 92 Q14

94. A train left Uckfield at 09:40 and arrived in London at 11:17
    How long did the journey take?

    Answer: .... (2)

    November 91 Q7

95. Mrs Concor left Heathrow Airport at 09:50 and arrived in Glasgow at 11:05
    How long was the flight?

    Answer: .... (2)

    January 91 Q5

96. Mrs Smith visits London.
    Her train leaves Oxford at 09:08 and arrives in London at 10:10
    She takes 25 minutes to drive to Oxford station, and 10 minutes to park her car.
    She allows 15 minutes to buy her ticket.

    (i) At what time does she leave home in the morning?

    Answer: .... (3)

    She returns on a train leaving London at 17:45

    (ii) How much time does she spend in London?

    Answer: .... hours .... minutes (2)

    Her train journey back to Oxford takes the same time as the morning train.

    (iii) At what time does she arrive in Oxford?

    Answer: .... (3)

    November 93 Q17

97. John ran a race in 59.4 seconds and Mary ran the same race in 48.6 seconds.

   (i) Who won the race?

   Answer: .... (1)

   (ii) How much faster was the winner?

   Answer: .... seconds (2)

   January 97 Q5

98. It took Jennifer 2 hours 30 minutes to cycle 40 kilometres.

   (i) How far did she cycle in half an hour?

   Answer: .... km (2)

   (ii) How far did she cycle in one hour?

   Answer: .... km (1)

   January 98 Q4

99. The lights from two lighthouses flash at exactly the same instant.
    The lights flash at intervals of 20 seconds and 25 seconds respectively.
    After how many seconds will they flash again at the same time?

   Answer: .... seconds (4)

   November 91 Q17

100. Mr Winton travels from Oxford to London.

   His train leaves at 07:45 and arrives at 09:00

   (i) How long does his train journey take?

   Answer: .... (2)

   He returns on a train which leaves London at 17:55
   It takes 1 hour 10 minutes.

   (ii) At what time does he get to Oxford?

   Answer: .... (2)

   November 97 Q15

101. Here are the journey times for some children:

name	distance travelled	time taken
Susan	20 km	6 hours
Jenny	2000 km	2.5 hours
John	40 km	5 hours
Ian	650 km	8 hours

If all the journeys were made without long delays, how do you think each of these children travelled? You can choose from walking, cycling, motoring or flying (in an aeroplane).

   Answer: Susan ....

   Jenny ....

   John ....

   Ian .... (4)

   January 96 Q15

102. John was born on 31 August 1985.

His brother Sam was born on 31 January 1987.

(i) Who is older?

Answer: .... (1)

(ii) By how many months is he older?

Answer: .... months (2)

January 96 Q3

103. Kate's holiday is from 26 April to 17 May inclusive.

How many days' holiday does she have?

Answer: .... days (2)

January 90 Q2

104. John is 15 years old today.

What is the date of his birth?

Answer: .... (2)

November 90 Q8

105. Laura was taken into hospital on 23 October.

She spent ten nights in hospital before returning home.

On which date did she leave hospital?

Answer: .... (2)

106. Many historians believe that Jesus Christ was born in the year 4 BC!

If this is correct, in which year did he have his twelfth birthday?

(Note: there was no year zero. 1 BC was followed by AD 1!)

Answer: AD .... (2)

107. These drawings show the times at which Laura goes to bed and gets up in the morning during the holidays.

(i) Write these times as 12-hour times.

Answer: goes to bed .... (1)

gets up .... (1)

(ii) Write these times as 24-hour times.

Answer: goes to bed .... (1)

gets up .... (1)

(iii) For how long is Laura in bed?

Answer: .... hours .... minutes (2)

(iv) For how long is Laura 'up' before she goes to bed again the next evening?

Answer: .... hours .... minutes (2)

108. Grandma has asked Alice's family to lunch and would like them to arrive at 12:00

They allow one and a half hours for the journey and ten minutes to buy petrol.

(i) At what time should they leave home?

Answer: .... (2)

The family leave Grandma's house at 16:40

Their journey home takes one hour and thirty-five minutes.

(ii) At what time do they get home?

Answer: .... (2)

January 95 Q6

109. Emma leaves home at 10:45 on Wednesday 12 February and returns at 15:30 on Friday 14 February, after staying with her friend Petra.

For how long was Emma away from home?

Answer: .... hours .... minutes (3)

110. The length of Sarah's puppy has increased from 30 cm to 45 cm in the months of June and July.

   (i) What is the increase in length?

   Answer: .... cm (1)

   (ii) Explain why it is difficult to measure the length of a puppy.

   Answer: ....

   .... (2)

   (iii) On the sketch below, draw a suitable line representing the growth of Sarah's puppy.

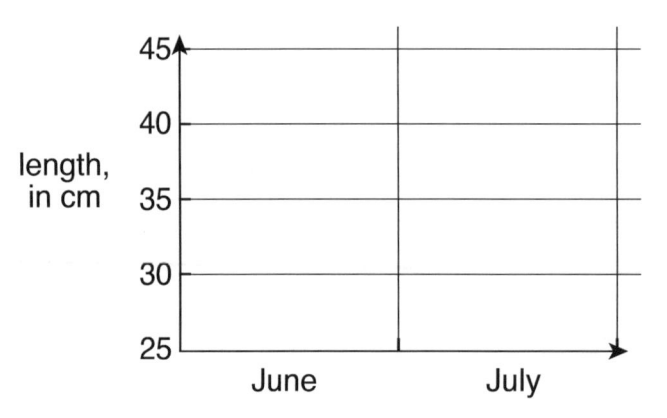

   (2)

   Sarah's father tells her that measures, such as the length of a puppy, are continuous.

   (iv) Explain what that means.

   Answer: ....

   .... (2)

111. This drawing of a minnow is approximately nine cm long.

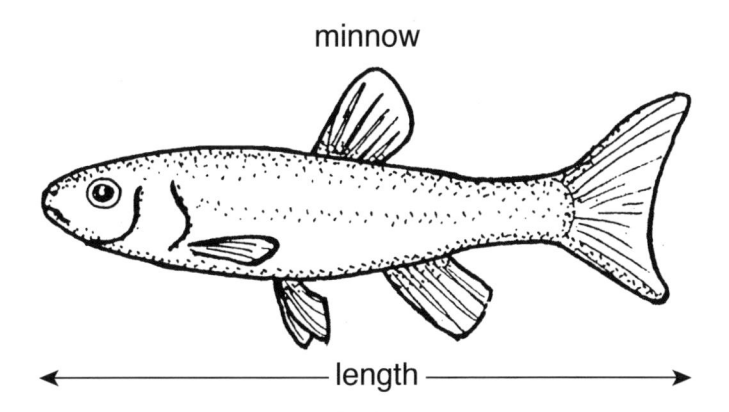

minnow

← length →

This line segment is nine cm long.

⊢─────────────────────────────────────⊣

(i) Explain why the measurement of the line segment is really only approximate.

Answer: ....

.... (2)

(ii) Measure, as accurately as you can, the lengths of these drawings of animals.

(a) slug

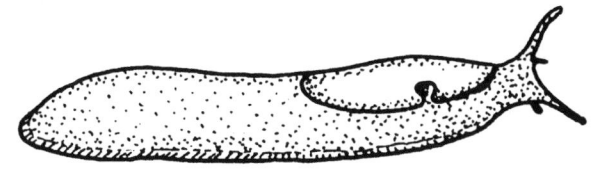

Answer: .... cm (1)

(b) crayfish

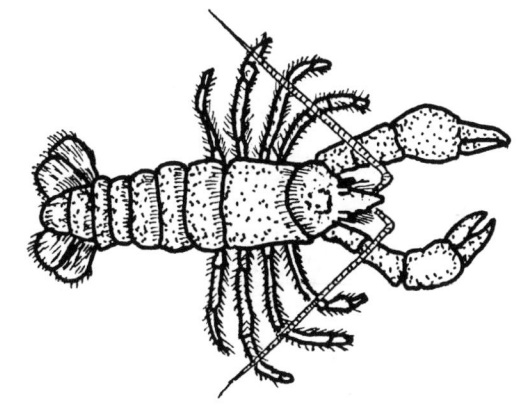

Answer: .... cm (1)

112. These drawings show three identical glass jars.

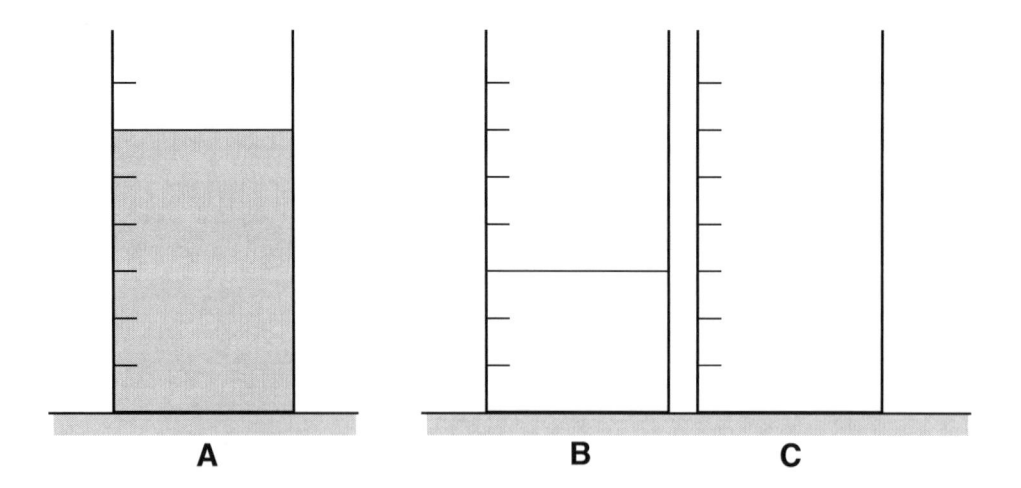

Some of the water from jar **A** is poured into jar **B** as shown.

The rest of the water in jar **A** is poured into jar **C**.

(i) Complete the picture by drawing the level of the water in jar **C**. (2)

(ii) Explain why doing this in practice is not as straightforward as it would seem in part (i).

Answer: ....

.... (2)

113. (i) A lump of Plasticine with mass 500 grams (grammes) is used to make a model of mass 140 grams.

What mass of Plasticine is left over?

Answer: .... grams (1)

(ii) Explain why a real-life situation is not as straightforward as it would seem in part (i).

Answer: ....

.... (2)

B Shape: knowing the properties of 2-D and 3-D shapes, including symmetry

1. Study these shapes.

   (i) Write **S** for a solid shape and **P** for a plane shape.

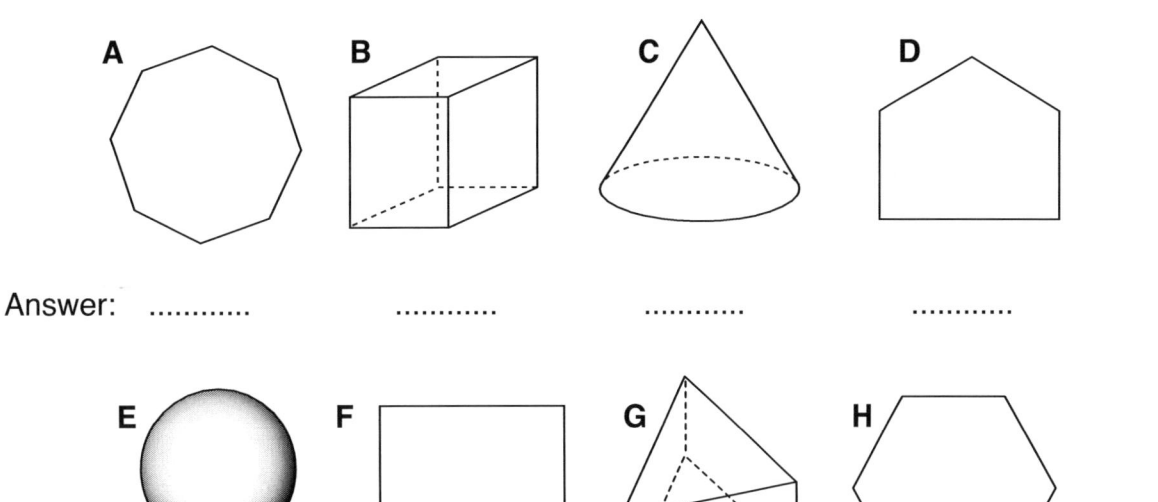

   A   **B**   **C**   **D**

   Answer: ....

   E   **F**   **G**   **H**

   Answer: ....   (4)

   (ii) Name shapes **A**, **C**, **E** and **G**.

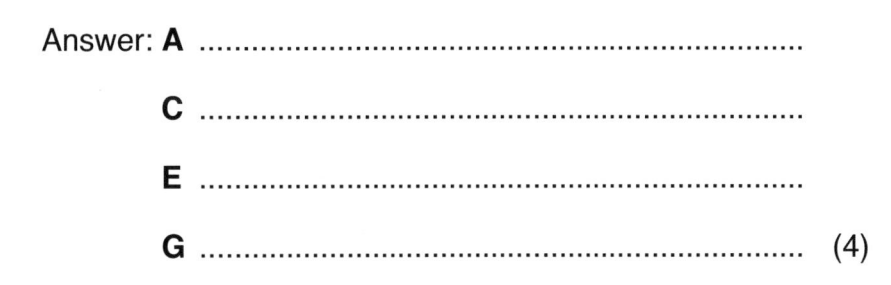

   Answer: **A** ....

   C ....

   E ....

   G ....   (4)

2. Name this solid.

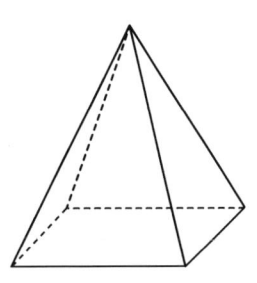

   Answer: ....   (2)

   November 92 Q6

3. Here is a list of the names of some shapes:

    square   cube   kite   rectangle

    triangle   circle   cylinder   pyramid

   (i) Using words from the list above, write down the names of these shapes.

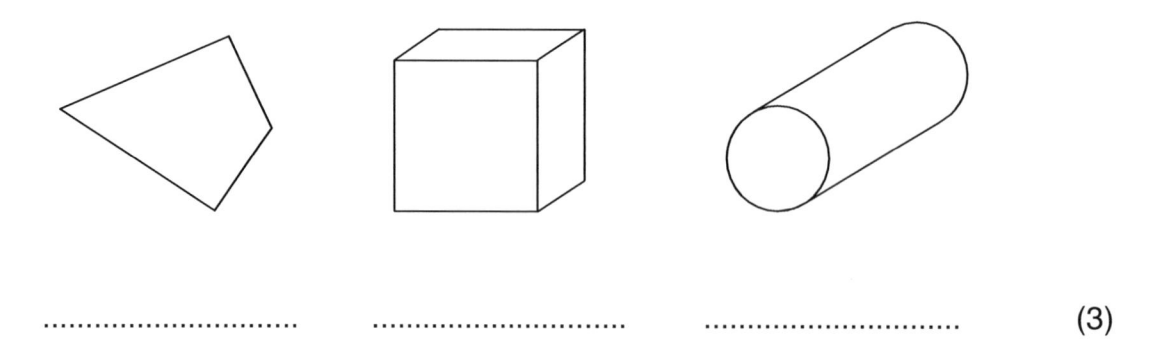

   ....   (3)

   (ii) Draw an isosceles triangle on the grid below.

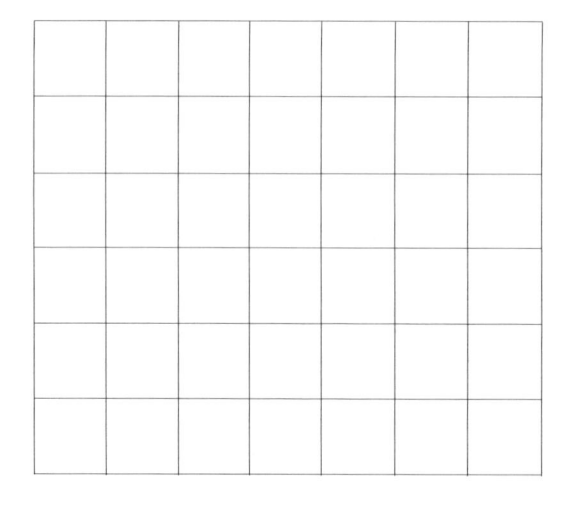

   (2)

   November 98 Q5(b)

4. How many sides has a pentagon?

   Answer: .... sides   (1)

   November 90 Q2

5. Name two shapes which are quadrilaterals.

   Answer: .... and ....   (2)

   January 92 Q8

6. How many sides of equal length has a rhombus?

   Answer: .... sides   (1)

   November 90 Q5

7. Complete the shape table below using these names:

   heptagon   quadrilateral   octagon   pentagon   hexagon

number of sides	name of polygon
3	triangle

   (5)

   January 91 Q12

8. Study shapes **A**, **B** and **C**.

   (i) What do **A** and **B** have in common?

   Answer: ....
   .... (2)

   (ii) What do **B** and **C** have in common?

   Answer: ....
   .... (2)

9. What is the name of this solid shape?

Answer: .... (2)

January 92 Q3

10.

(i) What sort of triangle is this?

Answer: .... (1)

(ii) Draw three lines to divide the triangle into four pieces of the same shape and size. (3)

February 94 Q15

11. Which of these shapes is a quadrilateral?

rhombus   **pentagon**   **hexagon**   **triangle**

Answer: .... (2)

January 90 Q4

B SHAPE ETC

12. Which is the odd one out in each of these groups of shapes?

(i) **square**   **hexagon**   **kite**   **circle**   **parallelogram**   **octagon**

Answer: .... because ....

.... (2)

(ii) **cube**   **cone**   **cylinder**   **trapezium**   **pyramid**   **prism**

Answer: .... because ....

.... (2)

13.

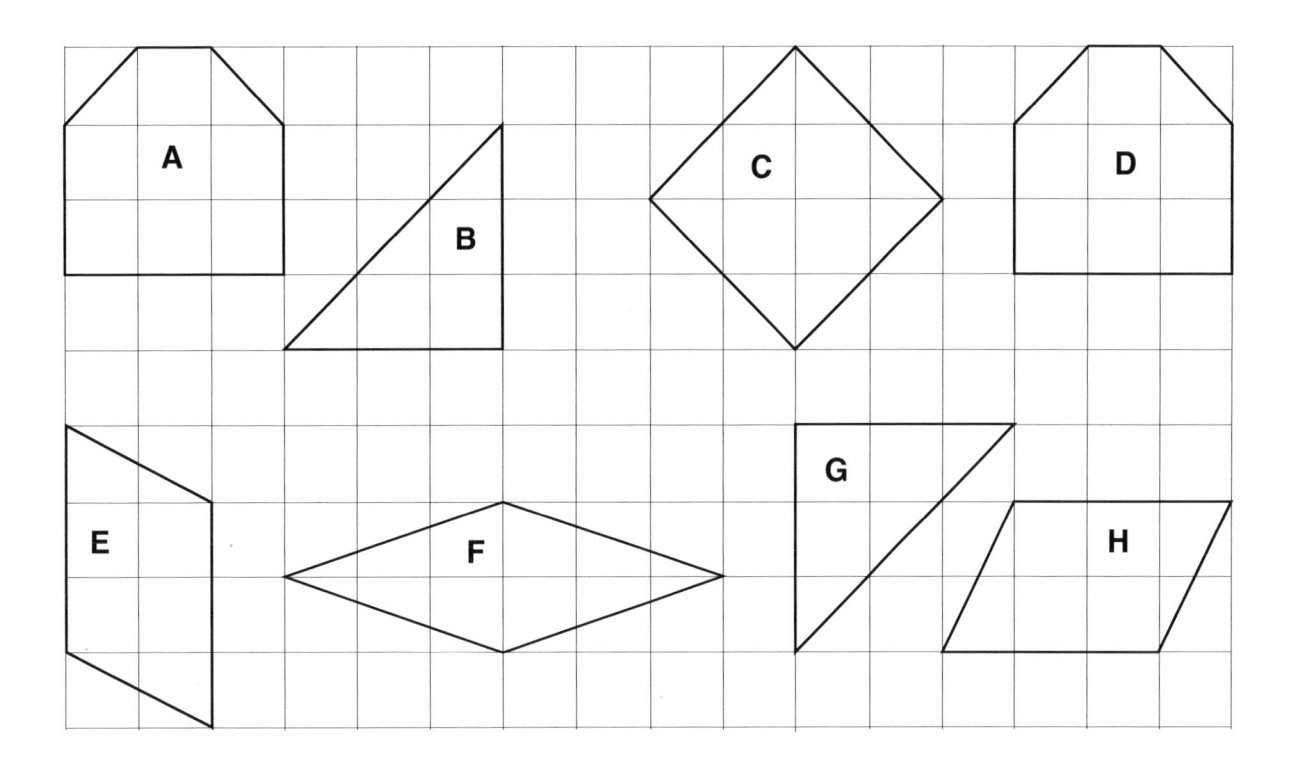

(i) Give the names of these shapes.

shape **A**   Answer: ....

shape **C**   Answer: ....

shape **F**   Answer: ....

shape **H**   Answer: ....

(4)

(ii) What sort of triangle is shape **B**?

Answer: ....

.... (2)

(iii) Fill in the missing letter to make this true:

Shape **A** and shape .... are congruent. (1)

(iv) There are two other pairs of congruent shapes.
Find one pair and fill in the missing letters.

Shape .... and shape .... are congruent. (2)

November 96 Q8

14. (i) Name these quadrilaterals.

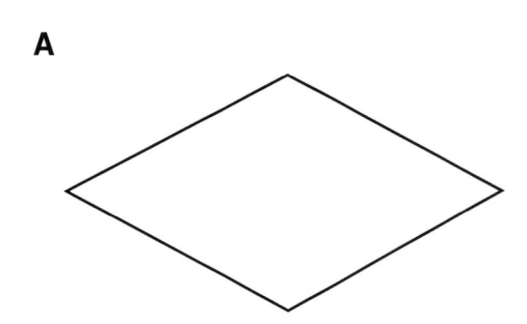

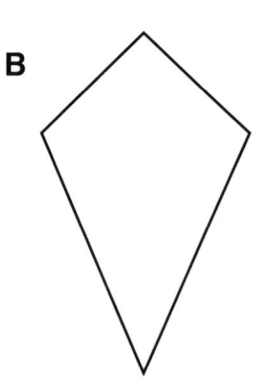

A

B

Answer: **A** .... Answer: **B** .... (2)

(ii) On each shape draw any lines of symmetry. (2)

(iii) Write the order of rotational symmetry of each of these shapes.

Answer: **A** .... Answer: **B** .... (2)

November 97 Q14

15. (i) Ben thought of a shape with three sides.
    It had one line of symmetry.
    What shape was it?

    Answer: .... (2)

(ii) Chris thought of a different shape.
    It was a shape with four sides.
    All its sides were equal in length.
    It had two lines of symmetry.
    What shape was it?

    Answer: .... (2)

January 97 Q7

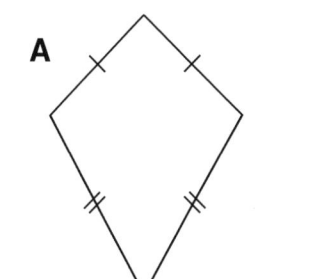

16.

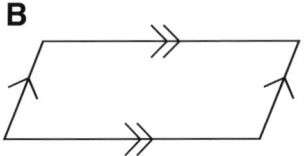

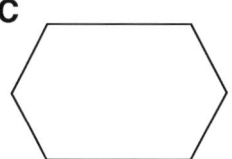

    A   B   C

   (i) Name each shape.

                                          Answer: **A** .... (1)

                                          Answer: **B** .... (1)

                                          Answer: **C** .... (1)

  (ii) (a) Which of the shapes **A**, **B** and **C** have reflective symmetry?

                                          Answer: .... (1)

      (b) Draw all the lines of symmetry on these shapes. (2)

 (iii) Which of the shapes **A**, **B** and **C** have rotational symmetry?

                                          Answer: .... (2)

January 96 Q8

17.

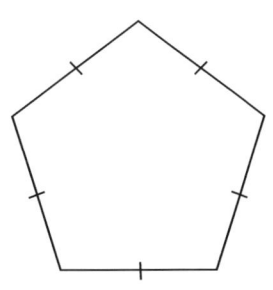

   (i) Name this regular shape.

                                          Answer: .... (1)

  (ii) Draw all its lines of symmetry. (2)

 (iii) Complete the following statement:

     This shape has rotational symmetry about its centre point of order .... (2)

Specimen 94 Q8

18. (i) Name these shapes.

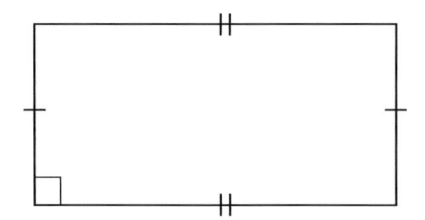

   Answer: .... Answer: .... (2)

   (ii) Draw all the lines of symmetry on these two shapes. (2)

   November 94 Q6

19.

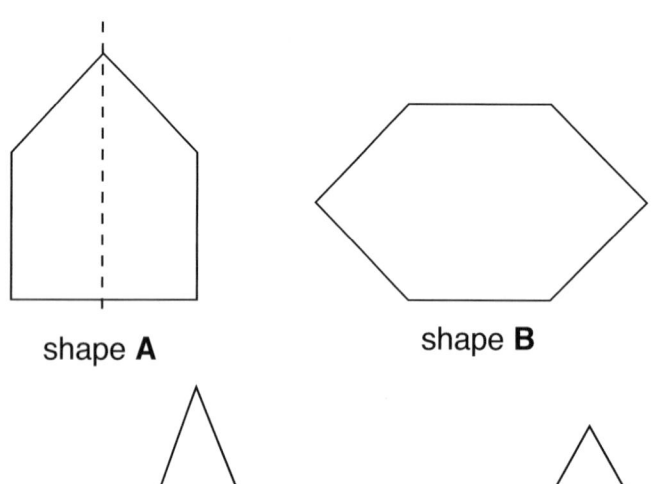

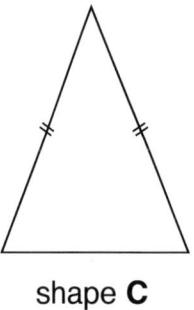

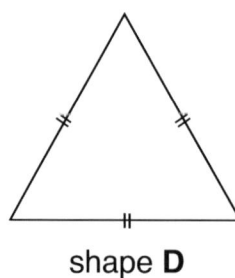

   shape **A**　　　shape **B**

   shape **C**　　　shape **D**

   (i) Name shapes **A** and **B**.

   shape **A** .... (1)

   shape **B** .... (1)

   (ii) What kind of triangle is **C**?　　Answer: .... (1)

   (iii) Shape **A** has one line of symmetry.
   Draw in all the lines of symmetry of the other shapes. (3)

   November 92 Q19

20. (i) Name this quadrilateral.

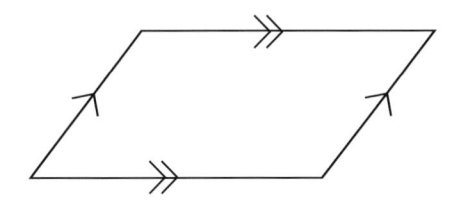

   Answer: .... (1)

   (ii) Mark on the quadrilateral

   (a) the acute angles using the letter *a* (1)

   (b) the obtuse angles using the letter *b*. (1)

   November 93 Q5

21. (i) Name these quadrilaterals.

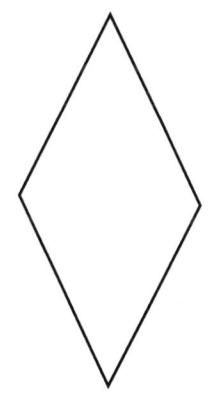

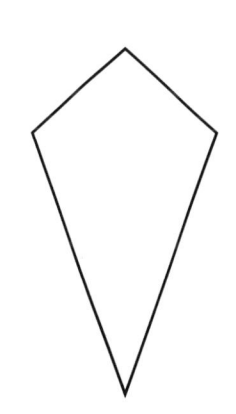

   .... (2)

   (ii) On each shape, mark with an **A** all acute angles and with an **O** all obtuse angles. (2)

   November 95 Q6

22. Draw on this shape all its lines of symmetry.

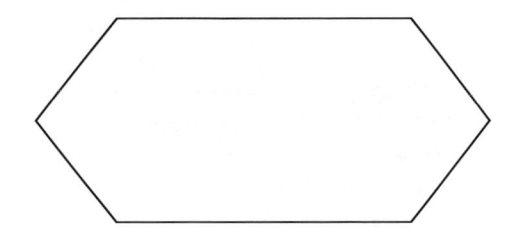

   (2)

   November 93 Q3

   107

23. Look at the following designs:

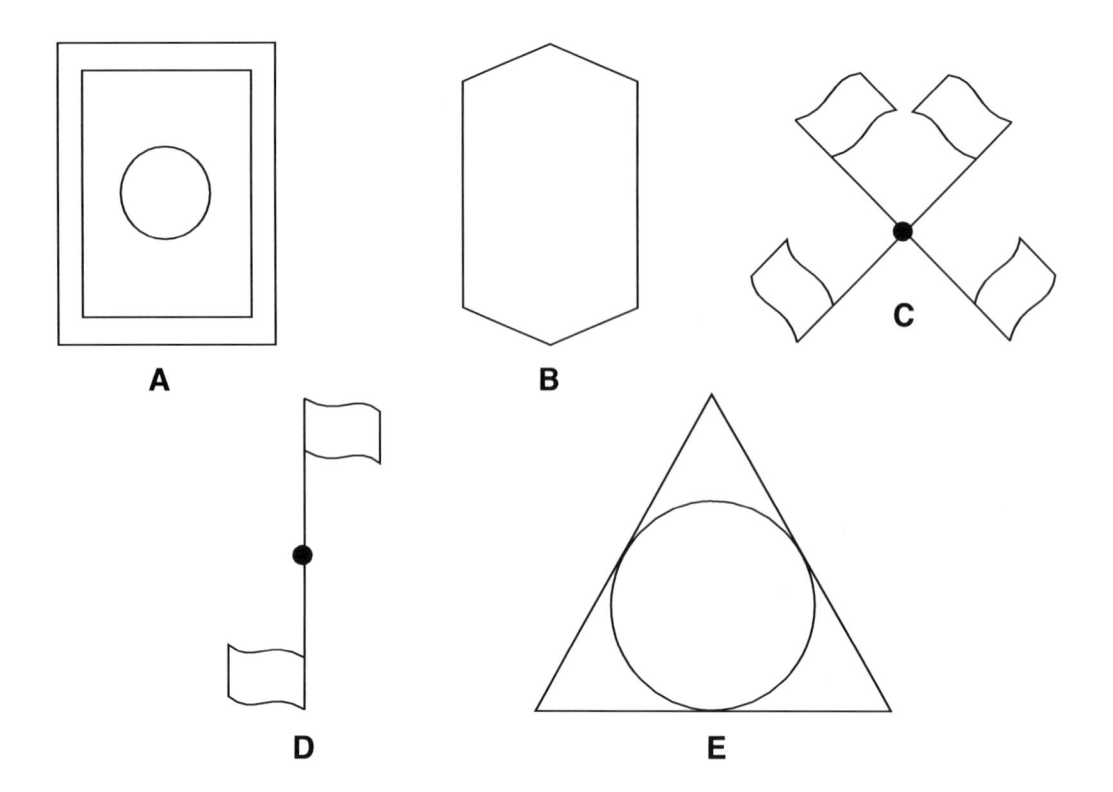

A **B** **C**

D **E**

(i) Which of the designs have line symmetry?

Answer: .... (3)

(ii) Which of the designs has rotational symmetry of order 1?

Answer: .... (1)

November 98 Q5(a)

24. (i) Draw the line of symmetry (fold line or mirror line) on this 'ink devil'.

(2)

(ii) (a) Draw all the lines of symmetry on these 'cutouts'.

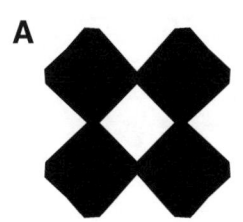

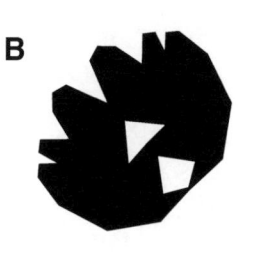

A   **B**

(3)

(b) How many times was the paper folded for cutout B?

Answer: .... (1)

25. (i) Draw in the lines of symmetry of these shapes.

All the straight lines are the same length, and the circles are all the same size.

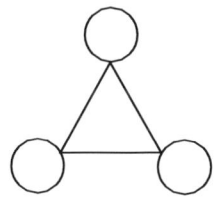

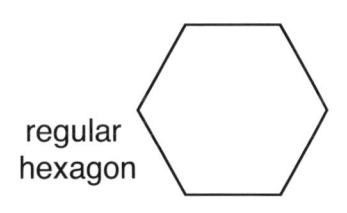

regular hexagon

(5)

(ii) The dotted lines are the lines of symmetry of a shape which is partly drawn. Sketch the complete shape on the diagram below.

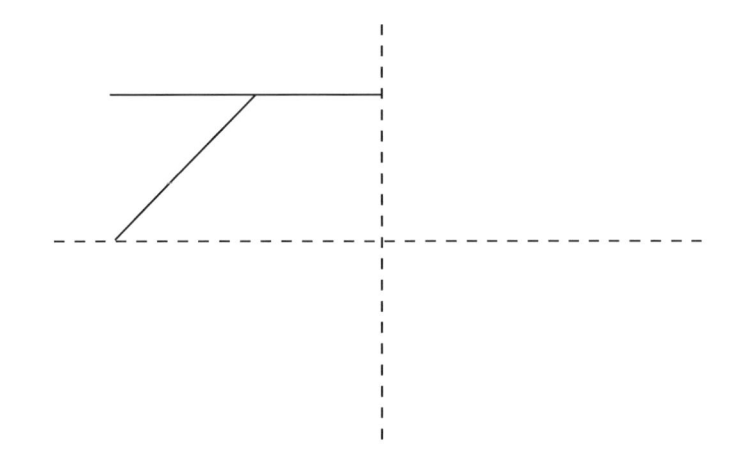

(5)

(iii) What is the name of the shape below?

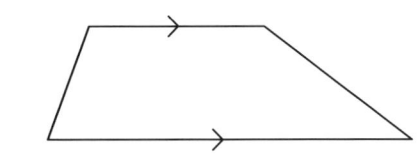

Answer: .... (2)

November 90 Q19

26. (i) On the shapes below, draw all the lines of symmetry.

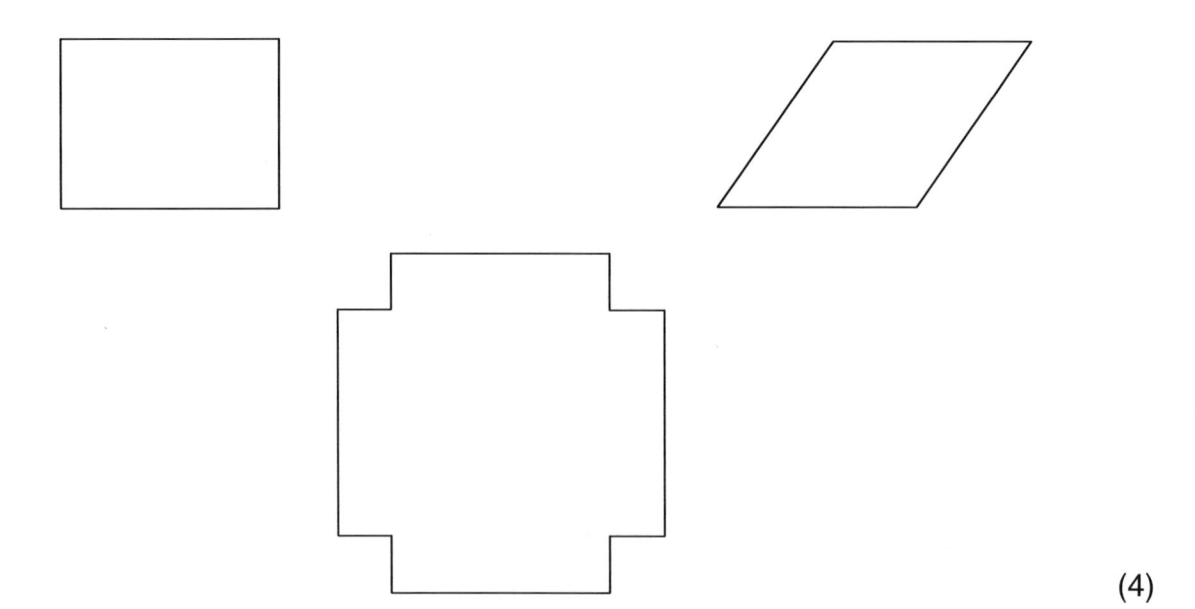

(4)

(ii) On the grid, draw three quadrilaterals which have just one line of symmetry.

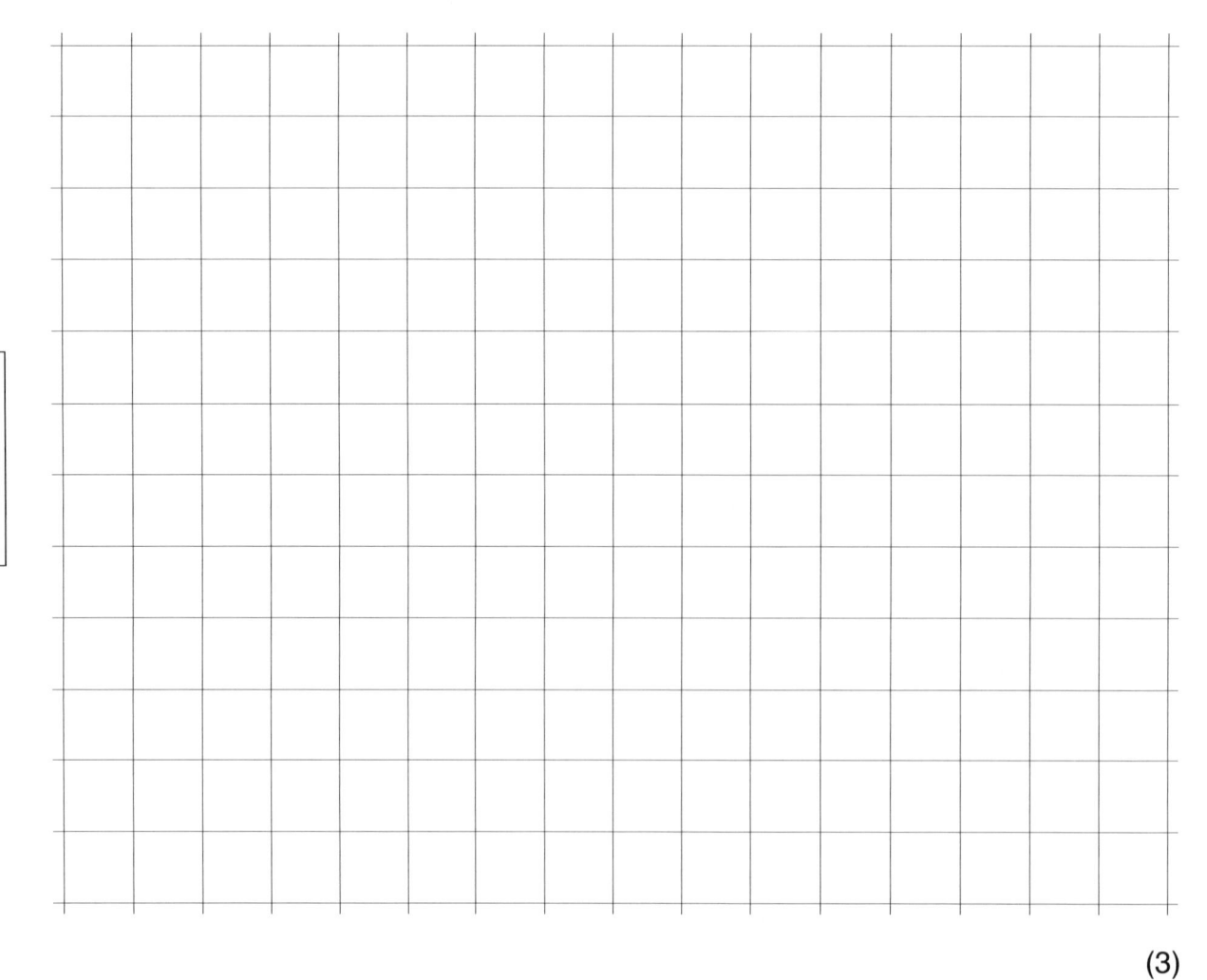

(3)

February 94 Q16

27. (i) (a) Name the set to which all of these shapes belong.

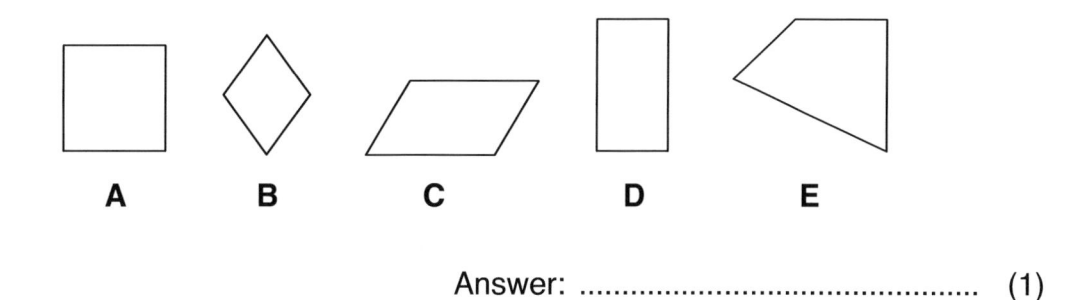

    A   B   C   D   E

    Answer: .... (1)

    (b) Complete the statements.

    Shape **B** is a ....

    Shape **C** is a ....

    Shape **A** has .... lines of symmetry.

    Shape **C** has .... lines of symmetry.

    Shape **D** has rotational symmetry of order ....

    The diagonals of shape **B** are .... to one another.

    (6)

(ii) On the grid below, draw the reflection of each of the shapes in the line *AB*.

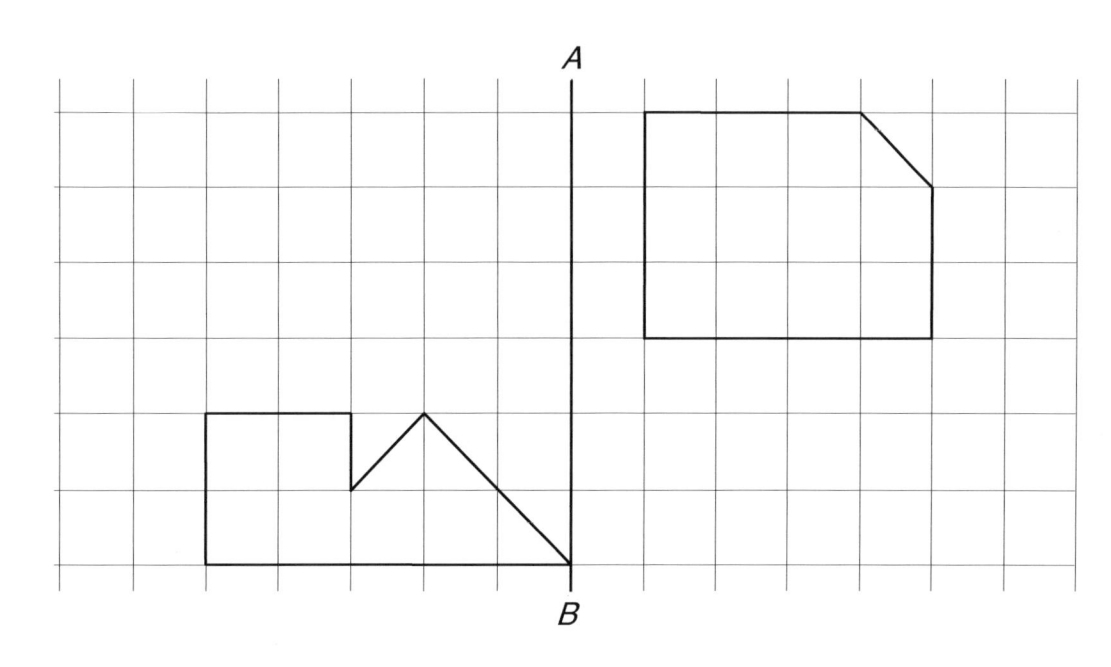

(3)

January 98 Q11

28. Draw all the lines of symmetry on these plane shapes.

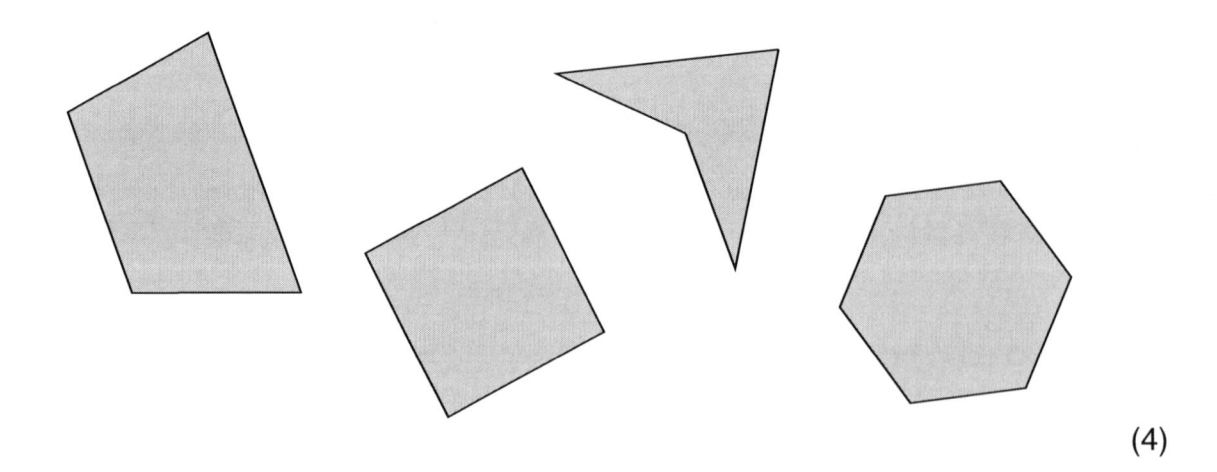

(4)

29. In the drawings below, the mirror lines are dotted.
    Draw the reflection of each shape in the mirror line.

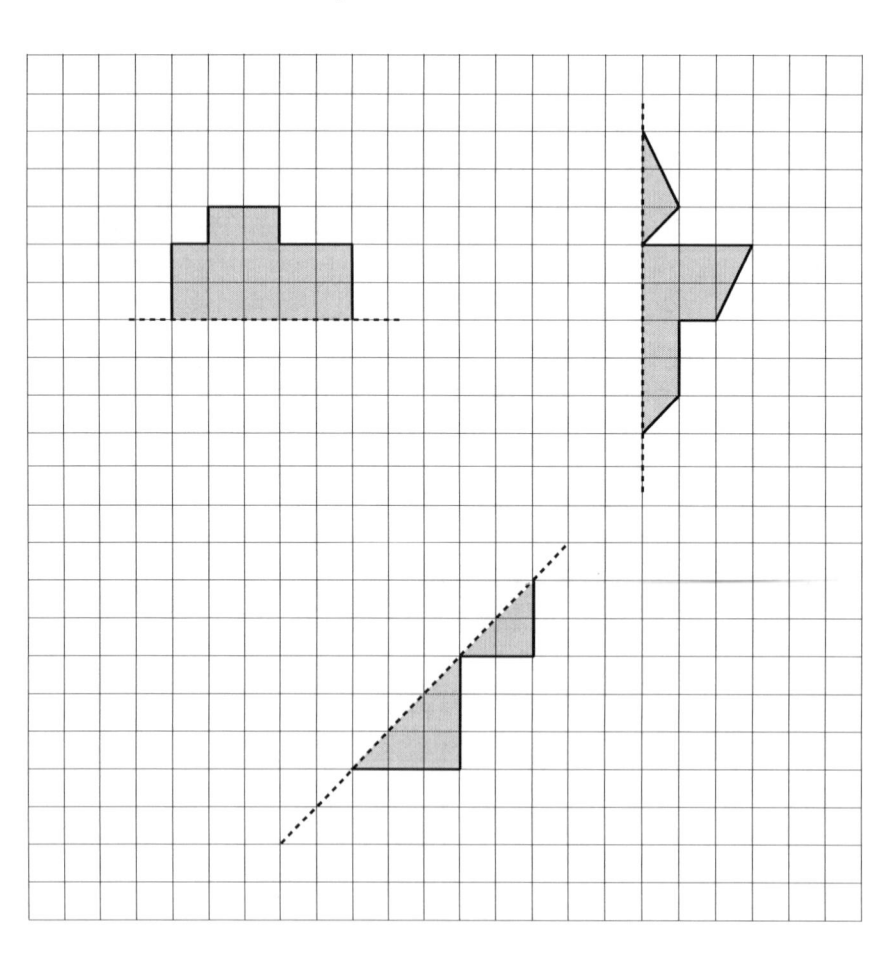

(6)

November 96 Q11

(Note: More questions on reflection will be found on pages 158 to 159.)

112

30. Study these shapes.

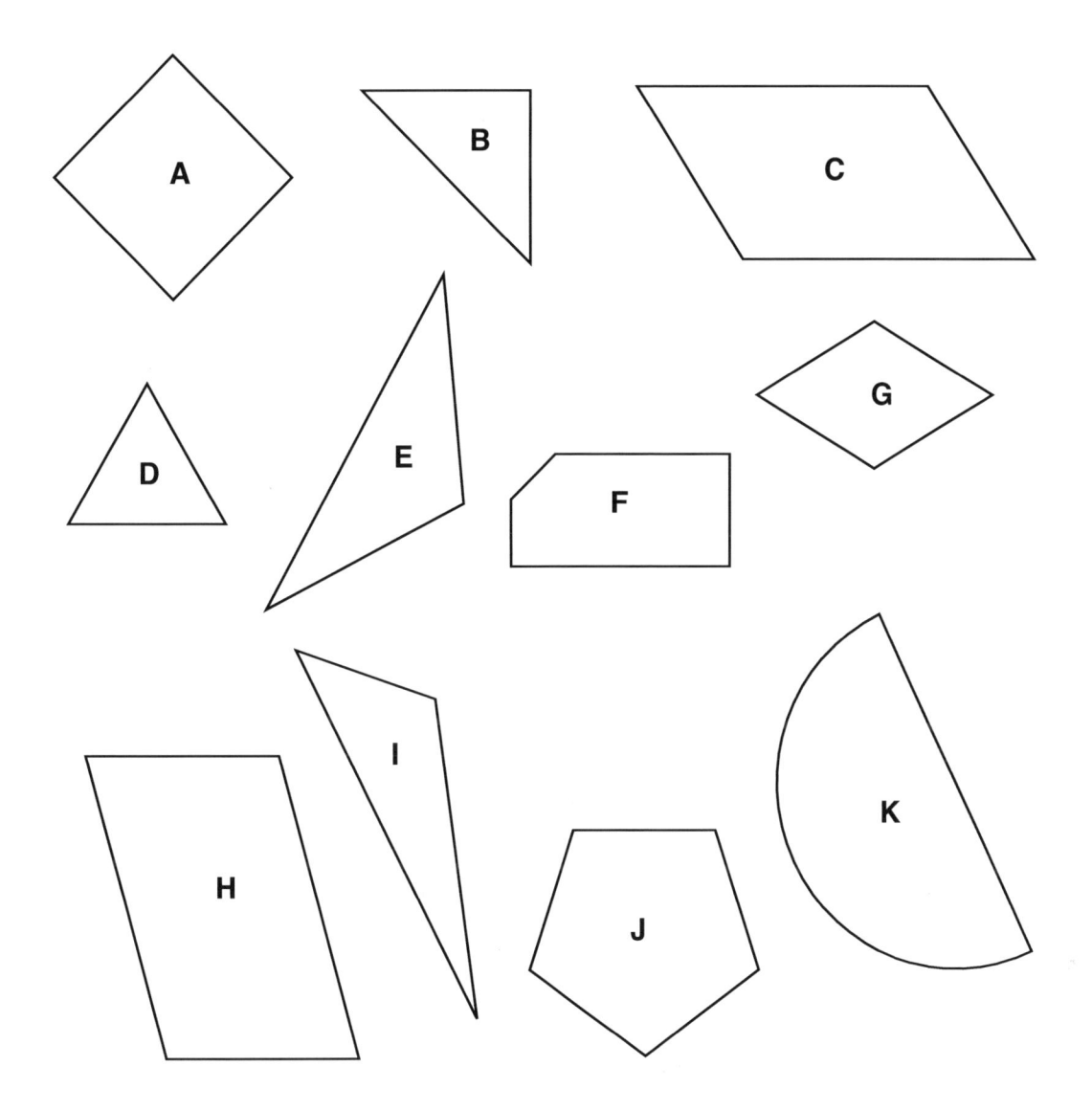

(i) Which shapes have no lines of symmetry?

Answer: .... (2)

(ii) Which shapes have rotational symmetry?

Answer: .... (2)

(iii) Which shapes contain at least one right angle?

Answer: .... (2)

31. Solid shape **A** has reflective symmetry. (It has **two** planes of symmetry.)
    Solid shape **B** does **not** have reflective symmetry.

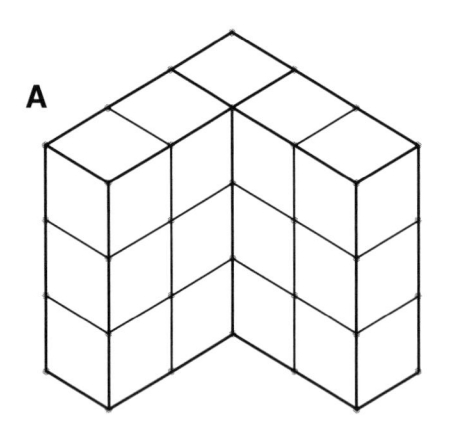

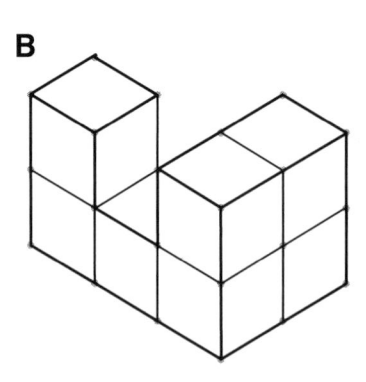

    (i) Which of the shapes **C**, **D** and **E** has reflective symmetry?

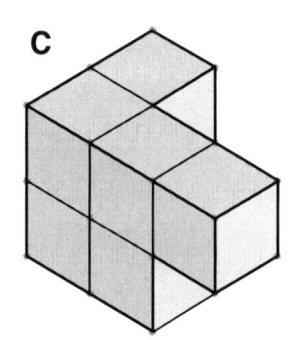

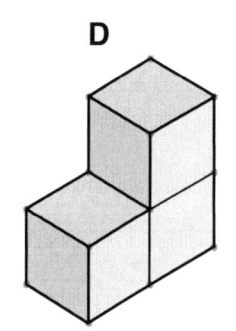

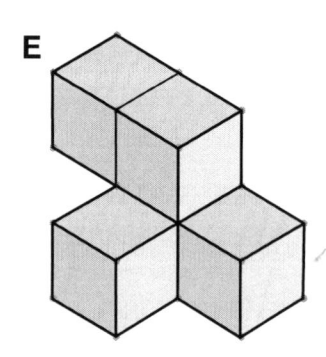

    Answer: .... (2)

    (ii) On the dotted grid below, draw a solid which has reflective symmetry.

    (2)

32. This diagram shows a 4-cm square which has been cut into five pieces.

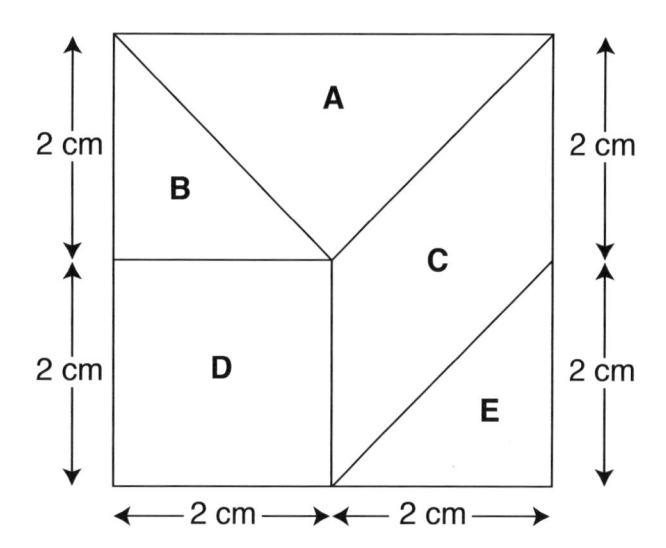

(i) Fill in the letters to complete the following statements.

   (a) Shape .... is a square.

   (b) Shape .... is a parallelogram. (2)

(ii) Different pieces will fit together to form new shapes.

   (a) Which two pieces can form a square?

   Answer: .... (2)

   (b) Name any two pieces which can form a trapezium.

   Answer: .... (2)

   (c) Which two pieces can form a triangle?

   Answer: .... (2)

   (d) Name any three pieces which can form a rectangle.

   Answer: .... (2)

January 93 Q16

33. This drawing shows a hexagon divided to make a square and two right-angled isosceles triangles.

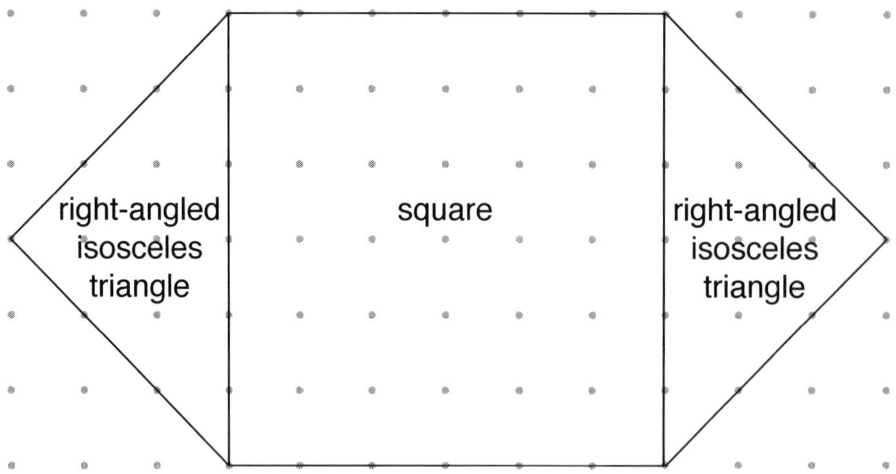

right-angled isosceles triangle   square   right-angled isosceles triangle

(i) Show how the same hexagon can be cut into a square and two congruent parallelograms.

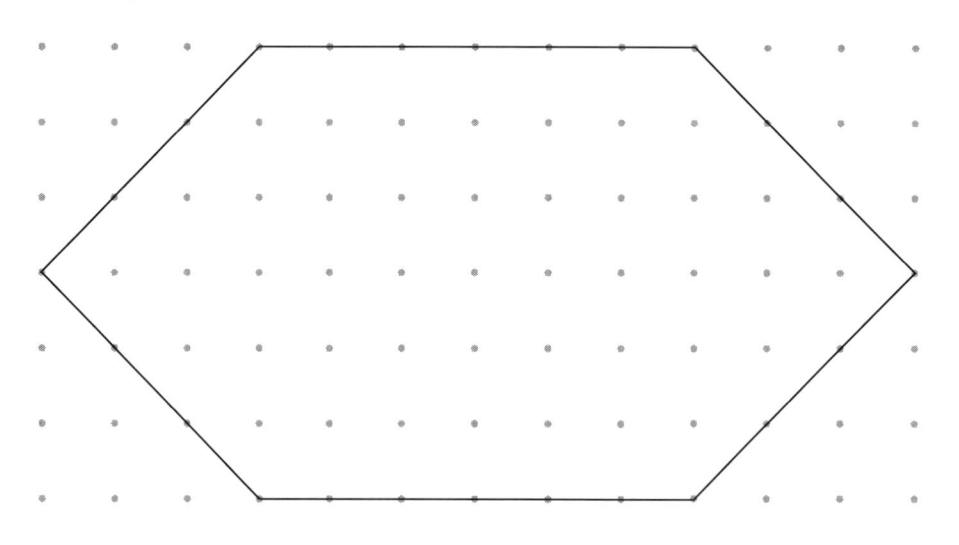

(3)

(ii) Show how the same hexagon can be cut into a parallelogram, a right-angled isosceles triangle and an isosceles trapezium.

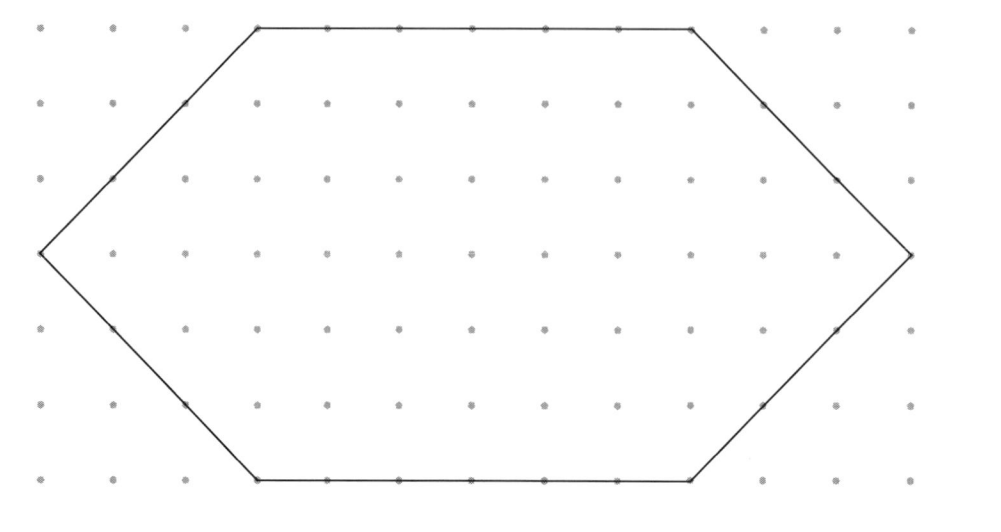

(3)

(iii) Show how to cut the hexagon into two congruent trapezia, a rectangle and two congruent triangles.

(3)

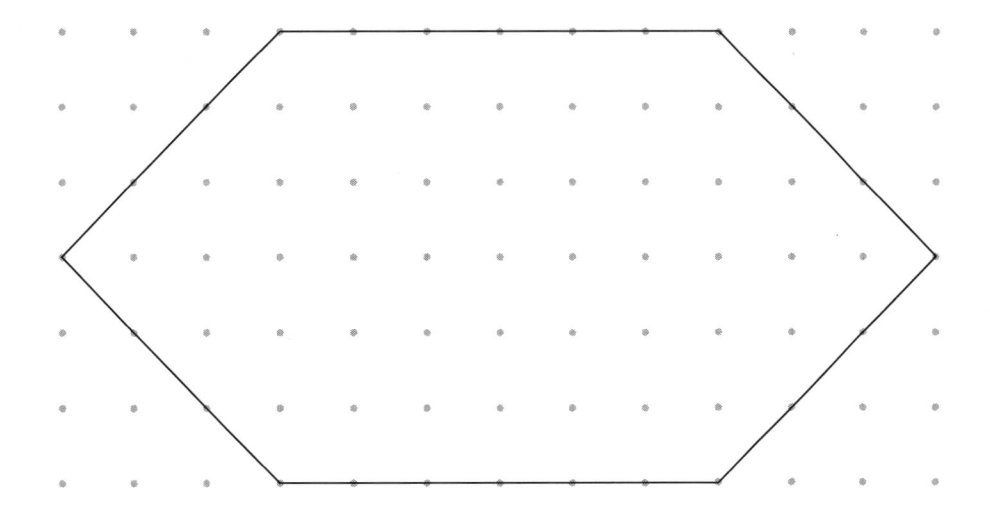

(iv) Now make up two examples of your own.

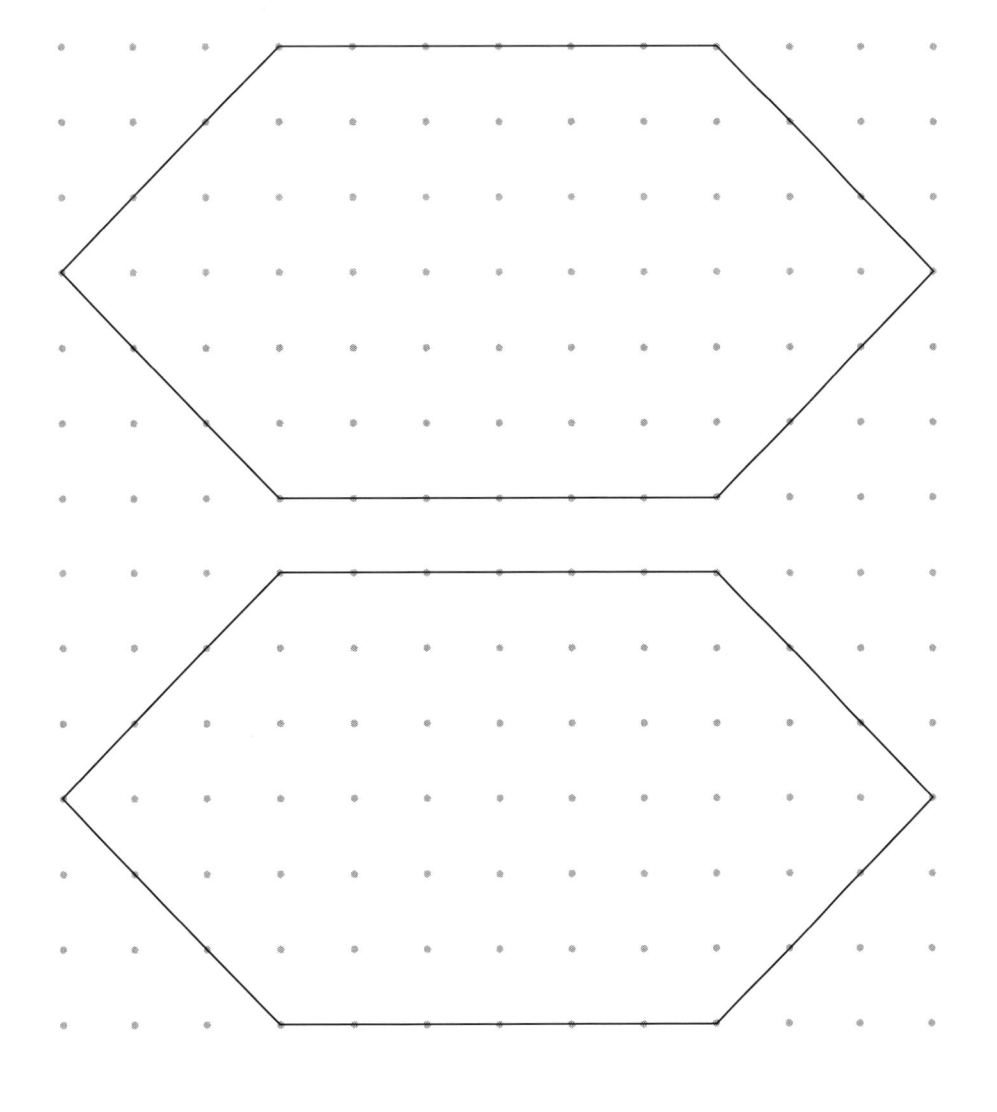

(5)

34. This equilateral triangle has been cut into 12 pieces.

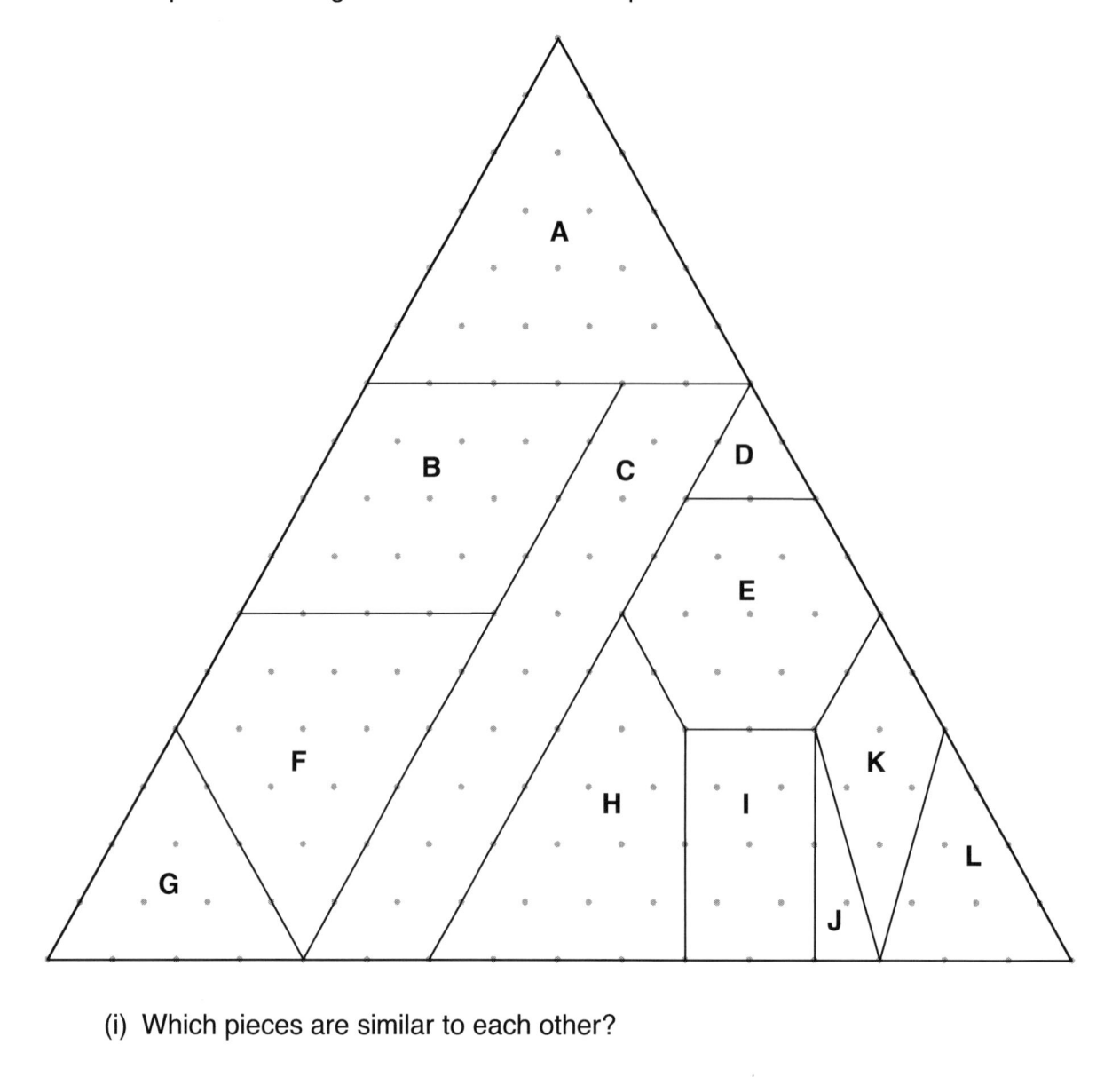

(i) Which pieces are similar to each other?

Answer: .... (2)

(ii) Which pieces have no symmetry at all?

Answer: .... (2)

(iii) Which two pieces fit together to make a pentagon which has one line of symmetry?

Answer: .... (2)

(iv) Which three pieces fit together to make an equilateral triangle of side 10 cm?

Answer: .... (2)

35. This diagram shows a net for making an ordinary die.

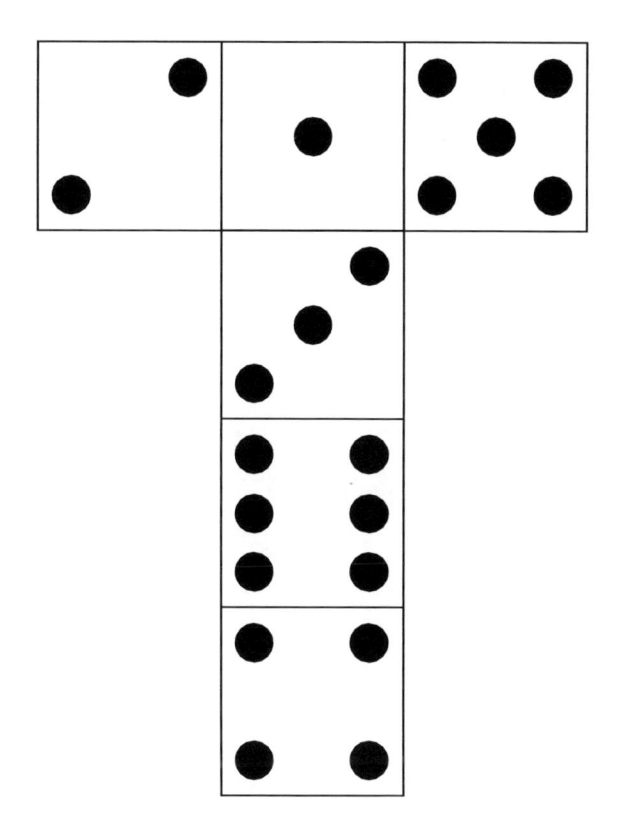

(i) How many faces does the die have?

Answer: .... (1)

(ii) When the die is made, which number will be opposite

(a) 2   Answer: .... (1)

(b) 3?   Answer: .... (1)

(iii) On the die, which numbers will be on faces touching the face with 6 on?

Answer: .... (2)

36. This cuboid is made of centimetre cubes.

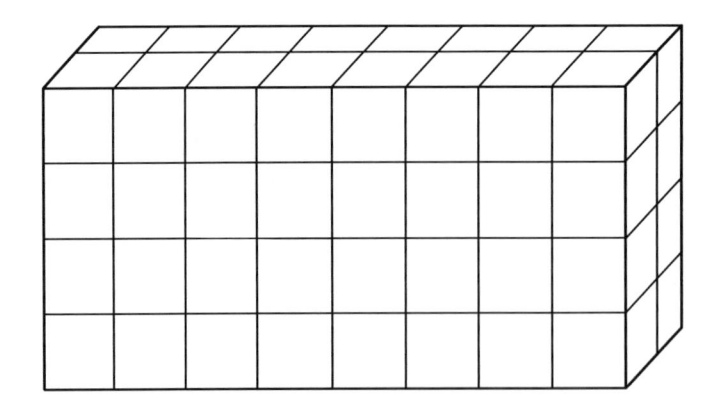

(i) How many centimetre cubes are used?

Answer: .... (2)

Jane needs a box which will hold half this number of cubes.

(ii) What would be the volume of this box?

Answer: .... cm³ (1)

Bob has 24 cubes and he decides to make a box, with a lid, to hold them.
He makes the length of his box 4 cm and the width 2 cm.

(iii) What will be the height of his box?

Answer: .... cm (2)

(iv) On the grid of centimetre squares draw the net of Bob's box.

(3)

SHAPE ETC
B

(v) What is the area of the net of Bob's box?

Answer: .... cm² (3)

January 98 Q10

37. (i) Which of these nets would make a cuboid?

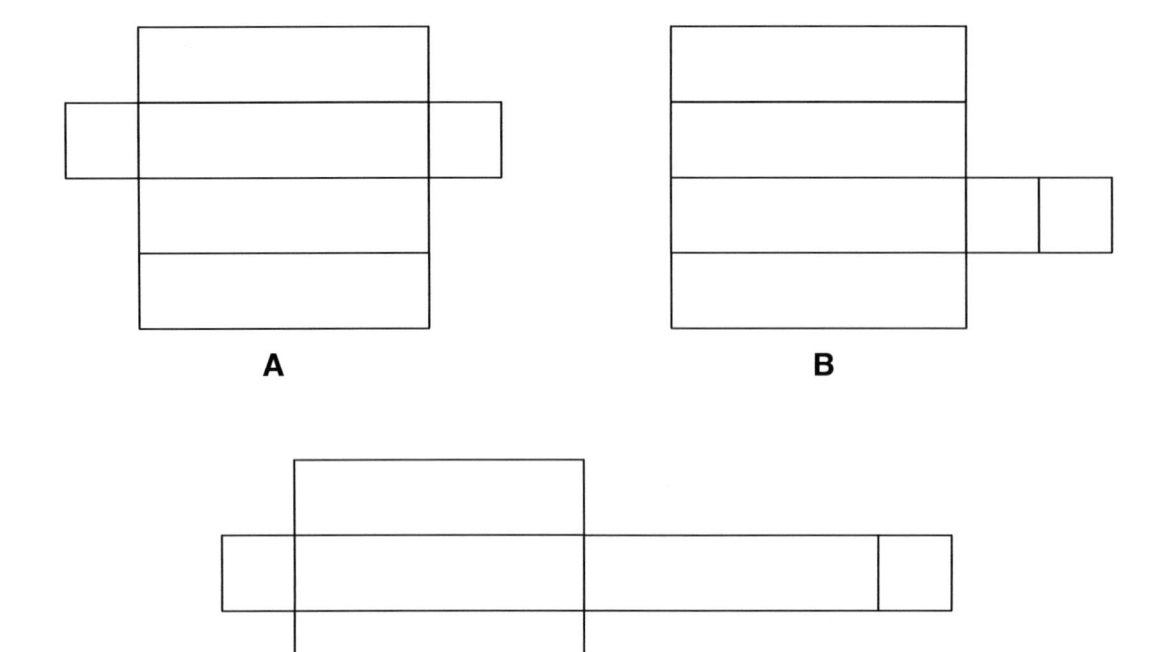

A

B

C

Answer: .... (3)

(ii) Sketch another net of the cuboid.

(3)

38. The box in the diagram is a cuboid measuring 2 cm by 3 cm by 4 cm.

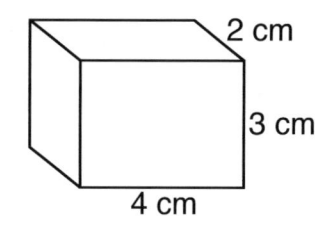

3 cm
2 cm
4 cm

Using the grid below, draw a net of the cuboid.

(4)

January 96 Q13

39. (i) On the grid below, draw a net of a cuboid measuring 3 cm by 5 cm by 2 cm.

(5)

(ii) How many centimetre cubes could you pack inside this cuboid?

Answer: .... (2)

(iii) Suggest the measurements of other cuboids which could hold exactly the same number of centimetre cubes.

Answer: ....

....

.... (3)

November 94 Q18

40. A hollow decoration like this is to be made from coloured plastic.
    All the edges are 6 cm long.

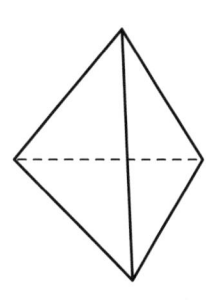

    (i) What is the name of this three-dimensional shape?

    Answer: .... (2)

    (ii) Using the grid below, draw accurately the net of the decoration.

(3)

November 93 Q18

41. On this dotted grid, draw the net of a tetrahedron, of which the base is shown.

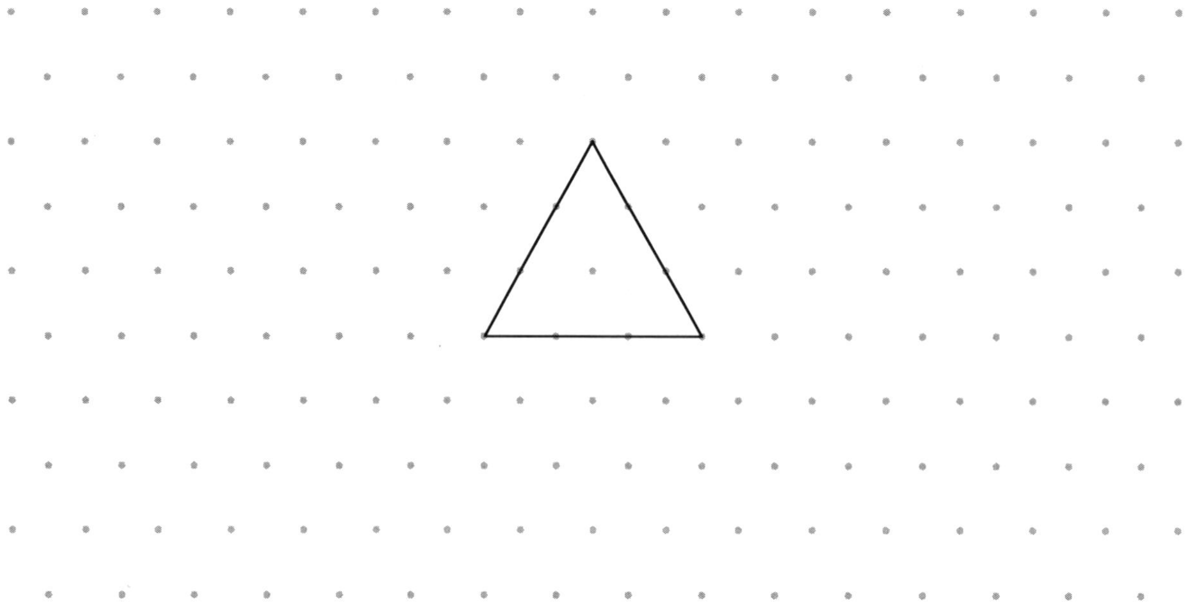

(3)

November 97 Q12

42. (i) Draw freehand a sketch of the solid shape which could be made from this net.

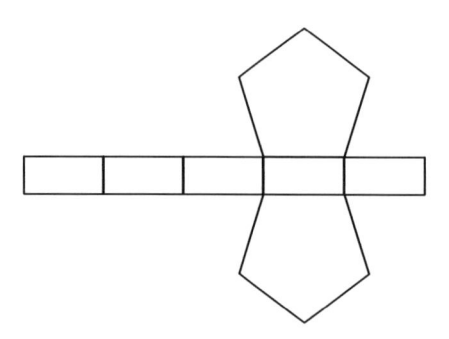

(3)

(ii) Name the solid.

Answer: .... (2)

B SHAPE ETC

126

C **Space**: understanding position, including co-ordinates; understanding direction, angle; movement

1. Write the co-ordinates of the points A to H, for example B (4, 5).

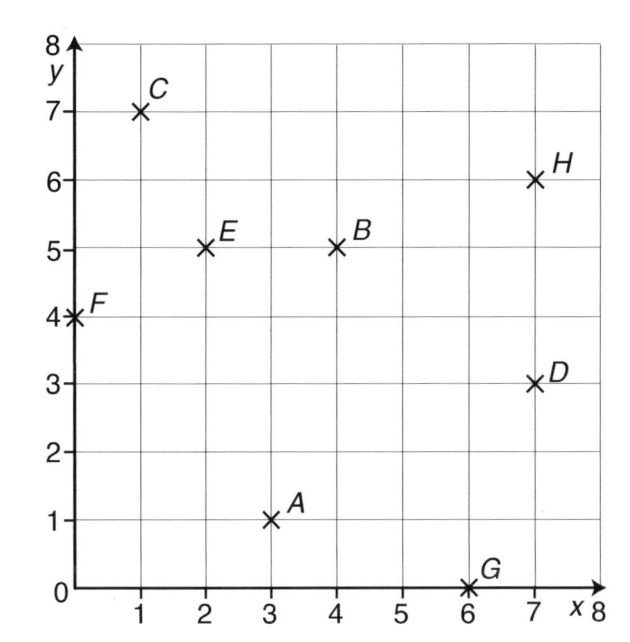

   Answer:

   A (............ , ...)

   B (............ , ...)

   C (............ , ...)

   D (............ , ...)

   E (............ , ...)

   F (............ , ...)

   G (............ , ...)

   H (............ , ...)   (8)

2.

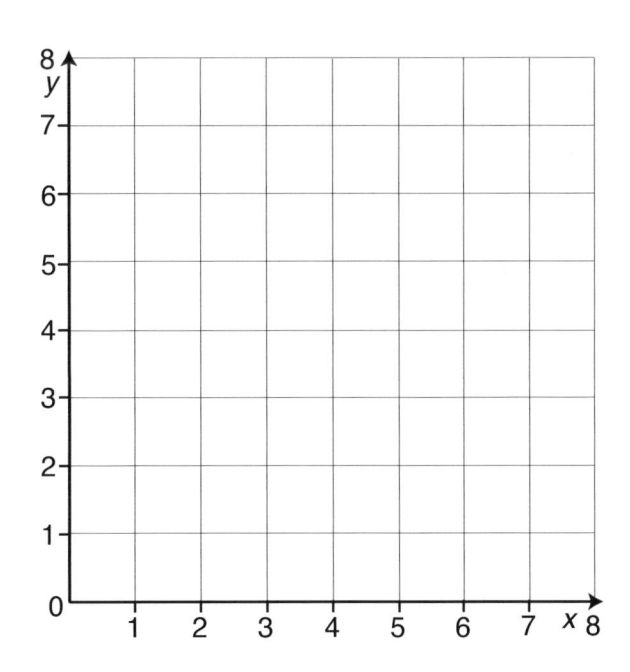

   (i) Plot and label the points A (1, 4), B (5, 5) and C (6, 1) on the grid. (3)

   (ii) A, B and C are three corners of a square.
        Draw the complete square and label the fourth corner D. (2)

   (iii) Write down the co-ordinates of D.   Answer: (............ , ...) (2)

   November 98 Q4

3. The point A (3, 5) is plotted on this grid.

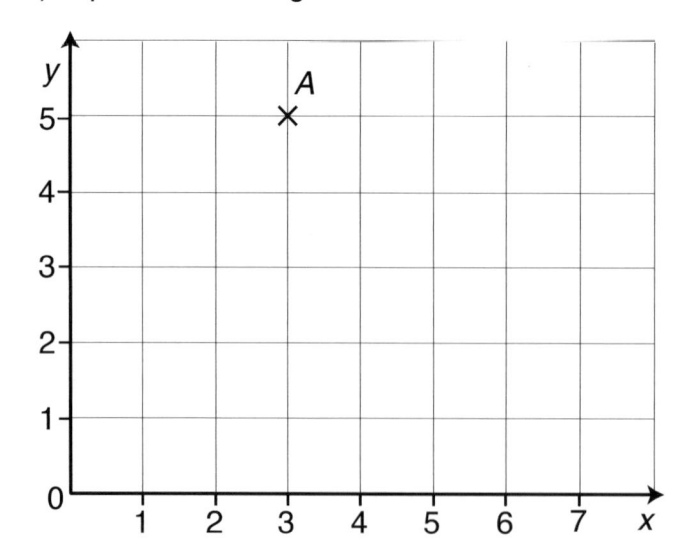

 (i) Mark the points B (1, 4) and C (3, 1) on the grid. (2)

 (ii) Mark another point D on the grid so that ABCD is a kite. Join ABCD. (2)

 (iii) Write down the co-ordinates of point D.

 Answer: (............ , ...) (1)

November 97 Q5

4. (i) Write the co-ordinates of the vertices of the rhombus ABCD.

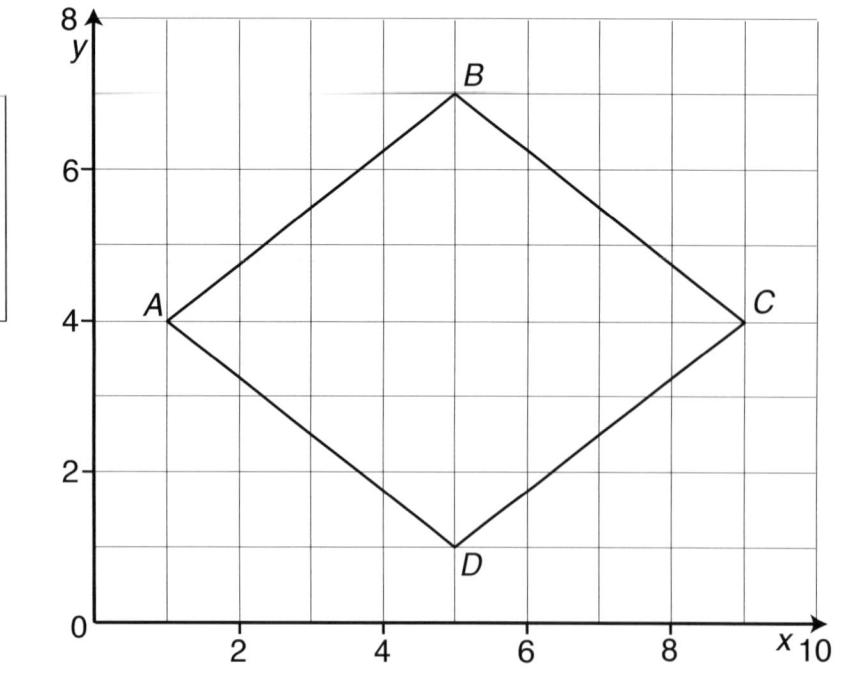

Answers:

A (............ , ...)

B (............ , ...)

C (............ , ...)

D (............ , ...) (4)

 (ii) Write the co-ordinates of the midpoint of ABCD.

 Answer: (............ , ...) (1)

5.

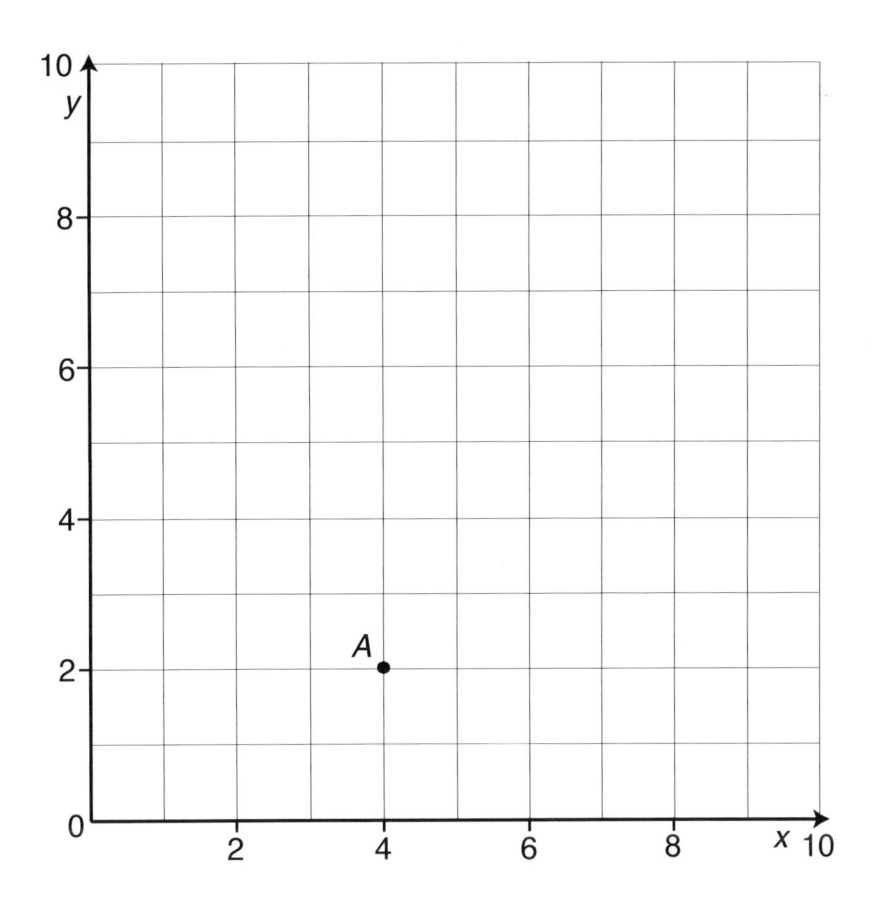

The point A (4, 2), is marked on the grid above.

(i) Plot the points B (7, 5) and C (5, 7).
Join AB and BC. (2)

ABCD is a rectangle.

(ii) Plot the point D and join AD and CD. (2)

(iii) On the rectangle draw all the lines of symmetry. (2)

(iv) Does ABCD have rotational symmetry?

Answer: .... (1)

(v) What is the area of rectangle ABCD?

Answer: .... cm² (2)

January 97 Q15

6.

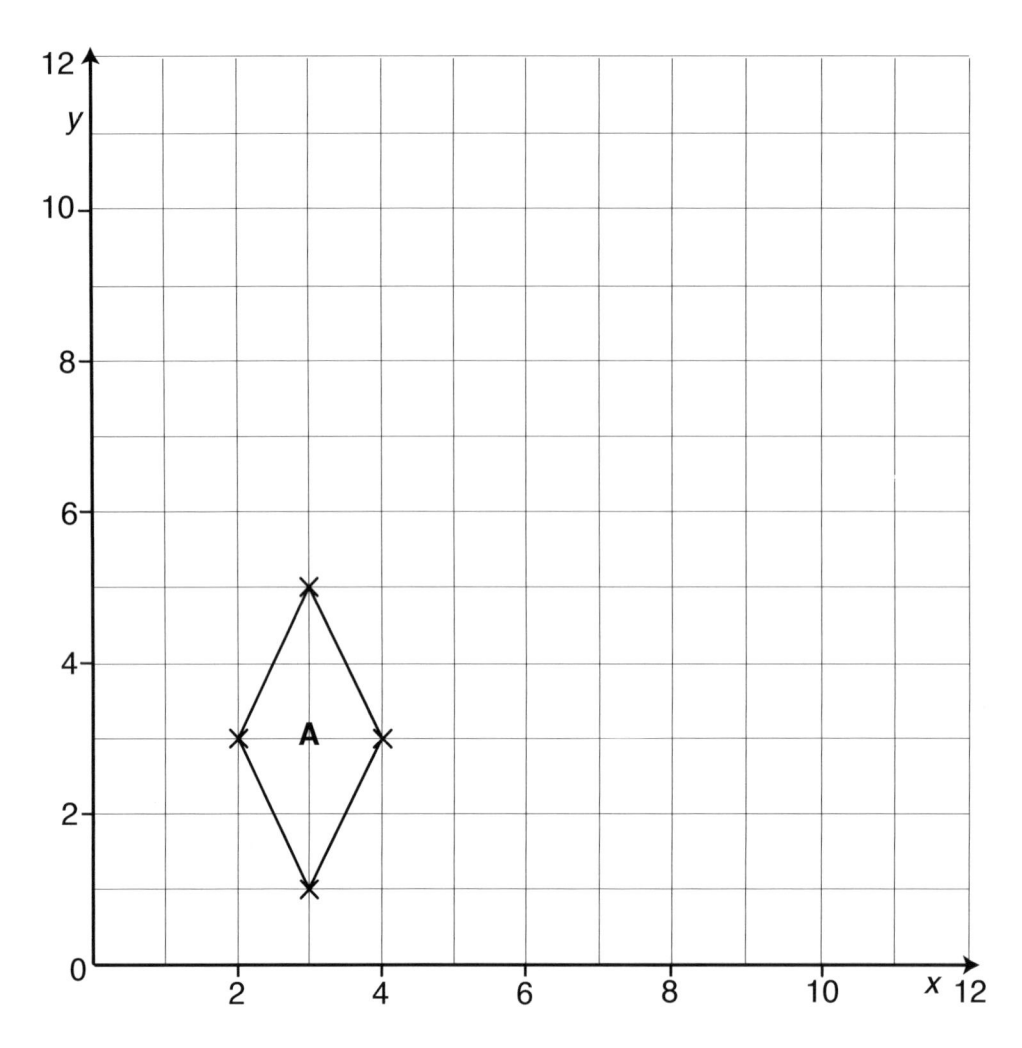

On the grid the points (3, 1), (4, 3), (3, 5) and (2, 3) have been joined. The shape has been labelled **A**.

(i) Plot and join the points (2, 7), (6, 7), (5, 10) and (2, 10). Label the shape **B**. (2)

(ii) Plot and join the points (10, 6), (12, 10) and (8, 10). Label the shape **C**. (2)

(iii) Complete the statements.

Shape **A** is a .... (1)

Shape **B** is a .... (1)

Shape **C** is an .... triangle. (1)

(iv) Draw all lines of symmetry on the shapes. (3)

(v) Complete the statement.

Shape .... has rotational symmetry of order 2 (1)

January 99 Q13

7. Answer these questions about the shape below.

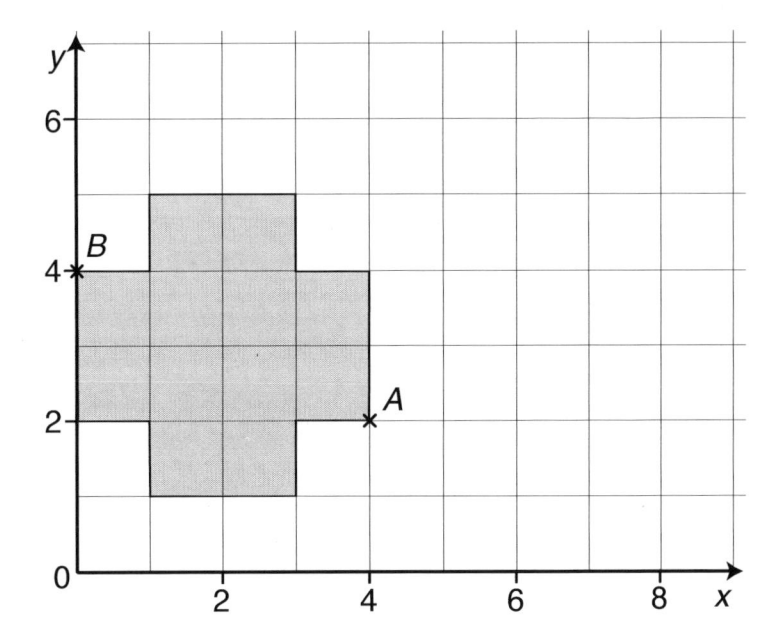

(i) What are the co-ordinates of the points marked A and B?

Answer: A (............ , ...) B (............ , ...) (2)

(ii) How many lines of symmetry does the shape have?

Answer: .... (1)

(iii) What is the order of rotational symmetry of the shape?

Answer: .... (2)

(iv) What are the co-ordinates of the centre of rotational symmetry?

Answer: (............ , ...) (2)

January 94 Q7

(v) What is the area of the shape?

Answer: .... cm² (1)

(vi) What is the perimeter of the shape?

Answer: .... cm (2)

8.

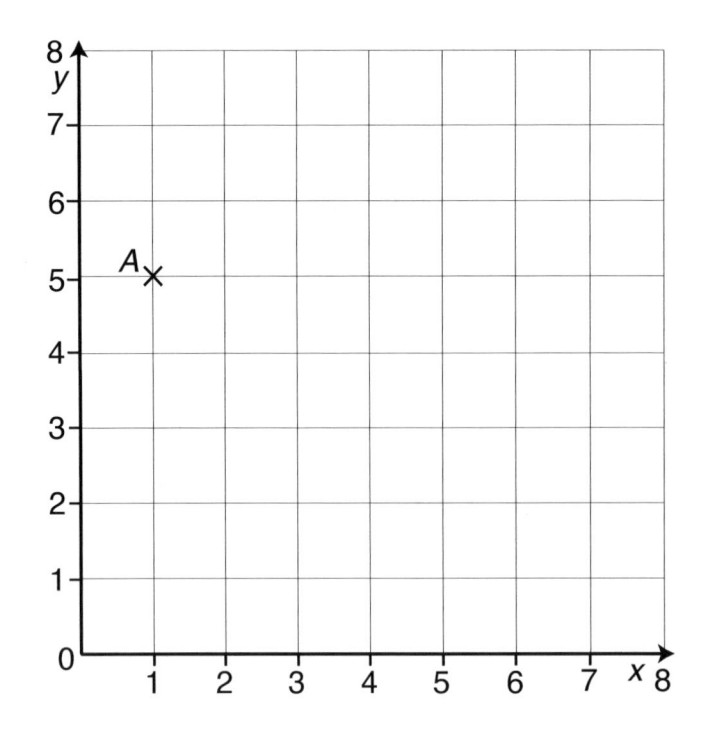

The point A (1, 5) is marked on the grid above.

(i) Plot the points B (1, 1), C (4, 1), D (6, 3) and E (4, 5). (4)

Join the points to make the shape ABCDE.

(ii) Name the shape you have drawn.

Answer: .... (1)

(iii) ED is perpendicular to CD.

Name two other sides which are perpendicular to one another.

Answer: .... and .... (1)

(iv) Name a pair of parallel sides.

Answer: .... and .... (1)

(v) On your shape draw any lines of symmetry. (2)

(vi) What is the area of shape ABCDE?

Answer: .... cm² (3)

January 95 Q10

9.

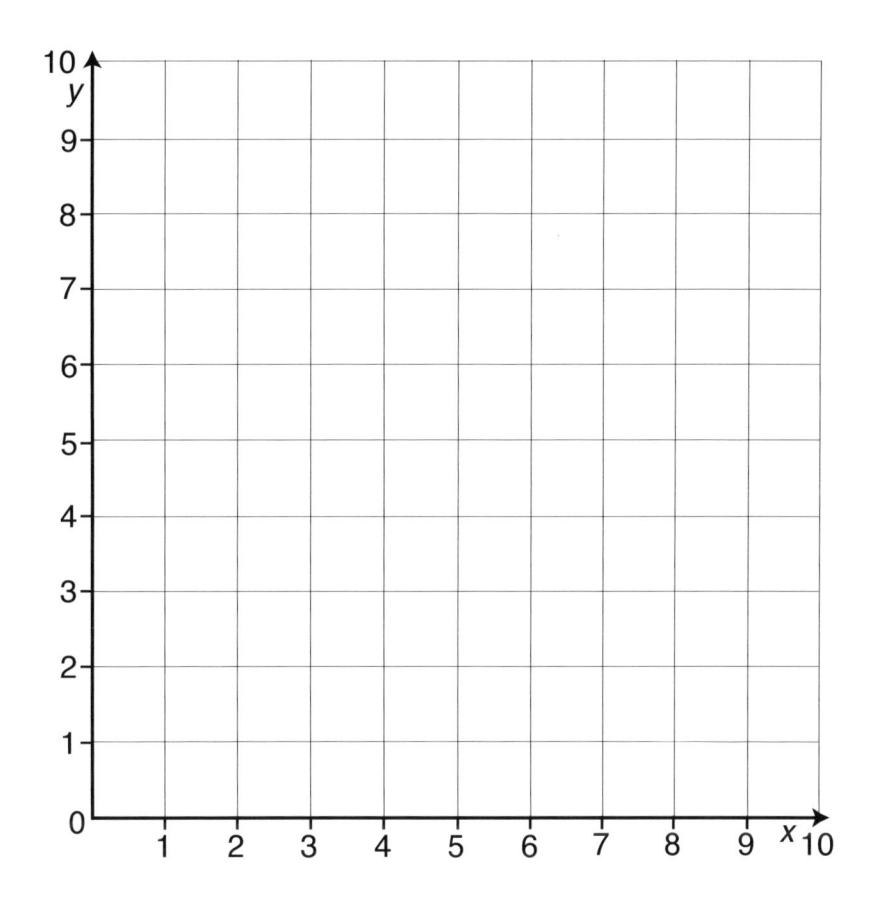

(i) Mark the points A (3, 1) and B (9, 7) on the grid. (2)
  Join the straight line AB.

(ii) Mark the point C (4, 6). (1)

(iii) Draw a straight line from C so that it is perpendicular to AB. (2)
  Join AC and CB.

(iv) Find the point D, on the grid, which completes a rhombus.
  What are the co-ordinates of point D?

Answer: (............ , ...) (2)

10.

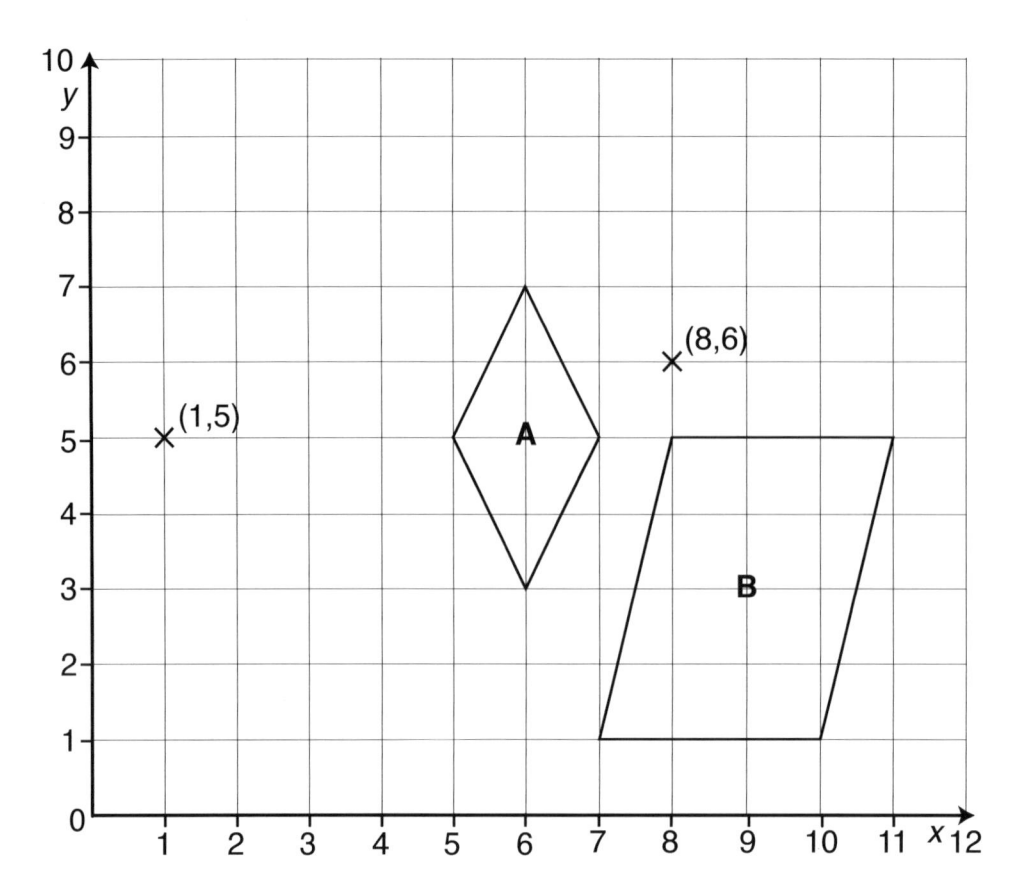

On the grid above, shapes **A** and **B** are drawn for you.

(i) Shape **A** is called a .... (1)

Shape **B** is called a .... (1)

(ii) The points (1, 5) and (8, 6) are plotted for you.

On the grid above, plot each set of co-ordinates and join them up as you go to make a shape.

Shape **C**, (1, 5); (4, 5); (4, 8); (1, 8)

Shape **C** is called a .... (2)

Shape **D**, (8, 6); (10, 6); (11, 8); (9, 9); (7, 8)

Shape **D** is called a .... (2)

Shape **E**, (1, 1); (4, 1); (4, 3)

Shape **E** is called a .... (2)

(iii) What is the area of each of these shapes?

B .... cm² **D** .... cm² **E** .... cm² (6)

(iv) What is the length of the perimeter of shape **C**? Answer: .... cm (1)

(v) What are the co-ordinates of the centre of shape **A**?

Answer: (.........., ...) (1)

January 95 Q18

11.

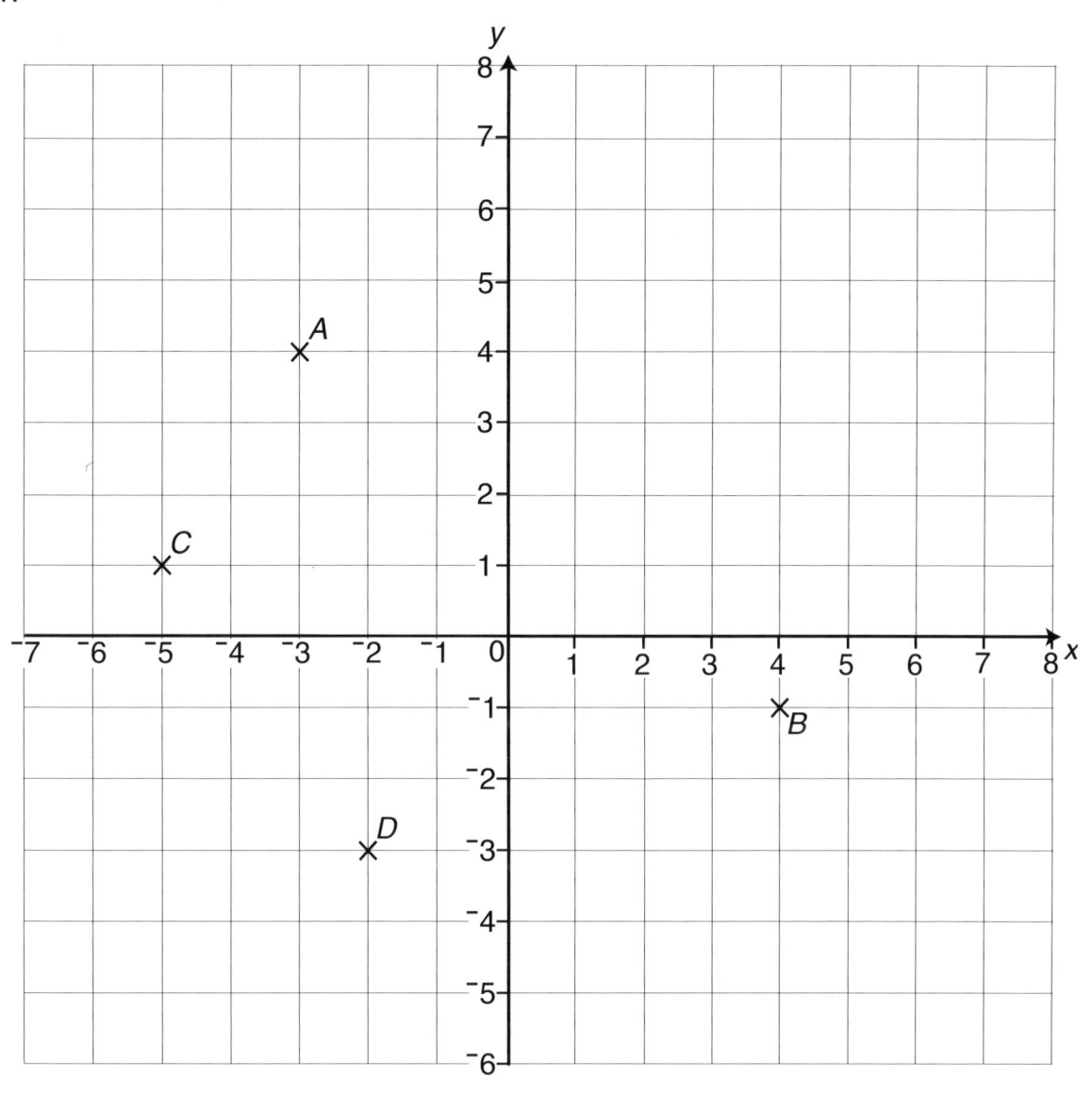

On this grid the point A has co-ordinates (⁻3, 4).

(i) Write the co-ordinates of the points B, C and D.

Answer: B (............ , ...) (1)

Answer: C (............ , ...) (1)

Answer: D (............ , ...) (1)

(ii) On the grid, plot and label the points

E (5, 6),   F (5, ⁻4),   G (⁻4, 6)   and   H (⁻6, ⁻4).

(4)

12.

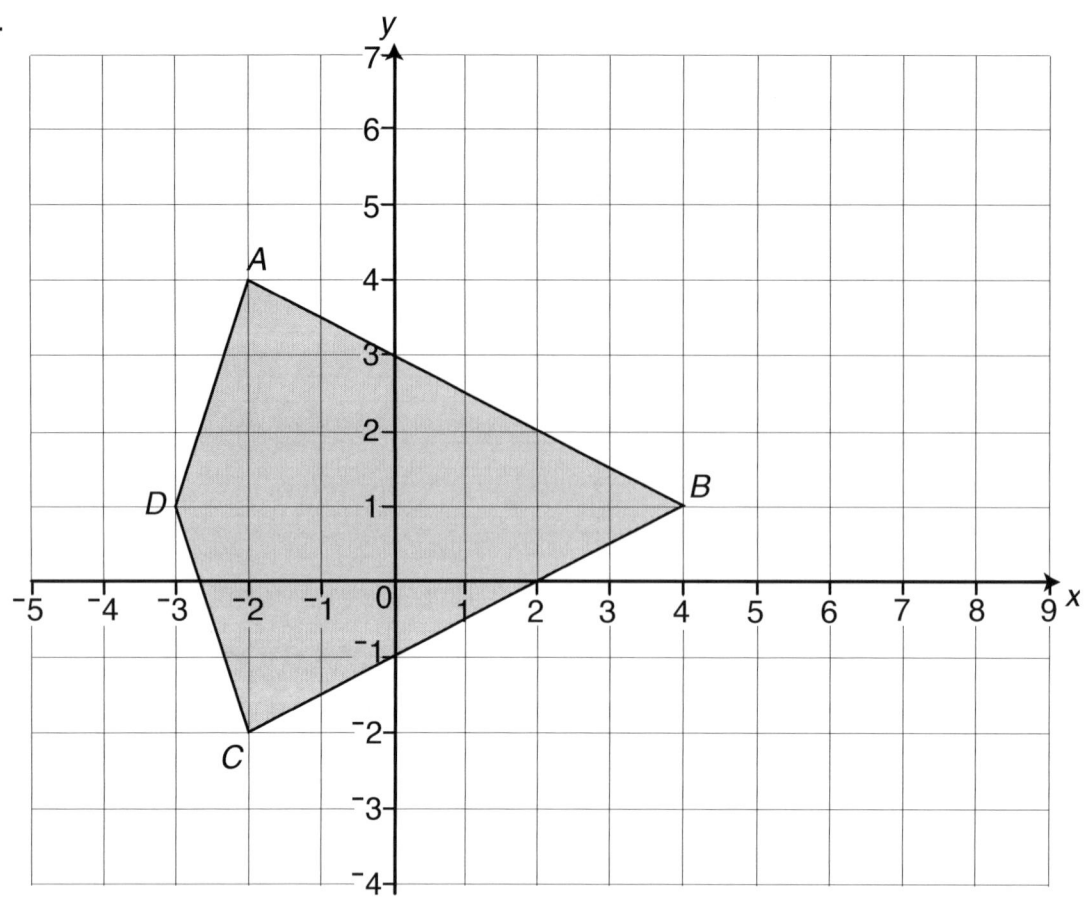

(i) (a) Write the co-ordinates of the points A, B, C and D.

Answer: A (............ , ...) (1)

Answer: B (............ , ...) (1)

Answer: C (............ , ...) (1)

Answer: D (............ , ...) (1)

(b) Name shape ABCD.   Answer: .... (1)

(ii) (a) Draw shape PQRS with co-ordinates P (6, ⁻2), Q (5, 2), R (6, 6) and S (7, 2). (2)

(b) Name shape PQRS.   Answer: .... (1)

13. (i) Label the directions shown on the compass drawing.
    The arrow points north.

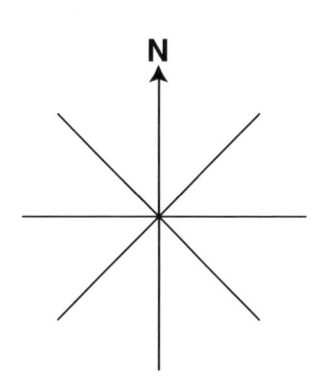

    (2)

    (ii) I face northeast when going down the path from my front door.
    I then turn 90° clockwise.
    In which direction am I now facing?

    Answer: .... (1)

    (iii) Later, I turn clockwise through one and a half right angles.
    I end up facing southwest.
    In which direction was I facing before turning?

    Answer: .... (3)

    January 96 Q12

14. A man is facing east.
    (i) Through how many degrees clockwise must he turn so that he is facing west?

    Answer: .... ° (1)

    Three soldiers, standing side by side, are facing north.

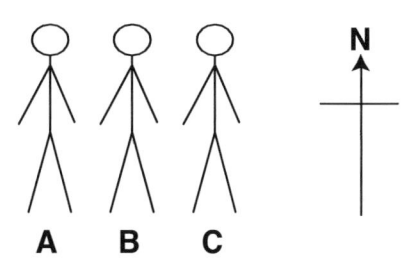

    Each soldier turns 270° anticlockwise.

    (ii) Which of the soldiers, **A**, **B** or **C**, is now standing in front of the other two soldiers?

    Answer: .... (2)

    Specimen 94 Q6

137

15. Draw lines to show the path taken by following these instructions.

go	3 cm N
then	2 cm W
then	1 cm N
then	5 cm E
then	3 cm S
then	2 cm E
then	1 cm N
then	4 cm W

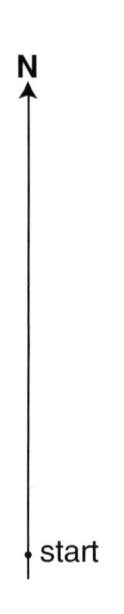

N

• start   (4)

16. The drawing shows the positions of two friends Anna *(A)* and Bella *(B)*.

N

scale: 1 cm represents 100 m

A•

•
B

(i) How far is Bella from Anna?

Answer: .... m   (1)

(ii) In which direction must Anna look, to face Bella?

Answer: ....   (1)

(iii) On the drawing, clearly mark the position of Colin *(C)* who is 350 metres NE of Anna. (2)

(iv) Mark the position of Dick *(D)* who is due W of Anna and due N of Bella. (1)

(v) How far is Dick from Colin?

Answer: .... m (2)

17.

scale: 1 cm to 1 cm

A spider *(S)* is 6 cm NE of the dot *P*.
A fly *(F)* is 5 cm W of the dot *P*.

(i) Mark and label the positions of the spider and the fly. (3)

(ii) How far is the spider from the fly?

Answer: .... cm (2)

18. Douglas is standing 20 metres NE of Corinne.

   (i) Complete this sentence.

   Corinne is standing 20 metres .... of Douglas. (1)

   Francisco is facing north.

   He turns through three right angles, clockwise.

   (ii) In which direction is he facing now?

   Answer: .... (1)

19.

FINISH HERE

START HERE

When tackling a cross-country course, competitors must not enter or even touch any of the marked obstacles.

Write instructions for the contestant so she can complete the course.

Each edge of a square represents 100 metres.

Use the instructions: FD (forward)   BK (back)
                        RT (right) 90°   LT (left) 90°

Answer: ....

....

....

....

....

.... (5)

Specimen 94 Q18

20. (i) Draw a line which is parallel to, and exactly 1.8 cm from, the line *XY*.

X————————————•————————————————Y
              Z

(1)

(ii) Draw a line which is perpendicular to *XY*, passing through *Z*. (1)

21. An angle is a measure of turn.

(i) Draw the new position of this line after it has been turned through one right angle about the dot.

(1)

(ii) Is this angle more or less than one right angle?

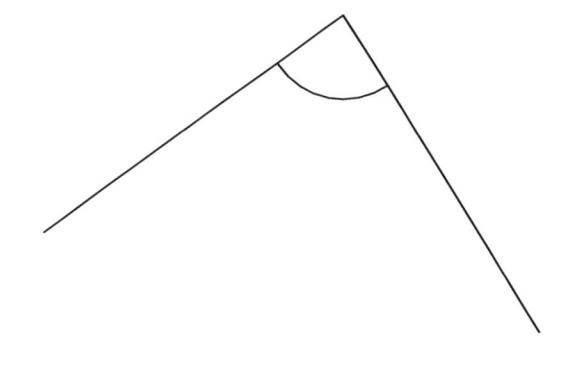

Answer: .... (1)

22. Name the types of angles (e.g. acute).

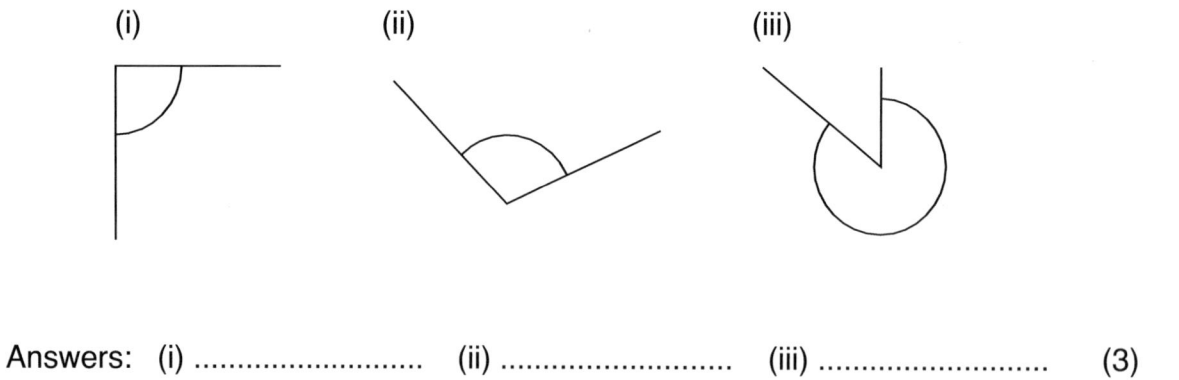

(i) (ii) (iii)

Answers: (i) .... (ii) .... (iii) .... (3)

23. Measure these angles.

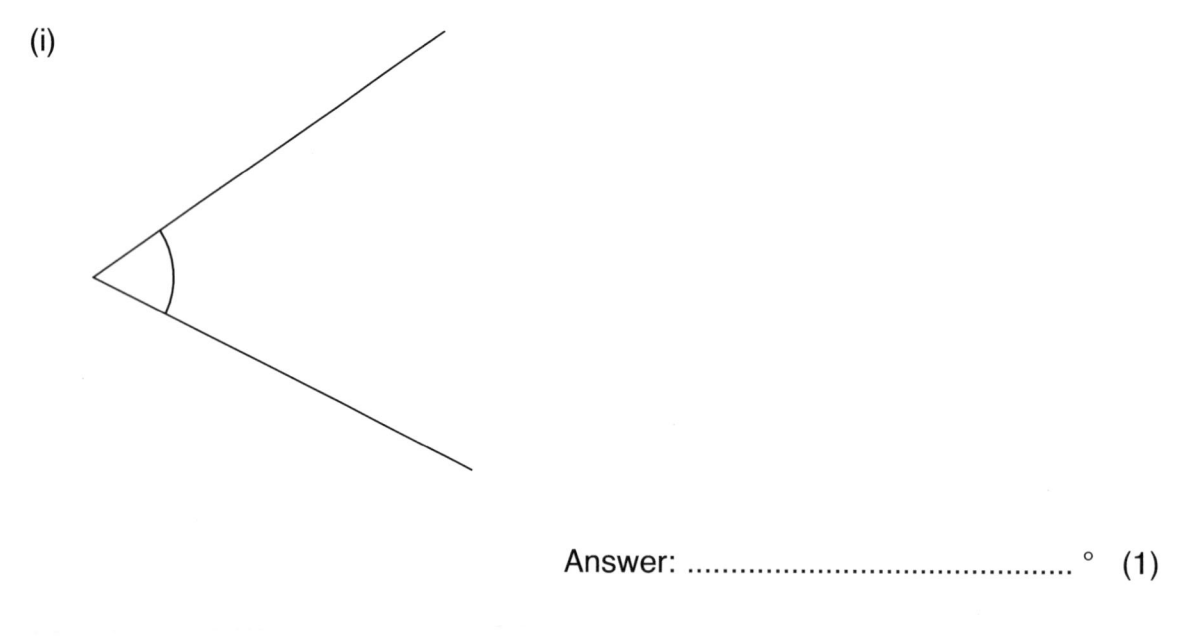

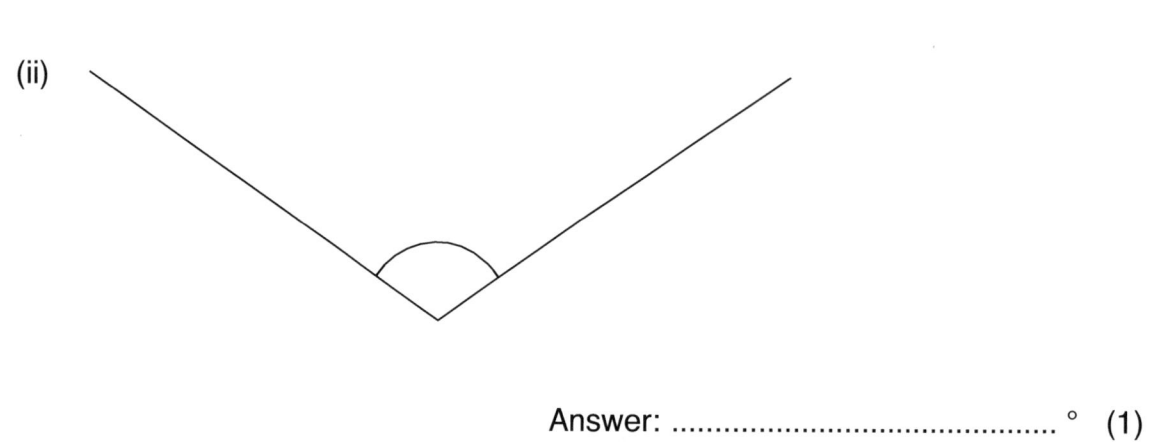

(i)

Answer: ....° (1)

(ii)

Answer: ....° (1)

24. Choose from the words listed below to complete these statements.

   acute   horizontal   obtuse   parallel   perpendicular   vertical

   (i) The surface of the water in a pond is ....

   (ii) At two o'clock, the smaller angle between the hands of a clock is

   ....

   (iii) When a pendulum stops swinging, it is ....

   (iv) A lamppost is usually .... to the ground.

   (v) Railway lines are .... to one another.

   (5)

   January 95 Q24

25. Draw a line which is perpendicular to the line *AB*.

   A ——————————————————————— *B*

   (2)

   November 93 Q7

26. (i) Write down an angle inside the shape *ABCDE* which is

   (a) obtuse   Answer: ....

   (b) right   Answer: ....

   (c) acute   Answer: ....

   (d) reflex   Answer: ....

   (4)

   (ii) Write down the name of this shape.

   Answer: .... (1)

   November 91 Q13

27. What kind of angle is this?

Answer: .... angle (2)

January 92 Q10

28. (i) Measure this angle.

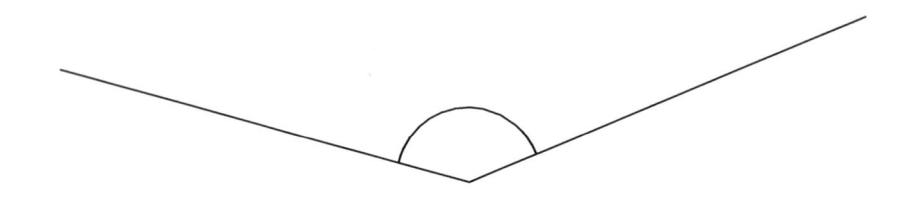

Answer: .... degrees (1)

(ii) What type of angle is it?

Answer: .... (1)

November 96 Q3

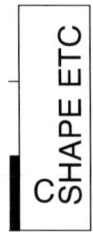

29.

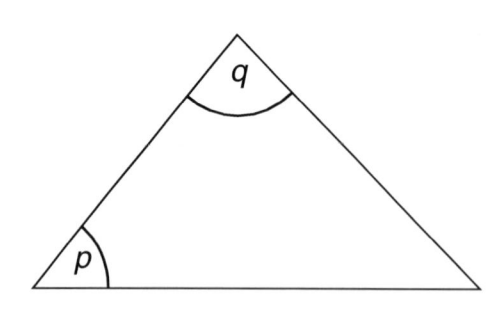

Measure the angles marked p and q in the diagram.

Answer: p = ...° (2)

q = ...° (2)

144

30.

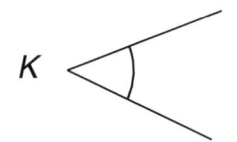

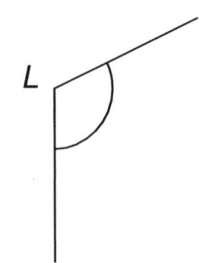

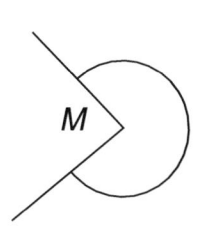

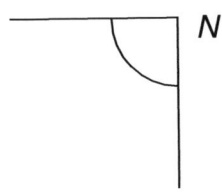

Angle K is an acute angle of about 45°
Describe the other angles in a similar way, without measuring them.

angle L is .... angle of about .... °

angle M is .... angle of about .... °

angle N is .... angle of .... °

angle O is .... angle of about .... °

(6)

January 93 Q13

31. (i) When a hand of a clock moves from 3 to 6, through how many degrees does it turn?

Answer: .... degrees (2)

November 92 Q5

(ii) Which of these angles is the larger?

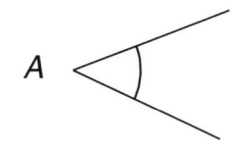

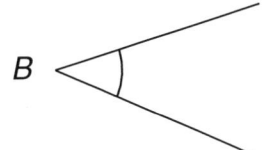

Answer: .... (1)

145

32. (i) Which type of angle is this?

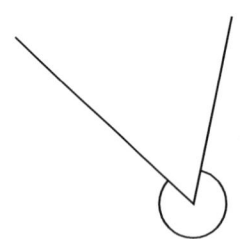

Answer: .... (1)

(ii) Measure the angle.

Answer: ....° (2)

33. Mary drew a triangle on coloured paper and cut it out.
She then tore off all the corners.

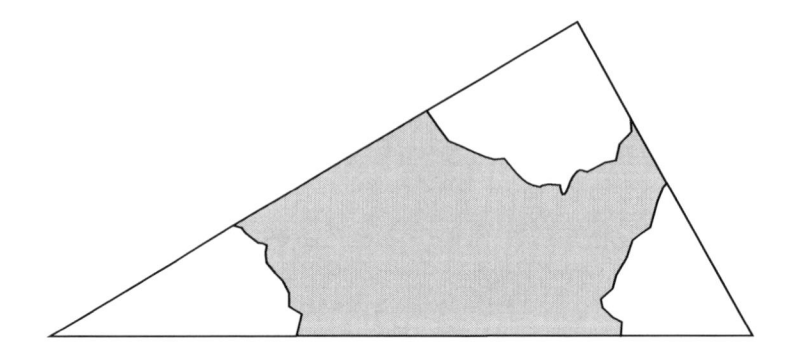

Mary then put the corners on her page like this.

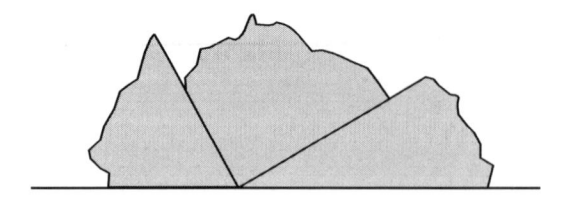

She said 'When I put the corners like this, look what happens!'
Which angle fact could Mary see?

Answer: ....

....

.... (2)

34. **Calculate** (do not measure) the angles *a*, *b*, *c* and *d*.

(i)

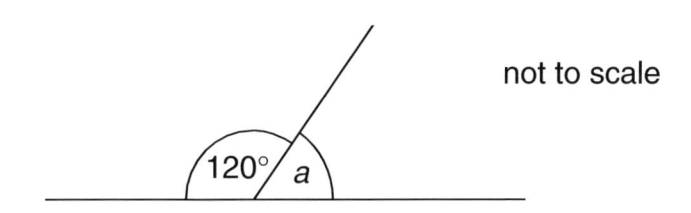

not to scale

Answer: *a* = ...° (1)

(ii)

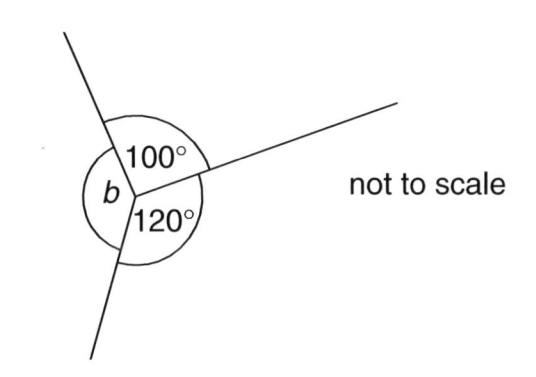

not to scale

Answer: *b* = ...° (2)

(iii)

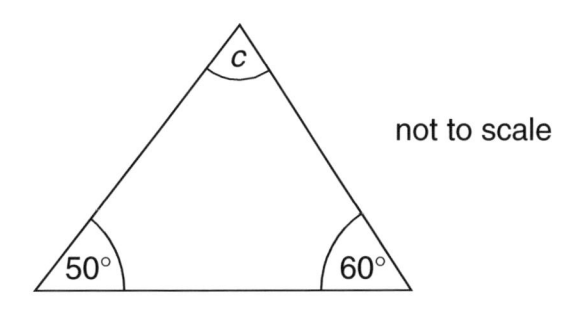

not to scale

Answer: *c* = ...° (2)

(iv)

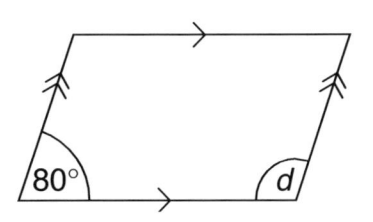

not to scale

Answer: *d* = ...° (2)

35. (i) Use compasses to construct a circle with centre *C*, of radius 2.8 cm. (1)

C.

(ii) Construct an arc of a circle, centre *C*, of radius 10 cm.
Draw only the part of the arc which lies inside the rectangle. (1)

36. (i) Draw accurately triangle *ABC*, where *AB* is 7.3 cm, *AC* is 10.9 cm and *BC* is 4.8 cm.

(4)

(ii) Measure angle *ACB*.

Answer: .... ° (2)

November 92 Q16

37. (i) Construct the triangle ABC, where AB is 8 cm, BC is 6.2 cm and AC is 3.7 cm.

(4)

(ii) (a) Measure the size of angle ACB.   Answer: .... ° (2)

(b) Is this angle acute, obtuse or reflex?   Answer: .... (1)

November 94 Q14

38. (i) Draw accurately triangle ABC, where AB is 8.3 cm, AC is 5.7 cm and BC is 8.9 cm.

(4)

(ii) Measure angle ACB.

Answer: .... ° (2)

November 97 Q10

39. (i) Construct a triangle whose sides measure 6 cm, 7 cm and 10 cm.

(5)

(ii) On your construction, mark with an *A* any acute angles, and with an *O* any obtuse angles.

(3)

Specimen 94 Q11

40. (i) Construct accurately the triangle *ABC* with *AB* = 6 cm, *BC* = 5 cm and angle *ABC* = 110°.

(4)

(ii) Measure and write down the length of *AC*.

Answer: .... cm (2)

November 91 Q18

150

41. (i) Draw accurately triangle *ABC*, where *AB* is 7.5 cm, *BC* is 9 cm and angle *ABC* is 70°

(4)

(ii) Which type of angle is angle *BCA*?

Answer: .... (1)

(iii) Measure the length of *AC*.

Answer: .... cm (1)

(iv) What is the length of the perimeter of triangle *ABC*?

Answer: .... cm (2)

January 99 Q9

42. (i) Draw, as accurately as you can, a triangle *ABC*, where *AB* measures 8.6 cm, *BC* measures 6.5 cm and angle *ABC* is 75°

(3)

(ii) Measure the angles *BAC* and *ACB*.

Answer: Angle *BAC* = ... ° (1)

Angle *ACB* = ... ° (1)

(iii) Measure the length of *AC*.

Answer: .... cm (1)

(iv) What is the length of the perimeter of the triangle *ABC*?

Answer: .... cm (2)

November 95 Q11

43. (i) Draw, as accurately as you can, a triangle *ABC*, where *AB* is 6.5 cm, *AC* is 7.2 cm and angle *BAC* is 90°

(4)

(ii) Measure the length of *BC*.

Answer: *BC* = ... cm (1)

(iii) What is the perimeter of the triangle *ABC*?

Answer: .... cm (2)

January 97 Q10

44. What is the perimeter of this triangle?

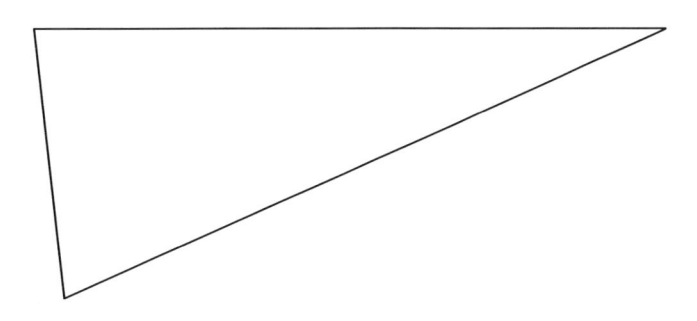

Answer: .... cm (3)

45. (i) Construct accurately the triangle *ABC*, where *AB* is 7.4 cm, angle *BAC* is 40° and angle *ABC* is 95°

(3)

(ii) Measure the length of line *AC*.

Answer: *AC* = ... cm (1)

January 95 Q13

46. Here is a constructed triangle:

PQ is 10 cm.

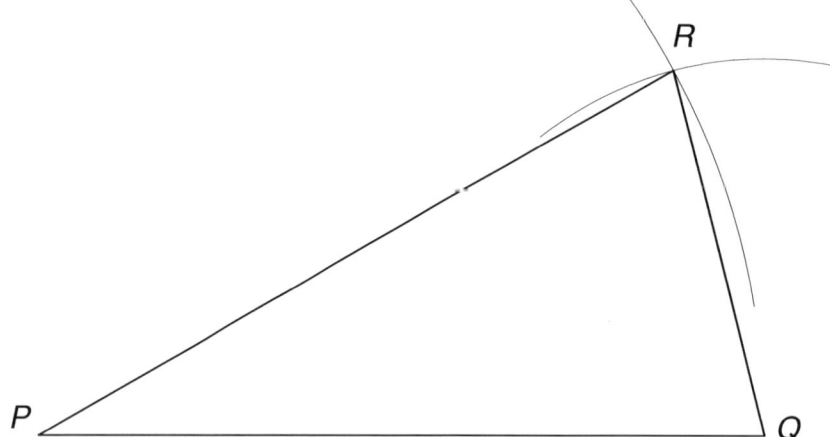

(i) (a) Which radius arcs have been constructed?

Answer: *PR* .... cm (1)

Answer: *QR* .... cm (1)

(b) What shape is triangle PQR?

Answer: .... (1)

(ii) (a) Mark the point S, the midpoint of PR and point T, the midpoint of PQ. Join ST. (1)

(b) What shape is the quadrilateral QRST?

Answer: .... (2)

47. (i) Draw, as accurately as you can, a triangle ABC, where AB is 8.3 cm, AC measures 6.8 cm and angle BAC is 60°

(4)

(ii) Measure the angle ACB and the length of BC.

Answers: angle ACB = ... ° (1)

BC = ... cm (1)

January 96 Q10

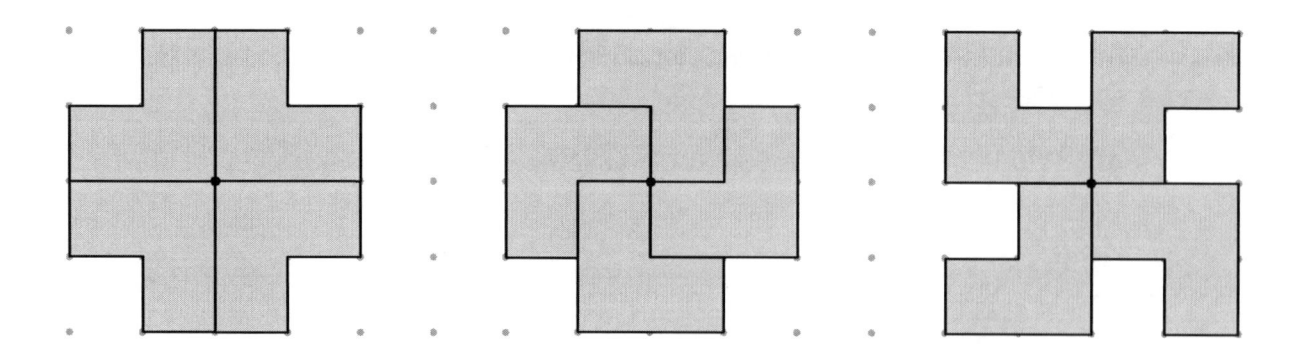

48. These diagrams show three different patterns which can be made when a simple shape is rotated (turned) through one right angle each time about one of its corners.

In this case, the simple shape is

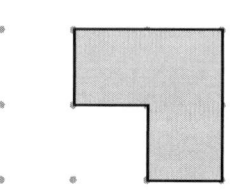

(i) Using the simple shape drawn below, make two similar patterns by rotating the shape through right angles about its corners.

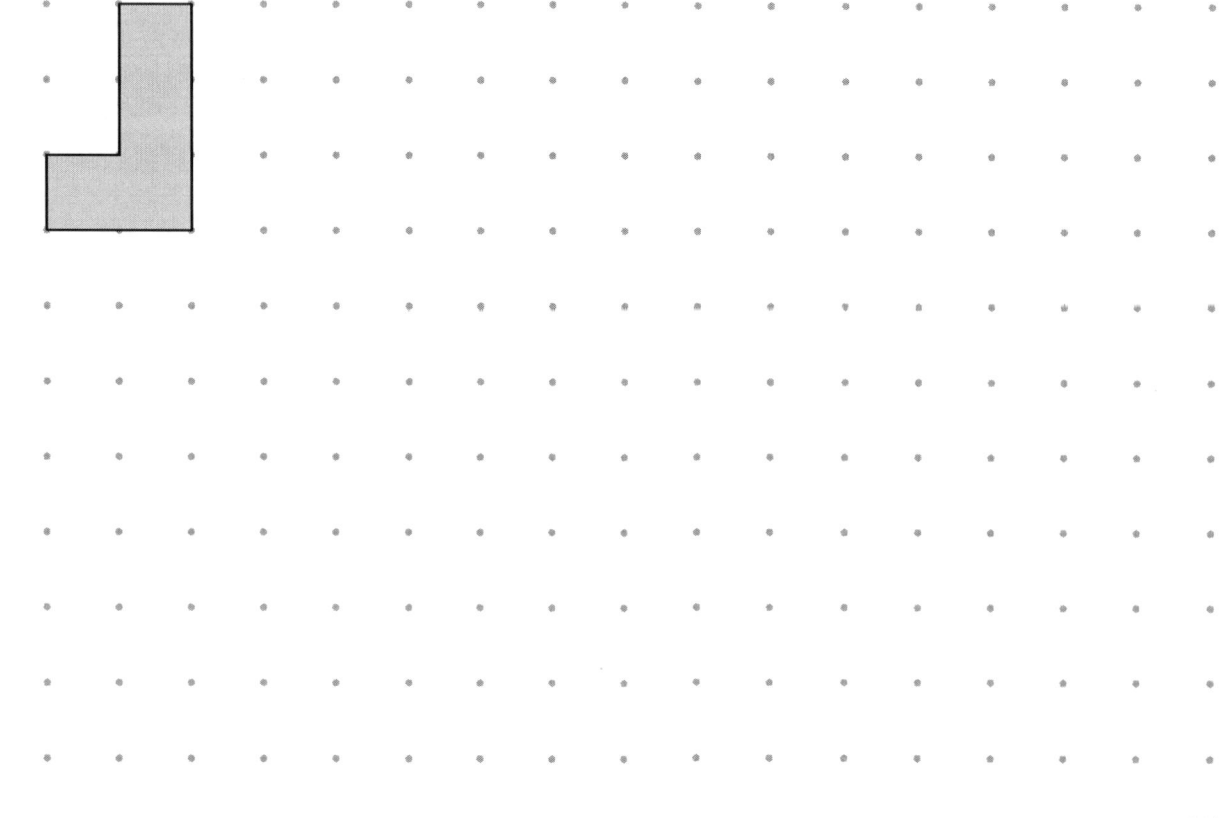

(4)

(ii) Make two patterns by rotating this shape through right angles about its corners.

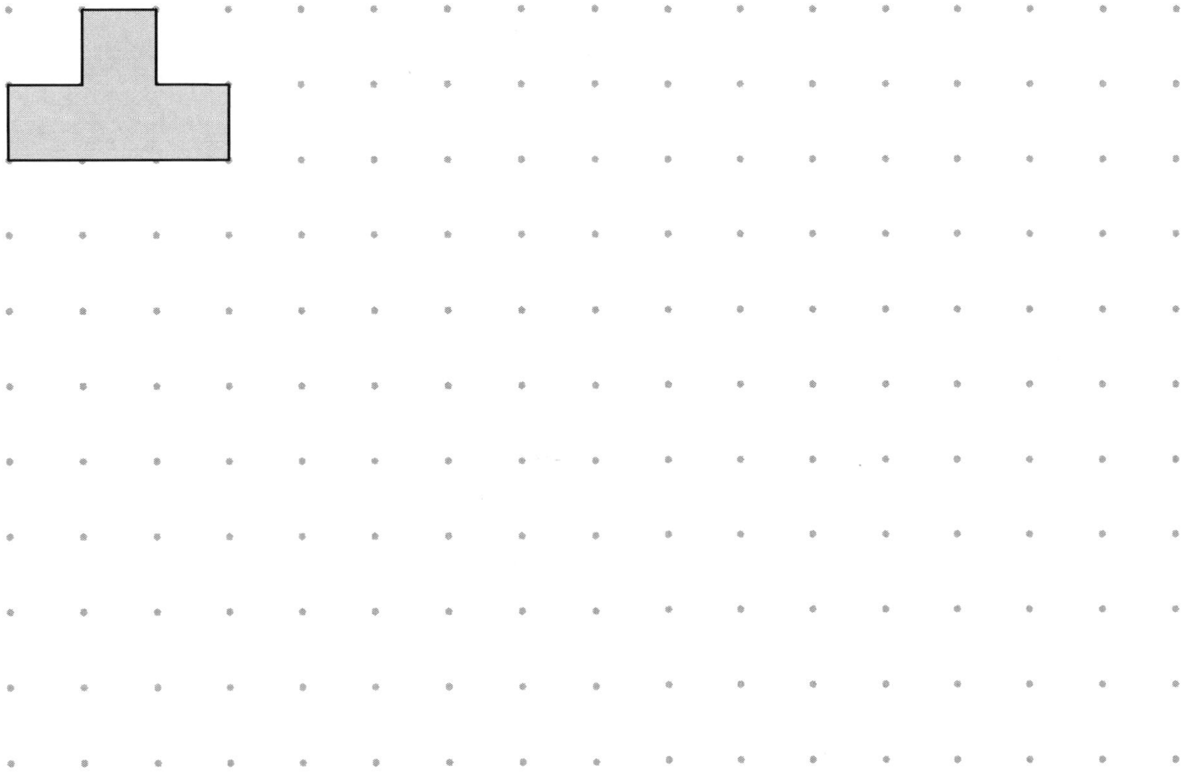

(4)

(iii) Make two patterns by rotating this shape through right angles about its corners.

(4)

49. In this question write one of the words

        reflection   **rotation**   **translation**

to describe the transformation when

(i) **A** is mapped (moved) onto **B**

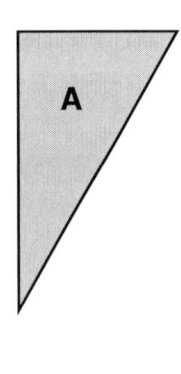

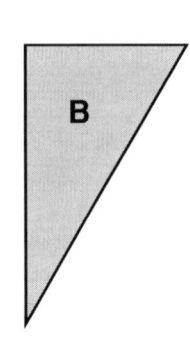

Answer: .... (1)

(ii) **C** is mapped onto **D**

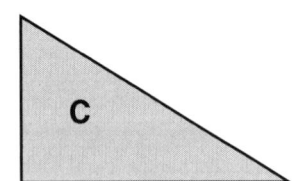

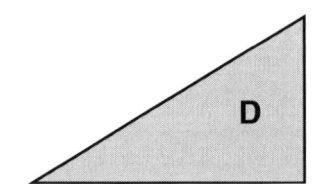

Answer: .... (1)

(iii) **E** is mapped onto **F**.

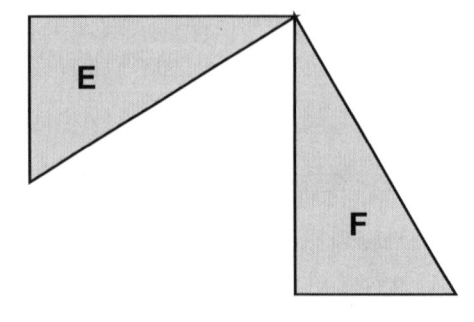

Answer: .... (1)

50. (i) Reflect the triangle in the line.

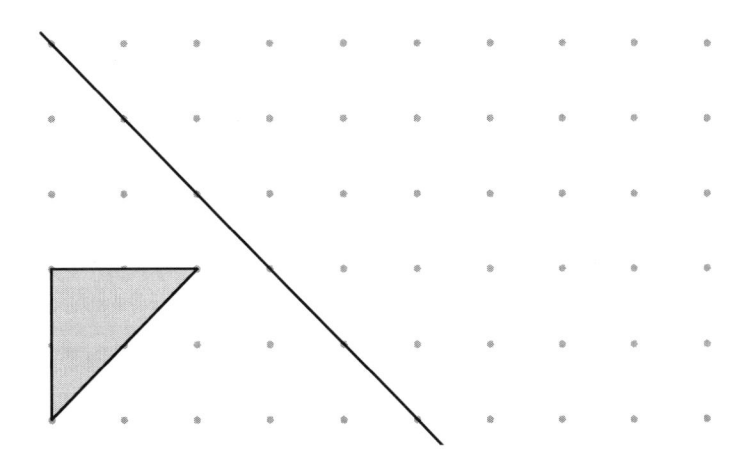

(2)

(ii) Rotate the shape through 90° anticlockwise about the large dot.

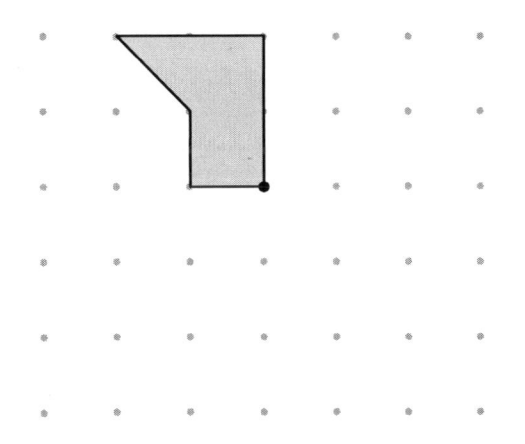

(2)

(iii) Translate the shape, 2 units left and 3 units up.

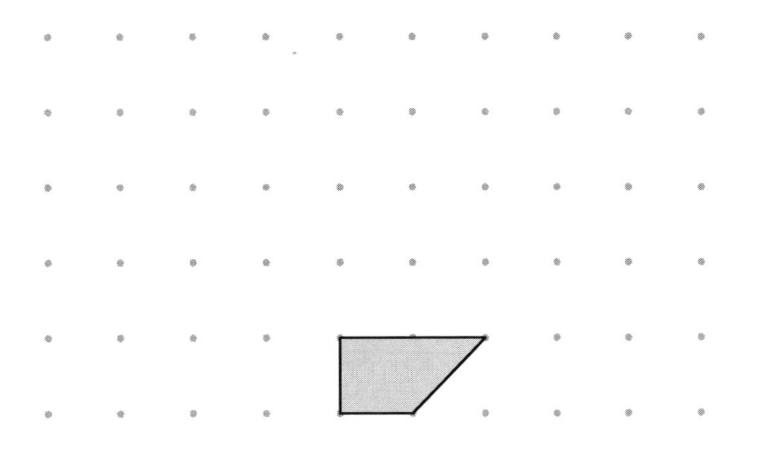

(2)

SHAPE ETC
SC

51. (i) Which shape is **not** congruent to shape **A**?

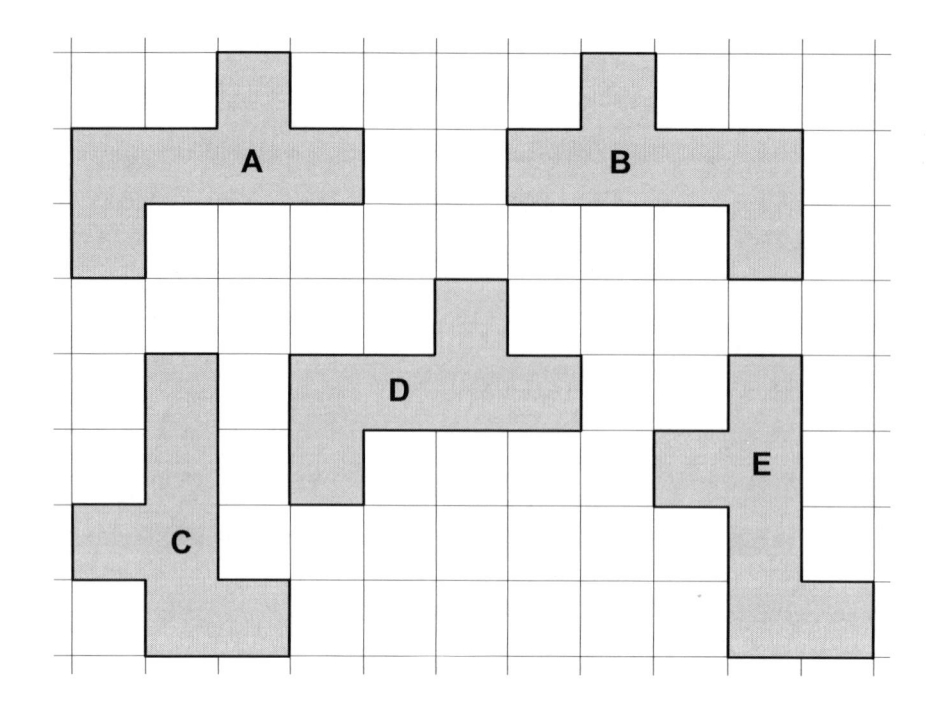

Answer: .... (1)

(ii) Explain your answer to part (i).

Answer: ....

....

.... (2)

52. Penny has these shapes:

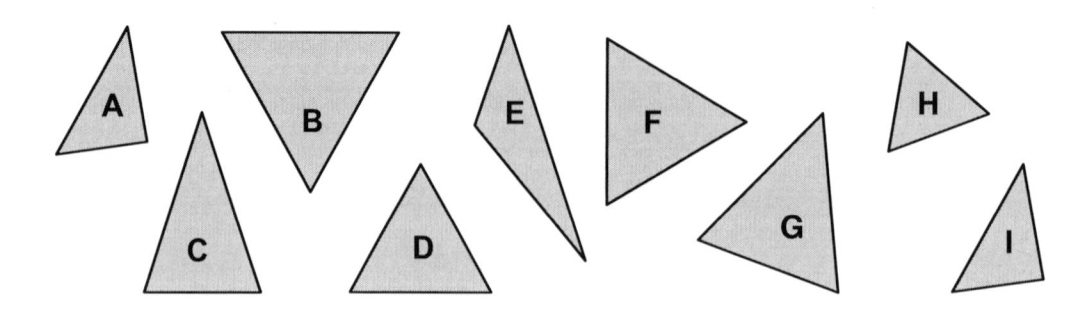

(i) Which shape is congruent to shape **A**?   Answer: .... (1)

(ii) Which shapes are similar to shape **B**?   Answer: .... (2)

160

53. Here is a part of a tessellation made up of tiles:

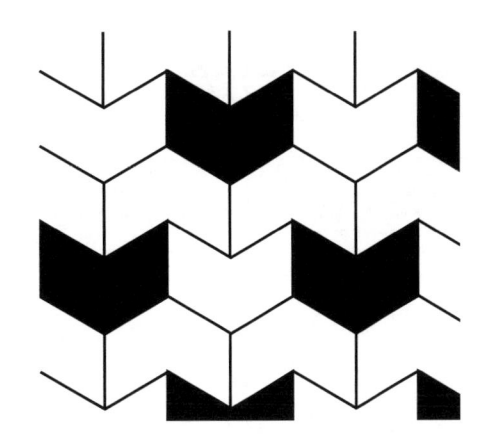

On the dotted grid below, draw a tessellation using the tile **A**.

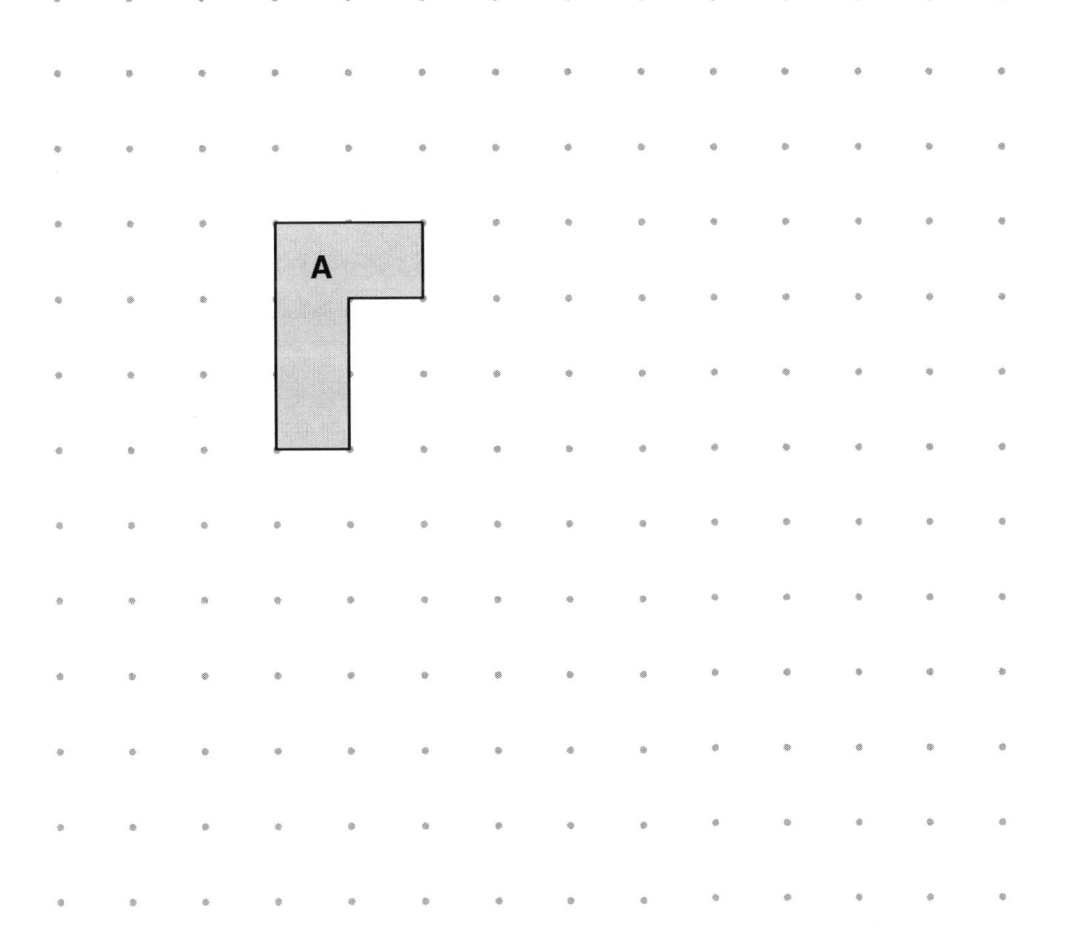

You do not need to fill the grid, but you should continue in all directions far enough for your pattern to be clear.

(5)

54. This diagram shows part of a tessellation made up of triangular tiles.

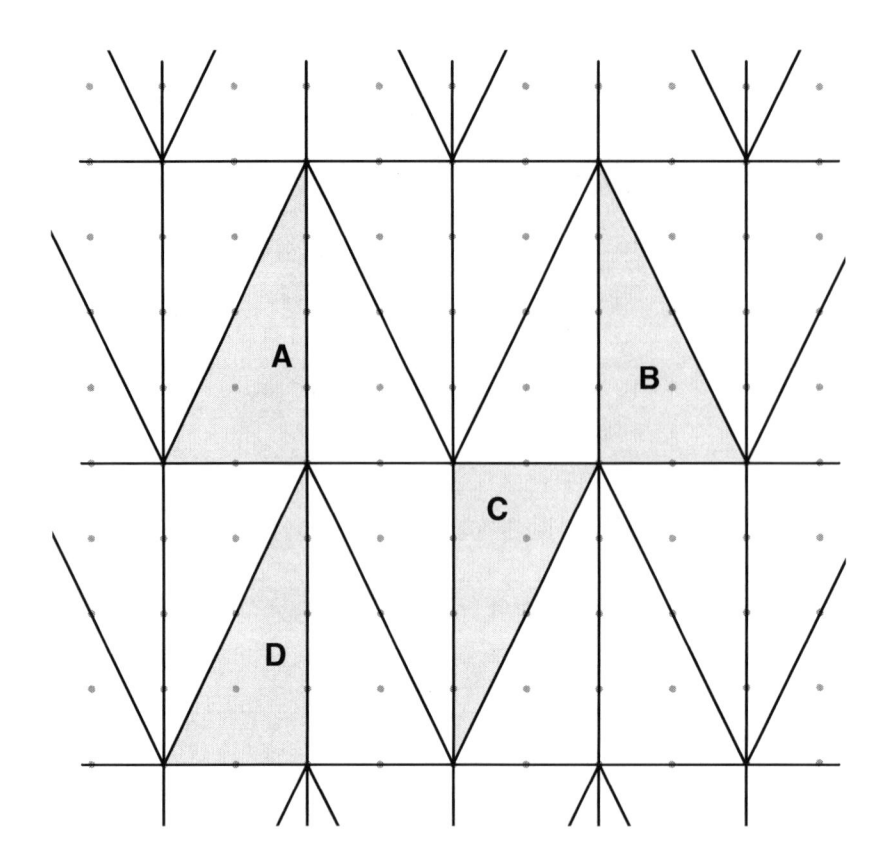

(i) Which transformation (reflection, rotation or translation) would map

(a) **A** onto **B** Answer: .... (1)

(b) **A** onto **C** Answer: .... (1)

(c) **A** onto **D**? Answer: .... (1)

(ii) Which word describes the relationship between triangles **A**, **B**, **C** and **D**?

Answer: .... (2)

STRAND 6: HANDLING DATA

A   **Data handling:** collecting, presenting and interpreting data

1. Sort these objects in two different ways by drawing loops round objects which are the same in some way.

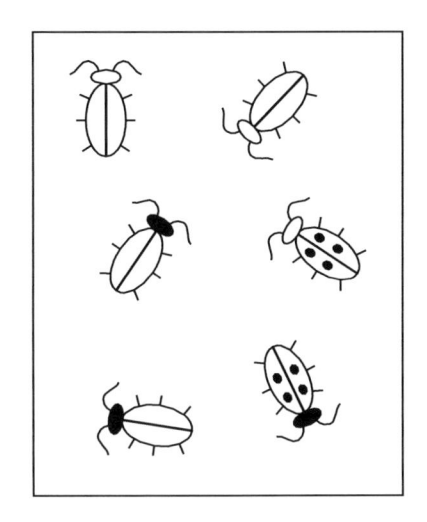

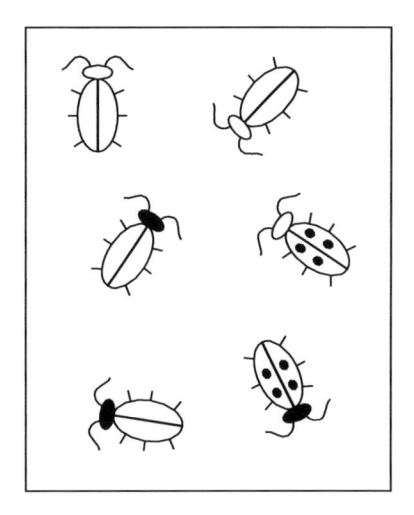

   (4)

2. Ben's uncle asks him what he would like for Christmas.

   He sends Ben this decision tree diagram.

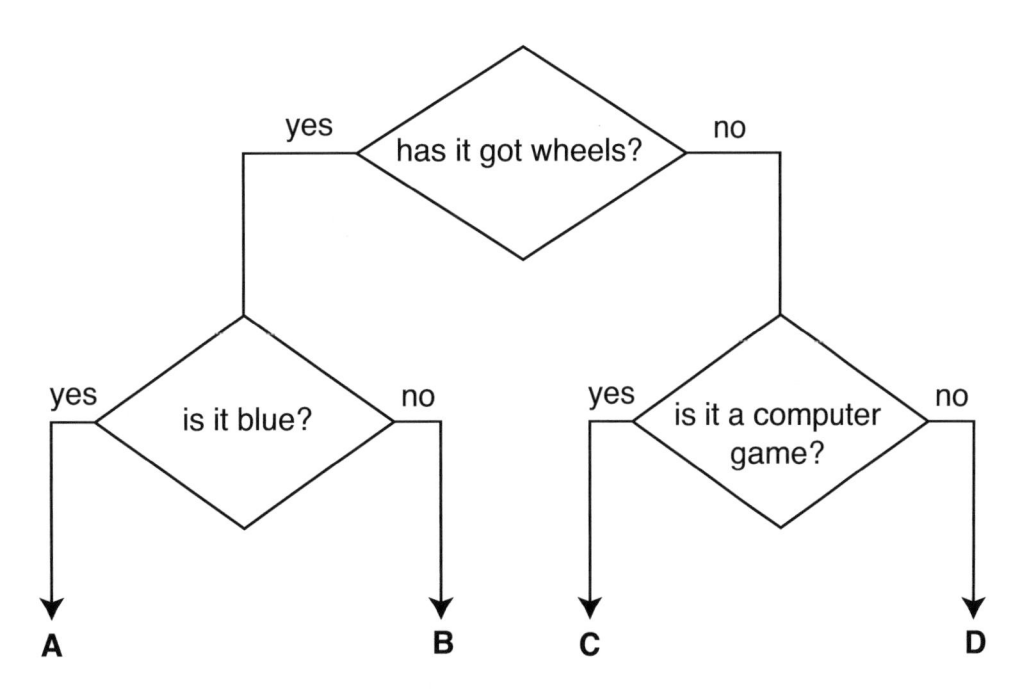

   Ben would like his uncle to give him a blue bicycle.

   Would it be **A**, **B**, **C** or **D** on his uncle's diagram?

   Answer: .... (2)

January 96 Q11

3. Sort these bears.

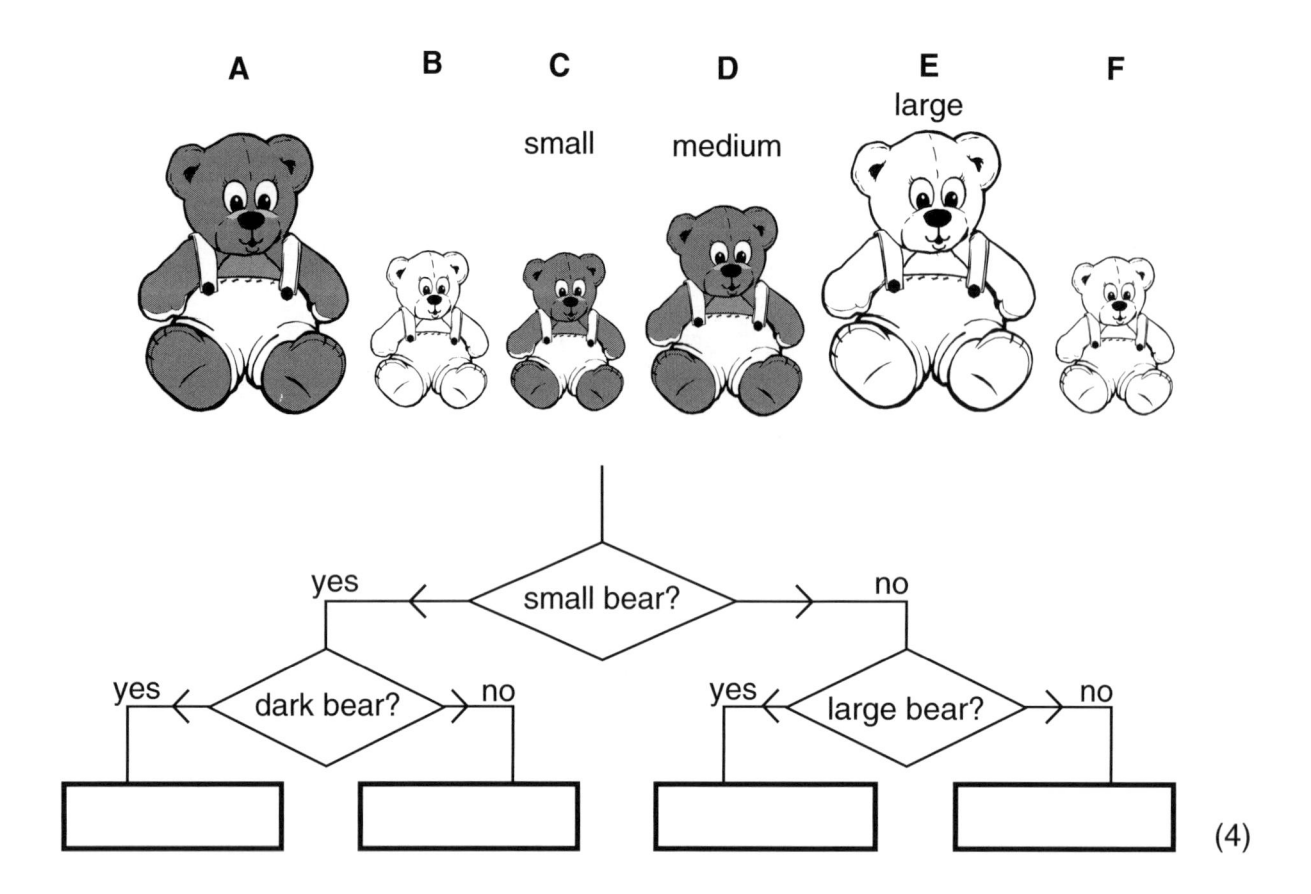

A B C D E F
        small medium large

```
           small bear?
      yes /          \ no
   dark bear?      large bear?
  yes /  \ no    yes /   \ no
  [   ] [   ]   [    ]  [    ]
```
(4)

4. Complete the details on the decision tree diagram.

(A and B have been done for you.)

Remember, always start at the top of the decision tree diagram for each object.

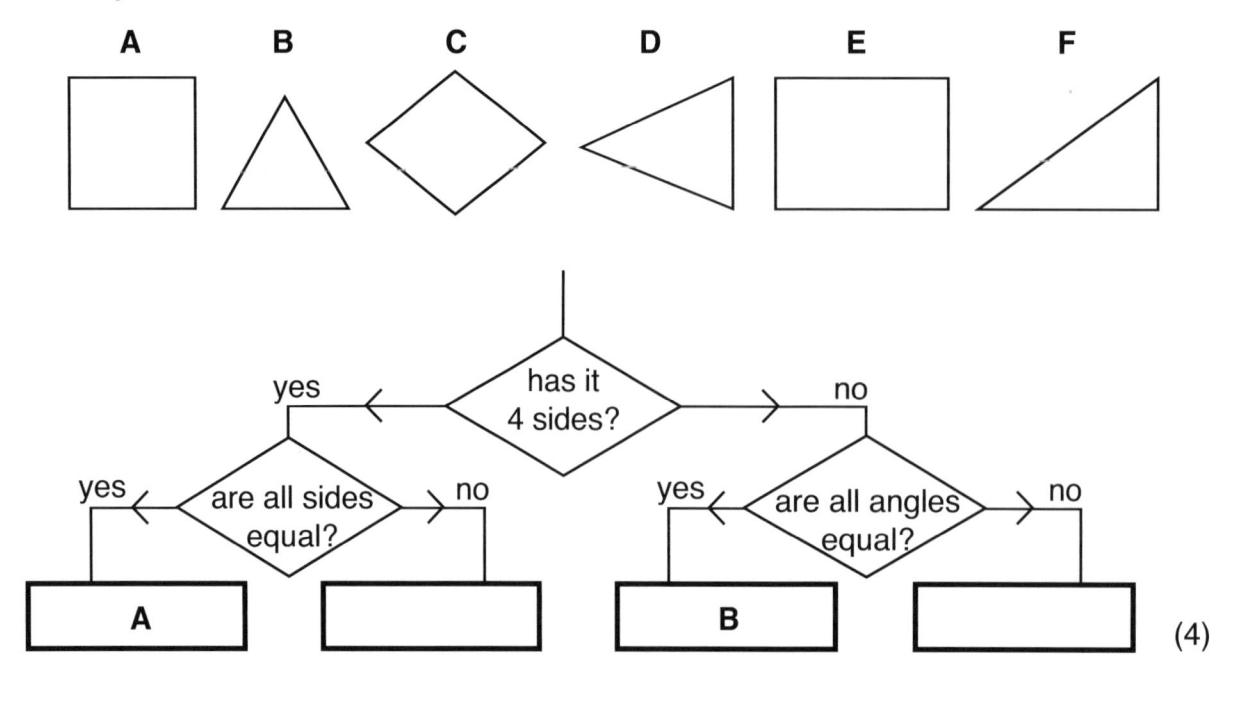

A B C D E F

```
              has it 4 sides?
        yes /              \ no
   are all sides equal?   are all angles equal?
   yes /    \ no          yes /       \ no
   [ A ]   [    ]         [ B ]      [    ]
```
(4)

5. Sort these numbers.

   (Start at the top with each number!)

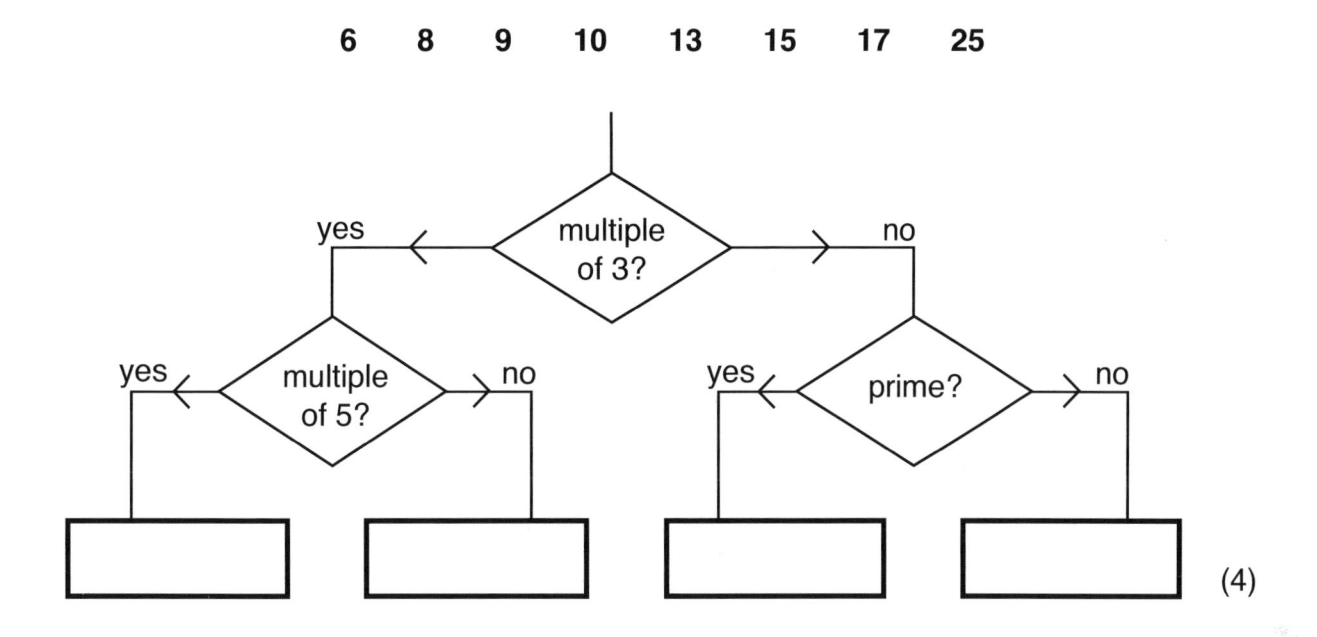

   6   8   9   10   13   15   17   25

   Decision tree:
   - multiple of 3?
     - yes → multiple of 5?
       - yes → [15]
       - no → [6, 9]
     - no → prime?
       - yes → [13, 17]
       - no → [8, 10, 25]

   (4)

6. Choosing from these questions, fill in the question boxes.

   Check **thoroughly** before you write on the decision tree diagram!

   all sides equal?   all angles equal?   4 sides?   one line of symmetry?

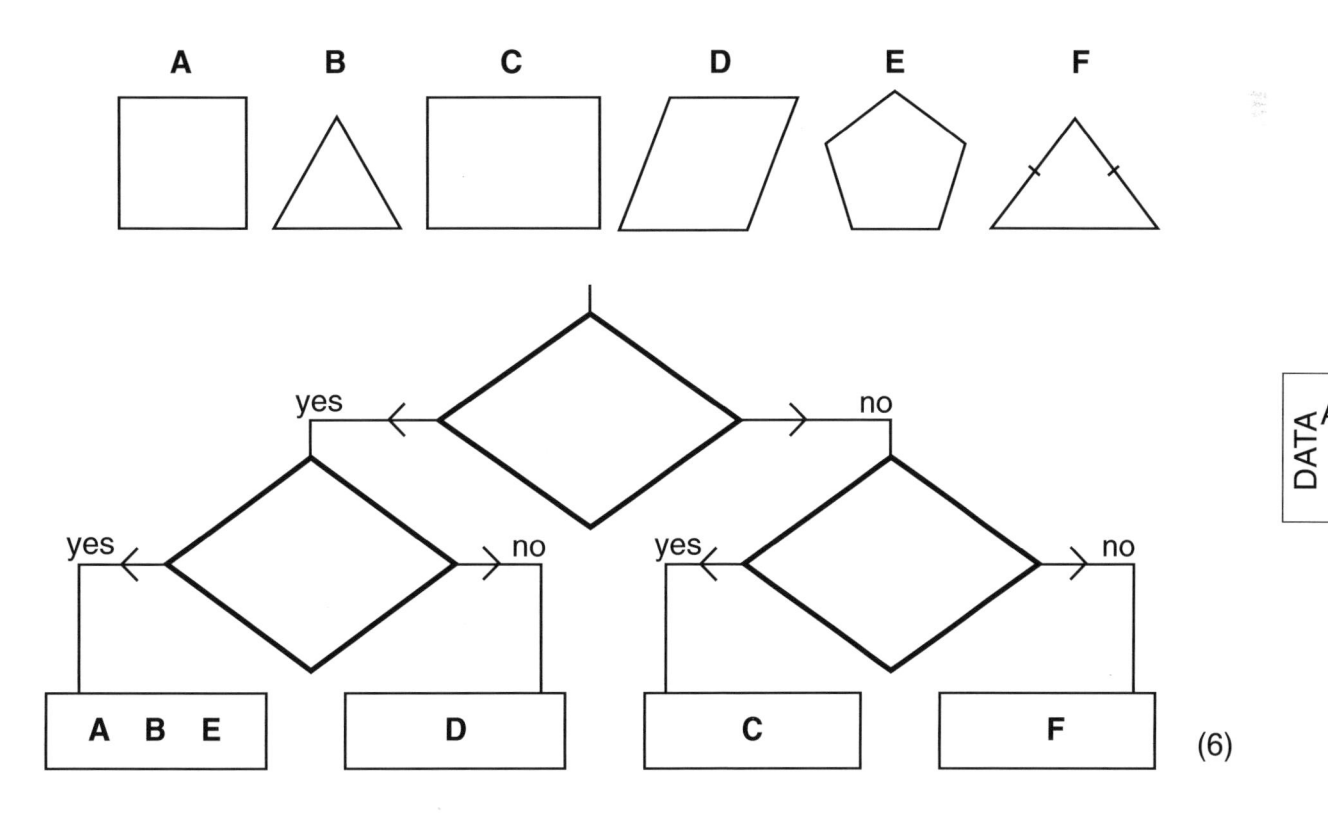

   Shapes:
   - A: square
   - B: triangle
   - C: rectangle
   - D: rhombus/parallelogram
   - E: pentagon
   - F: isosceles triangle

   Decision tree leading to:
   - yes/yes → A B E
   - yes/no → D
   - no/yes → C
   - no/no → F

   (6)

165

7. In a mapping diagram, a member of the first set is mapped onto one or more members of the second set.

A mapping diagram shows a relationship.

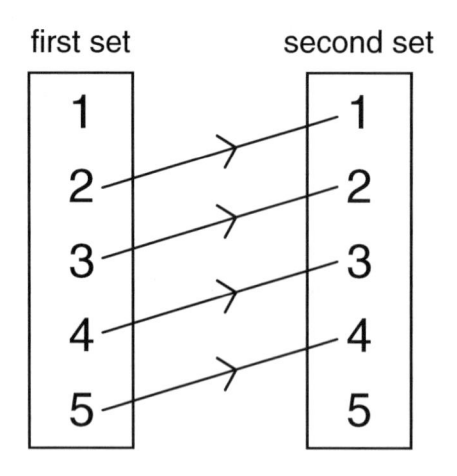

This mapping can be described in words as 'is one more than'.

(i) Draw arrows to show the mapping 'is one less than'.

(2)

(ii) Which mapping is shown here?

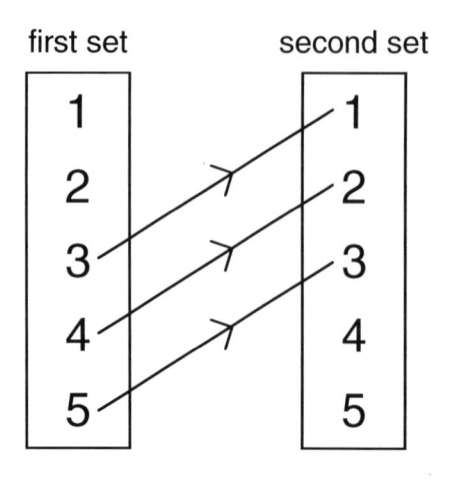

Answer: .... (2)

8. (i) Draw arrows to show the mapping 'has one more side than'.

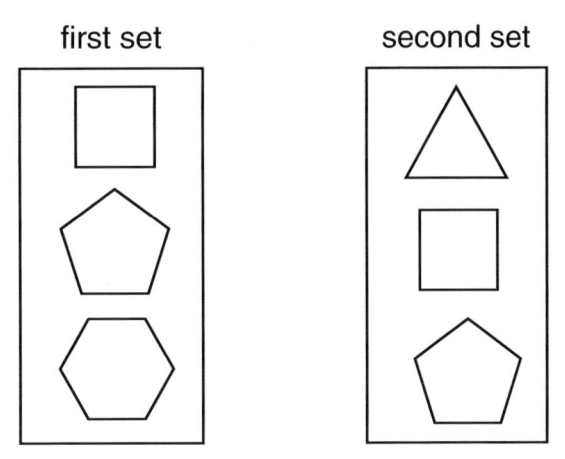

first set   second set

(2)

(ii) Complete this mapping of the relationship 'has more sides than'.

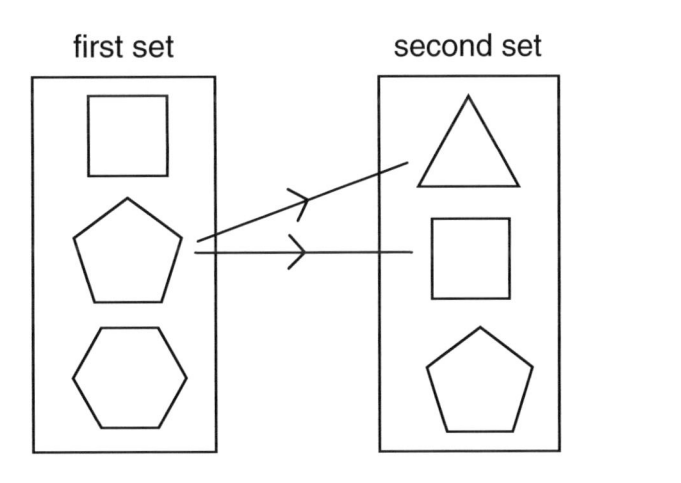

first set   second set

(2)

(iii) Draw arrows to show the mapping 'has two more sides than'.

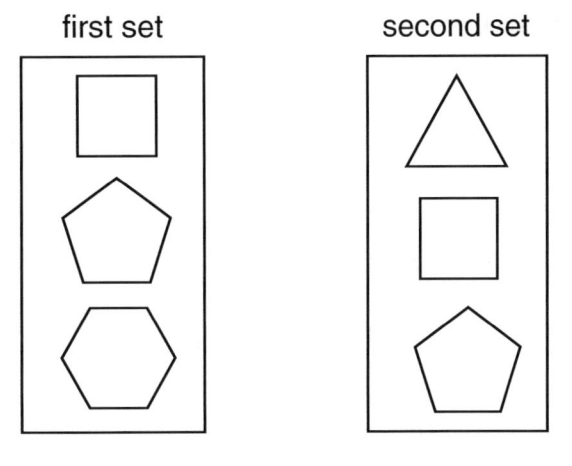

first set   second set

(2)

9. This data table shows some facts about six children.

name	age (years)	sex (M/F)	height (cm)	waist (cm)	mass (kg)
Anna	9	F	134	66	38
Ben	10	M	142	62	34
Colin	8	M	131	61	35
David	9	M	140	59	37
Ekwi	11	F	153	60	41
Fiona	10	F	138	63	33

(i) Who has the smallest height?   Answer: .... (1)

(ii) Who is the second heaviest?   Answer: .... (1)

(iii) Which nine year old has the larger waist measurement?

   Answer: .... (1)

(iv) How many girls are older than Colin?   Answer: .... (1)

The teacher keeps a record card for each child.

```
NAME:  Anna         AGE:  9
SEX (M/F):  F       MASS (kg):  38
HEIGHT (cm): 134    WAIST (cm):  66
```

(v) Study Anna's record card and then complete the record card for David.

```
NAME:  David        AGE:
SEX (M/F):          MASS (kg):
HEIGHT (cm):        WAIST (cm):
```
(2)

The record card for one of these children has been partly filled in.

(vi) Complete the card.

```
NAME: ..........................   AGE:  10
                                        ........

SEX (M/F):   M        MASS (kg): .........
           ............

HEIGHT (cm): ..........   WAIST (cm): .........
```
(2)

(vii) Gina is a nine-year-old girl who is one cm taller than Ben and two kg lighter than Fiona.

Her waist measurement is three cm more than Anna's.

Complete Gina's record card.

```
NAME:  Gina           AGE: .........

SEX (M/F): ..........   MASS (kg): .........

HEIGHT (cm): ..........   WAIST (cm): .........
```
(2)

10. This data table shows some facts about the Brown family.

name	wears glasses	brown hair	blue eyes	plays golf
Mum	✓	✗	✓	✗
Dad	✓	✓	✗	✓
Tom	✗	✗	✓	✓
Jane	✗	✓	✓	✗

(i) Who has blue eyes and brown hair?

Answer: .... (1)

(ii) Who plays golf but does not wear glasses?

Answer: .... (2)

11.

name	date of birth	height	eye colour	favourite sport	favourite TV programme
Janet	10.11.79	1.56 m	brown	hockey	Grange Hill
Simon	6.12.79	1.30 m	blue	soccer	Dr Who
Claire	23.2.79	1.34 m	blue	netball	Neighbours
Phil	4.1.80	1.45 m	green	tennis	Grange Hill
Polly	15.8.79	1.20 m	brown	swimming	Neighbours
Bob	9.4.79	1.25 m	blue	soccer	Grange Hill

Using the information table above, answer the following questions.

(i) Which children had brown eyes?

Answer: .... (2)

(ii) What percentage of the children had blue eyes?

Answer: ....% (3)

(iii) Who was the youngest?

Answer: .... (2)

(iv) How many years old was he or she in June 1990?

Answer: .... (2)

(v) How much shorter was Polly than Claire?

Answer: .... cm (2)

(vi) What is the name of the child who was smaller than Phil, older than Polly, had blue eyes and liked soccer best?

Answer: .... (2)

January 91 Q20

170

12. The table shows the number of people who went to a computer exhibition on five days.

	Monday	Tuesday	Wednesday	Thursday	Friday
adults	2147	3026	1721		5000
children	3927	5121	3000	2446	

On Thursday twice as many children as adults went to the exhibition.

On Friday three times as many children as adults went to the exhibition.

(i) Use this information to fill in the gaps in the table. (4)

(ii) What was the total number of children who attended the exhibition during the five days?

Answer: .... (4)

(iii) Approximately how many people, to the nearest thousand, attended the exhibition on Monday?

Answer: .... (2)

November 90 Q17

13. Alice has found four beetles.

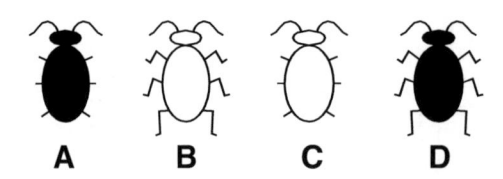

A B C D

(i) Write the letters in the correct regions of this Carroll diagram.
   (*A is done for you.*)

	long legs	not long legs
not black		
black		A

(3)

(ii) Write the letters in the correct regions of this Venn diagram.

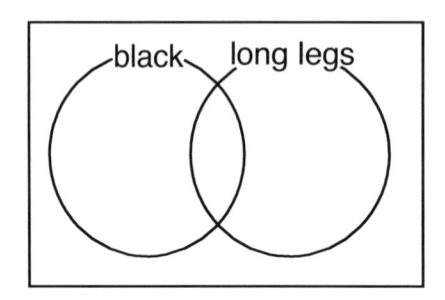

black   long legs

(4)

(iii) Complete this data table for Alice's beetles.

beetle	black	long legs
A	✓	✗
B		
C		
D		

(3)

172

14. The first nine counting numbers are

    1 2 3 4 5 6 7 8 9

    (i) Write each number in the correct region of this Carroll diagram.

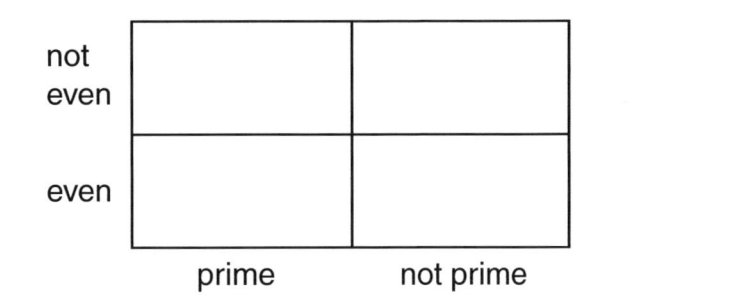

	prime	not prime
not even		
even		

    (4)

    (ii) Write each number in the correct region of this Venn diagram.

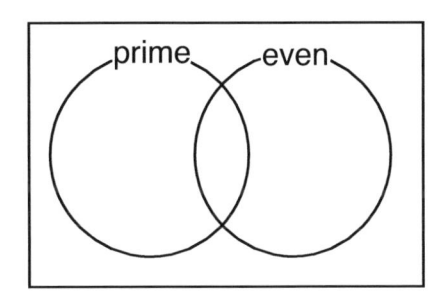

    (prime) (even)

    (4)

15. This Venn diagram shows the numbers of pupils.

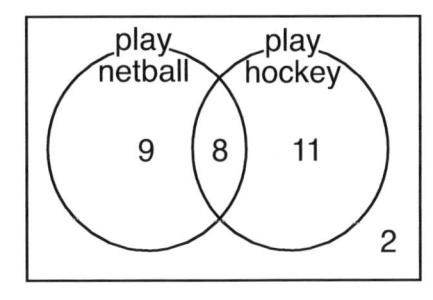

    play netball: 9, play hockey: 11, intersection: 8, outside: 2

    How many pupils do not play hockey?

    Answer: .... (2)

16. This Venn diagram shows the numbers of girls in a class who play the piano (set P) and the recorder (set R).

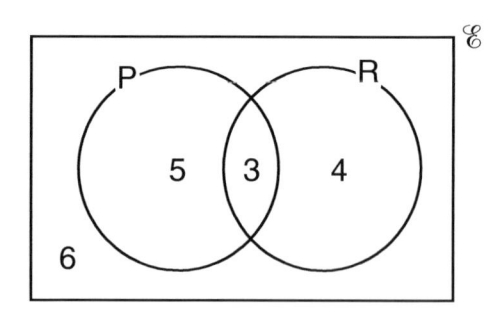

    (i) How many girls play the recorder and not the piano?

    Answer: .... girls (2)

    (ii) How many girls are in the class?

    Answer: .... girls (3)

    November 90 Q16

17. There were 15 people standing on a railway platform.

    Each carried a newspaper or umbrella or both.

    Ten people carried a newspaper and eight carried an umbrella.

    (i) Use this information to complete the Venn diagram, where N represents the set of people with a newspaper and U represents the set of people with an umbrella.

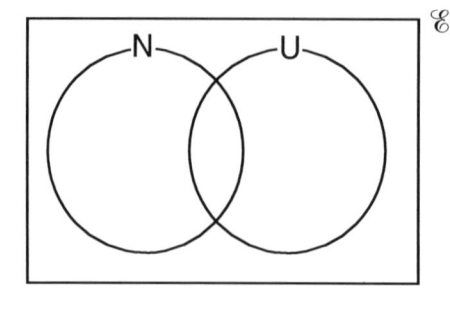

    (5)

    (ii) How many people carried both a newspaper and an umbrella?

    Answer: .... (1)

    November 91 Q19

18. Study the letters in these words.

triangle   square

(i) On the Venn diagram below write the letters of these two words in the correct regions.

Each letter **a e g i l n q r s t u** is to be written on the diagram **once** only.

These are the only letters of the alphabet which we are considering.

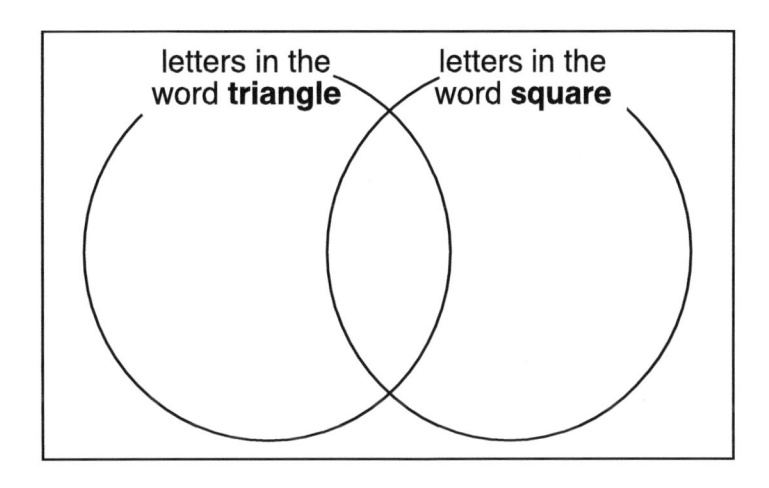

letters in the word **triangle**   letters in the word **square**

(4)

(ii) Which letters are in both words?   Answer: .... (2)

(iii) Which letters are in the word **square** but not in the word **triangle**?

Answer: .... (2)

19. This Carroll diagram shows some shapes.

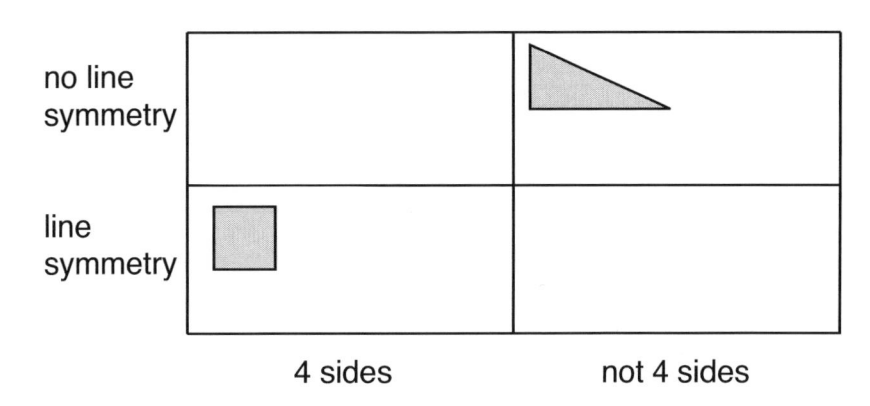

	4 sides	not 4 sides
no line symmetry		▲
line symmetry	■	

In the correct regions write **P** (parallelogram), **R** (rhombus) and **E** (equilateral triangle). (3)

175

20. Belinda has kept a tally of the numbers of sweets eaten by five of her friends in one week.

name	tally	total
Tina	|||| |||| |||| ||||	19
Sam	|||| |||| ||	....
Kerry	|||| |||| |||| |||| |||	....
Will	|||| |||	....
Jane	|||| |||| |||| |||| |||| ||	....

Tina has eaten 19 sweets.

(i) Complete the totals for the other four friends. (4)

(ii) How many sweets did the five friends eat altogether?

Answer: .... (2)

21. Four children, Alan, Bertie, Corrie and Debbie, played a game and recorded the winners by writing the first letters of their names.

A	B	D	B	A	C	B	B	D
B	A	A	D	B	B	C	C	A
C	C	A	D	B	D	B	A	C

(i) Complete the tally to show the number of wins by each child. (3)

	tally	total
Alan		
Bertie		
Corrie		
Debbie		

(ii) Write the numbers of wins in the 'total' column. (2)

22. At her party, Anna kept a record of all of the cups of cola drunk.
She drew this pictogram:

Key: one symbol **U** represents **1** cup

Anna	U U
Ben	U U U U U U U U U
Colin	U U U U
David	U U U U U U
Ekwi	U U U
Fiona	U

number of cups of cola drunk

(i) How many cups did Anna drink?

Answer: .... (1)

(ii) How many more cups did David drink than Ekwi?

Answer: .... (1)

(iii) How many cups were drunk altogether?

Answer: .... (2)

(iv) Name two people who drank seven cups between them?

Answer: .... and .... (2)

177

23. Alice and five friends have had an apple-eating contest.

    Alice has drawn this pictogram:

    Key: one symbol Ó represents **2** apples

Alice	Ó Ó Ó Ó Ó
Billy	Ó Ó Ó (
Clare	Ó Ó Ó Ó Ó Ó
David	Ó Ó Ó Ó Ó Ó (
Eleanor	Ó
Fefe	Ó Ó

    number of apples eaten

    (i) How many apples did Alice eat?

    Answer: .... (1)

    (ii) How many more apples did David eat than Fefe?

    Answer: .... (1)

    (iii) How many apples were eaten altogether?

    Answer: .... (2)

    (iv) Which two people ate 12 apples between them?

    Answer: .... and .... (2)

24. The diagram below shows how many cassettes of each type were sold in a shop in January.

Key: ☐ represents 20 cassettes

pop	☐☐☐☐☐☐☐☐☐☐☐☐☐
classical	☐☐☐☐☐☐☐
spoken	☐☐◸
country and western	
other	☐

(i) How many cassettes of pop music were sold?

Answer: .... (2)

The number of classical cassettes sold was double the number of country and western cassettes.

(ii) Fill in the diagram for country and western. (2)

(iii) Which type sold 50 cassettes?

Answer: .... (2)

(iv) How many cassettes were sold altogether?

Answer: .... (3)

(v) In December, 900 cassettes were sold.
   (a) How many more cassettes were sold in December than in January?

Answer: .... (2)

   (b) Suggest a reason why more were sold in December.

Answer: ....
   .... (2)

January 92 Q15

25. The chart below shows the number of cartons of orange drink sold from the school vending machine during a school week.

Key: ● represents 4 cartons

Monday	● ● ● ●
Tuesday	● ● ● ● ◖
Wednesday	● ● ●
Thursday	● ● ● ● ● ●
Friday	

(i) How many cartons of orange were sold on Monday?

Answer: .... (2)

20 cartons of orange were sold on Friday.

(ii) Show this on the chart. (2)

(iii) What is the total number of cartons sold during the week?

Answer: .... (3)

(iv) Estimate how many cartons would be needed for a school term of ten weeks.

Answer: .... (2)

November 90 Q21

26. The school has been given a gift of £300

The pictogram shows the prices of several things which would be useful.

camera	£ £ £ £ £ £ £ £
guitar	£ £ £ £ £
table-tennis table	£ £ £ £ £ £ £
staffroom armchair	£ £ £ £ £ £
encyclopaedias	£ £ £ £ £ £ £ £ £ £
stage lighting	£ £ £ £ £ £ £ £ £ £ £ £
cassette recorder	£ £ £ £

(i) If the cassette recorder costs £60, how much does each £ stand for on the pictogram?

Answer: £ .... (2)

(ii) Which two items together would cost exactly £300?

Answer: .... (5)

(iii) How much would be spent if the guitar, table-tennis table and cassette recorder were bought?

Answer: £ .... (3)

January 90 Q17

(iv) What is the largest number of items which could be bought with the £300, and what are they?

Answer: .... items (1)

The items are: .... (3)

27. In this block graph showing groups of people, one block represents one person.

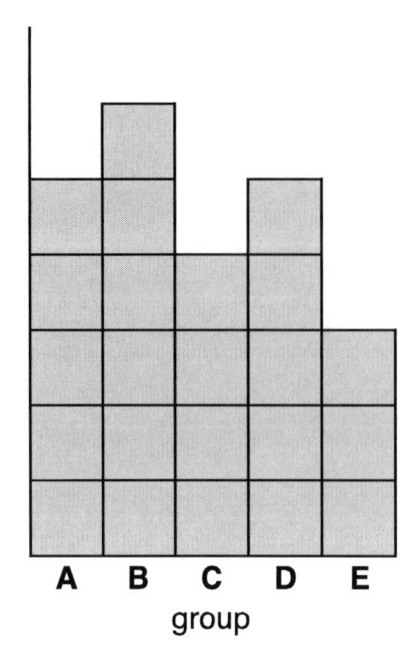

(i) How many people are represented in group **A**?

Answer: .... (1)

(ii) How many people are represented altogether?

Answer: .... (1)

(iii) How many more people are in group **A** than in group **E**?

Answer: .... (1)

(iv) Which group has the largest number of people?

Answer: .... (1)

28. Tommy has tipped some centimetre cubes in three colours onto the table.

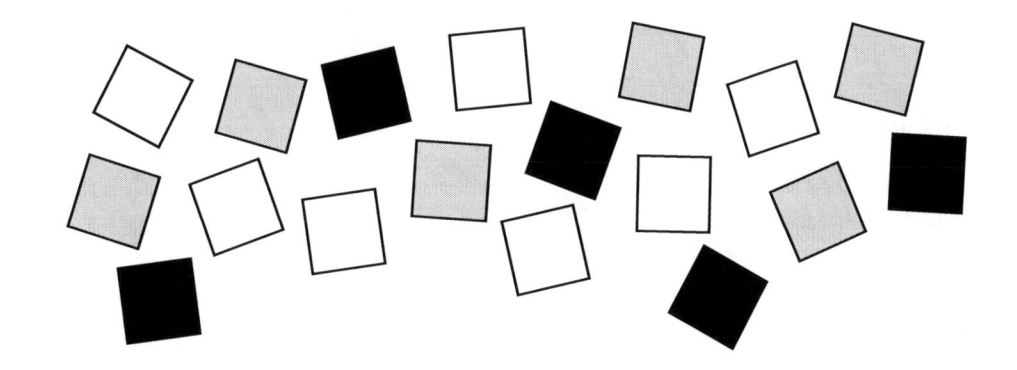

(i) On the square dotted grid below, complete the block graph to show Tommy's cubes.

(Three of the blocks have been drawn for you already.)

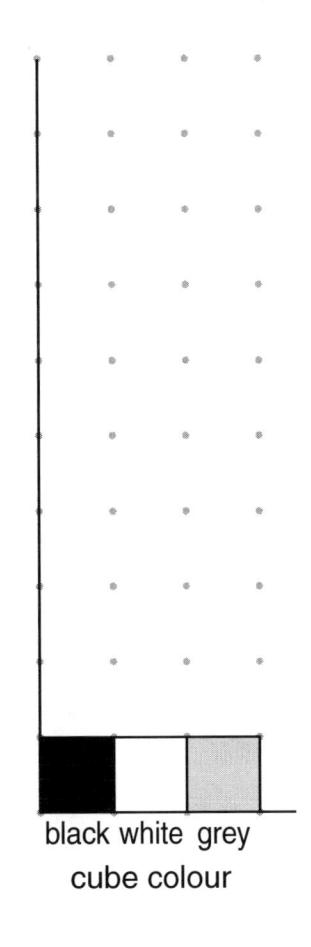

black white grey
cube colour

(3)

DATA A

At a football match there were 12 000 United supporters and 15 000 City supporters.

(ii) Suggest how you might show this as a block graph.

Answer: ....

.... (2)

183

29. Clare has 11 mice, four all black and five all white and two black and white. Her friends draw these diagrams to show this information.

Alice
Carroll diagram
(numbers of mice shown)

	black	no black
no white	4	0
white	2	5

Ben
Venn diagram
(numbers of mice shown)

black 4 (2) 5 white
0

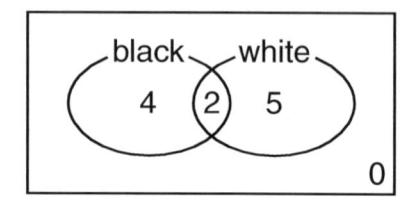

Carrie
pictogram
(one symbol represents one mouse)

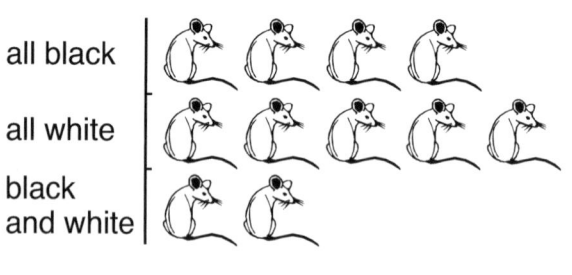

all black
all white
black and white

Danny
block graph
(one block represents one mouse)

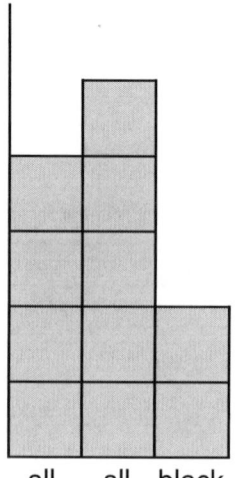

all black — all white — black and white
colour of mouse

Ellie

fraction diagram

| | all black | | | all white | | | black and white |

Study these five different diagrams and answer the questions.

(i) Why is there a zero in one region of the Carroll diagram?

Answer: ....

.... (2)

(ii) What do the Carroll diagram and the Venn diagram have in common?

Answer: ....

.... (2)

(iii) What do the pictogram and block graph have in common?

Answer: ....

.... (2)

(iv) Looking at the fraction diagram, what fraction of the mice are all white?

Answer: .... (1)

(v) If one of Clare's black mice escaped, what percentage of those remaining would be all black?

Answer: .... % (2)

DATA A

185

30. Sarah cut a pizza into eight equal pieces.

She ate one piece, her friend John ate three pieces and her dog Tubby ate the rest.

Sarah has drawn this diagram.

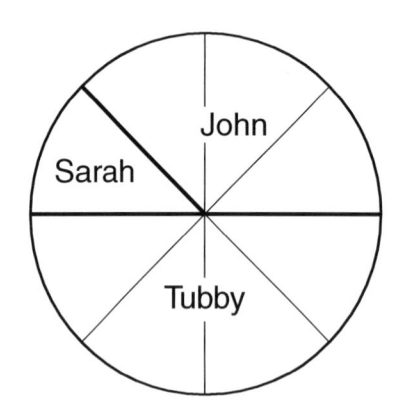

(i) What fraction of the pizza has been eaten by

(a) Sarah

Answer: .... (1)

(b) John

Answer: .... (1)

(c) Tubby?

Answer: .... (1)

(ii) What percentage of the pizza has been eaten by

(a) Tubby

Answer: .... % (1)

(b) Sarah?

Answer: .... % (2)

John has started to draw a fraction diagram to show how the pizza was shared.

(iii) Complete John's fraction diagram above. (2)

(iv) On the dotted grid below, draw either a pictogram or a block graph to show the same information.

(4)

(v) Which diagram (Sarah's, John's or your own) do you think is the most useful, and why?

Answer: .... diagram, because ....

....

.... (4)

31. Eight groups of children, **A** to **H**, went on a spider hunt.

They drew this block graph to record their results.

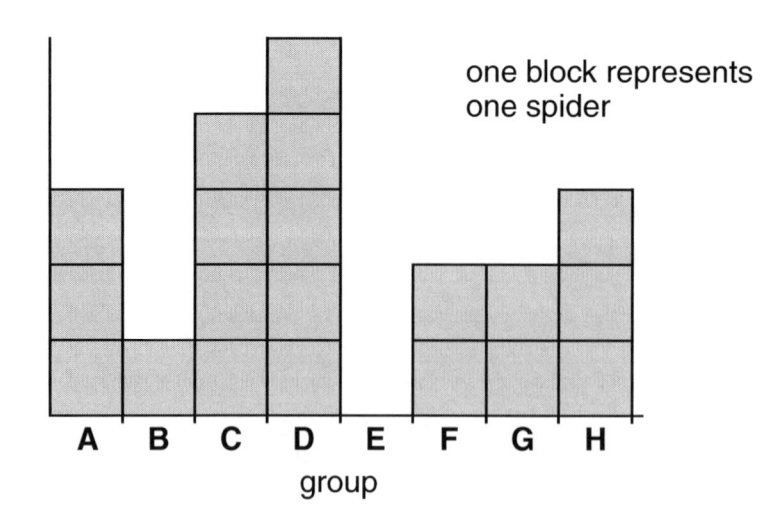

one block represents one spider

(i) (a) Which group found the most spiders?

Answer: .... (1)

(b) How many spiders did group **E** find?

Answer: .... (1)

(c) What was the total number of spiders found?

Answer: .... (2)

(d) How many groups found more spiders than group **F**?

Answer: .... (1)

Samantha suggested that a bar chart might be better than a block graph, and she drew the one shown at the top of the next page.

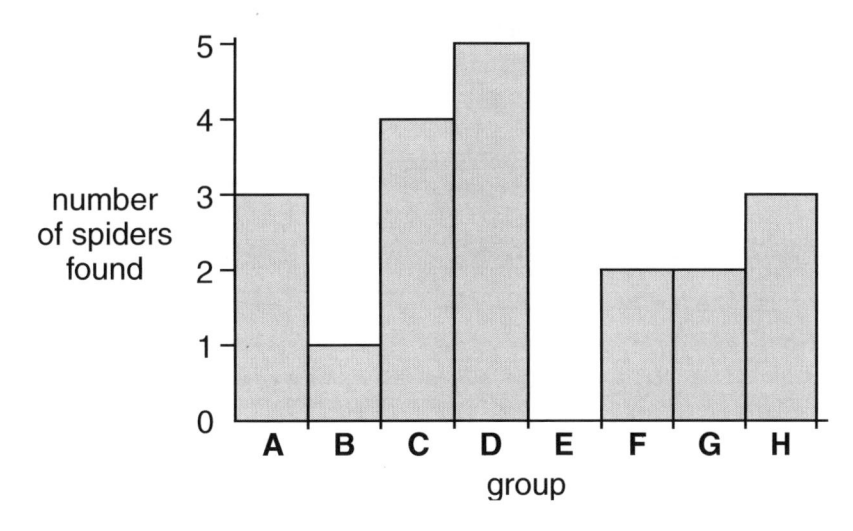

[Bar chart: y-axis "number of spiders found" from 0 to 5; x-axis "group" with bars A=3, B=1, C=4, D=5, E=0, F=2, G=2, H=3]

(ii) Suggest two ways in which this bar chart differs from the block graph on page 188.

1 .... (1)

2 .... (1)

(iii) Suggest one reason why a bar chart may be better in this study than

(a) a pictogram

Answer: ....

.... (2)

(b) a fraction diagram

Answer: ....

.... (2)

(c) a block graph.

Answer: ....

.... (2)

32. Ann has drawn this graph to show how some children travel to school.

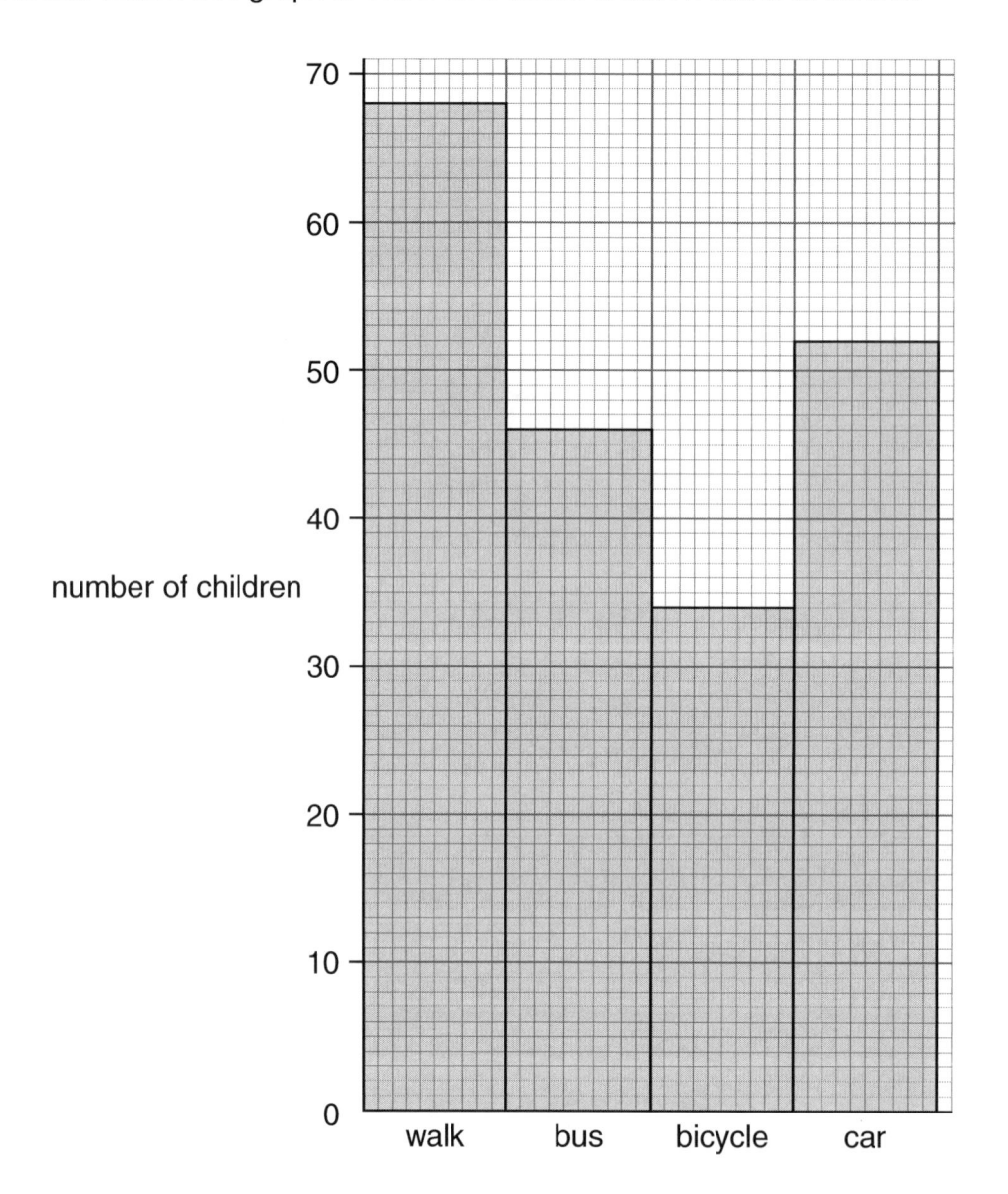

(i) What is the total number of children who took part in Ann's survey?

Answer: .... (3)

(ii) How many more children walk to school than are taken by car?

Answer: .... (2)

(iii) What fraction of these children travel to school by bus?
Give your answer in its simplest form.

Answer: .... (2)

(iv) What percentage of the children walk to school?

Answer: .... % (2)

(v) Complete this sentence:

Twice as many children .... to

school as .... to school. (2)

November 95 Q14

33. The table below shows the absences for each class in a school during one week.

class	Mon	Tue	Wed	Thu	Fri	total
1	2	1	0	1	0	4
2	3	2	1	2	1	9
3	0	2	3	2	4	....
4	2	3	3	1	1	10
5	1	....	0	2	20	....
total	8	11	7	....	26	....

(i) Fill in the blanks. (4)

(ii) What were the total absences for the whole school for the week?

Answer: .... (1)

(iii) Which class had perfect attendance on two days of the week?

Answer: .... (1)

One class visited a museum that week.

(iv) Which class was this?

Answer: .... (1)

(v) On which day was the visit to the museum?

Answer: .... (1)

(vi) Which class had fewest absences?

Answer: .... (1)

(vii) Complete the bar chart to show the total number of absences per day.

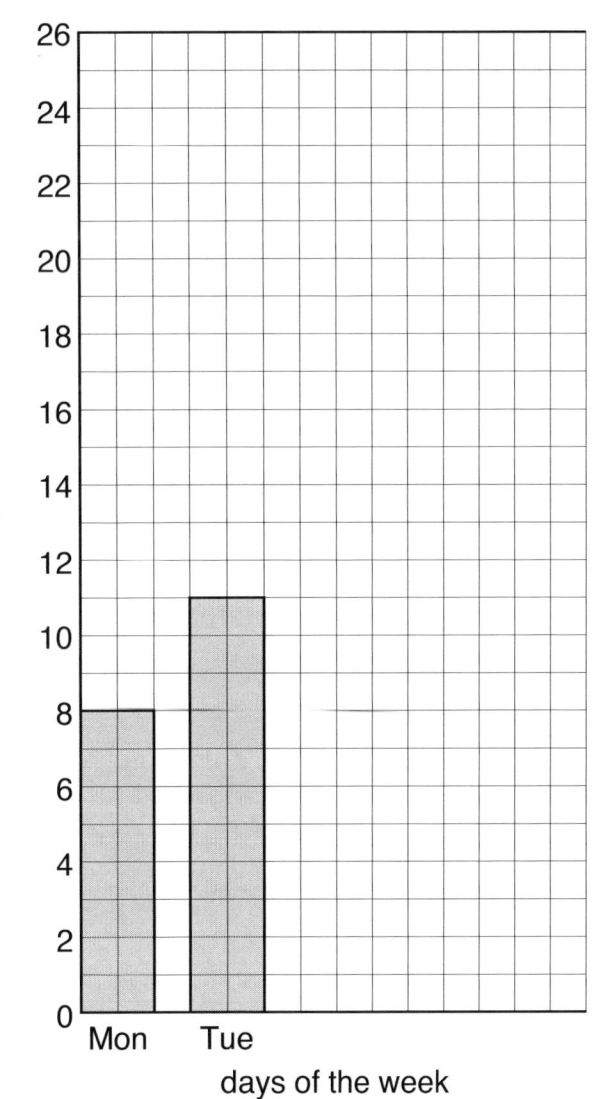

number of absences

Mon Tue

days of the week

(4)

November 91 Q14

34. The bar chart shows the number of mountain bikes a firm sold over a one-year period.

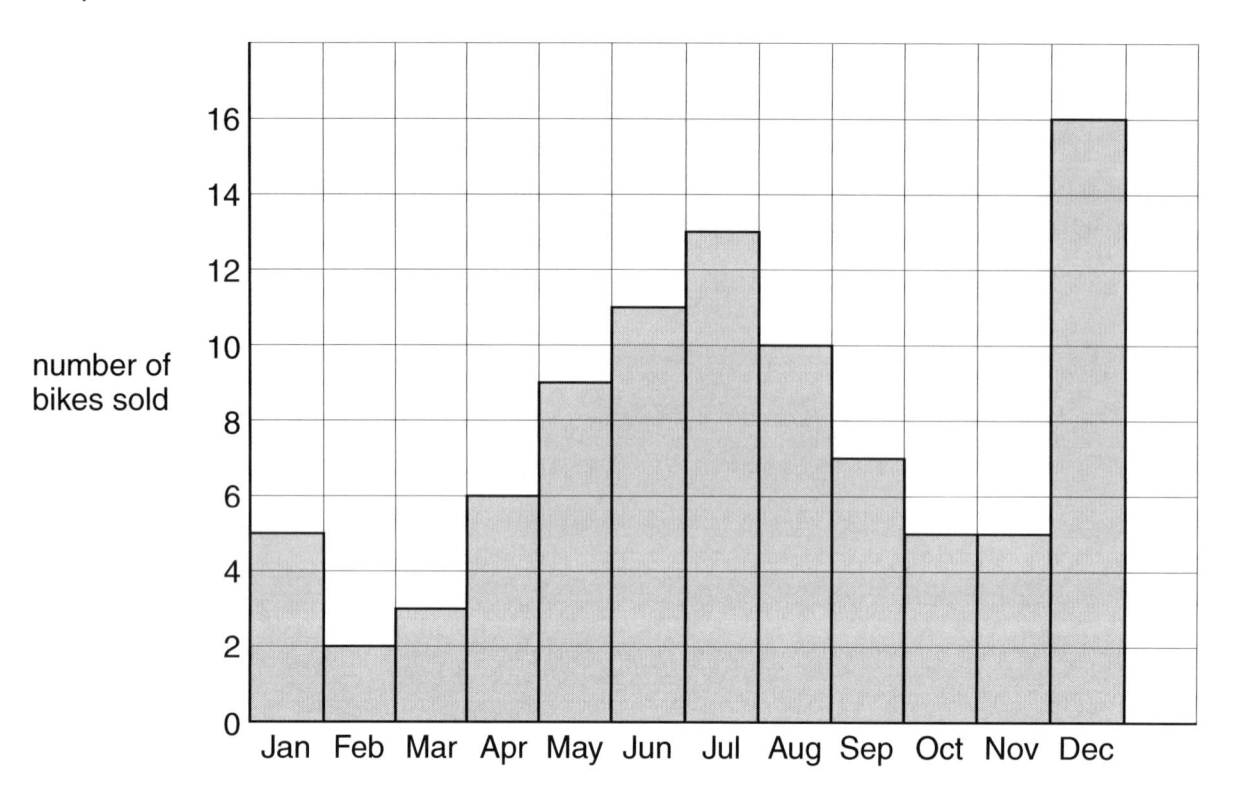

(i) In which month was the smallest number of bikes sold?

Answer: .... (1)

(ii) In which two consecutive months was the same number of bikes sold?

Answer: .... and .... (2)

(iii) How many bikes were sold altogether during these two months?

Answer: .... (2)

(iv) Suggest a good reason why sales leading up to July increased in the way shown.

Answer: ....

.... (2)

(v) (a) In which month was the greatest number of bikes sold?

Answer: .... (1)

(b) Why do you think this was so?

Answer: .... (1)

February 94 Q12

35. Mary's poodle has six puppies.

    The bar chart shows the masses of five of them.

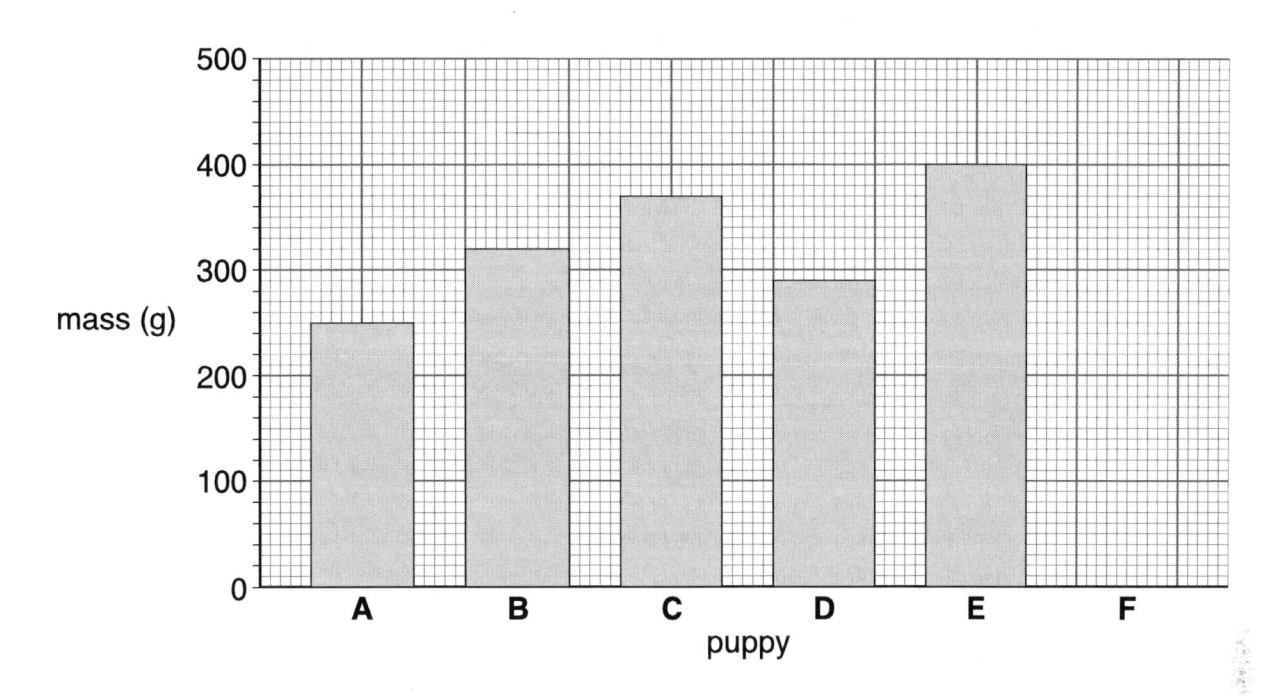

    Mary would like to keep puppy **B**.

    (i) What is its mass?

    Answer: .... g (2)

    (ii) Write the mass of puppy **A**

    (a) in g

    Answer: .... g (1)

    (b) in kg.

    Answer: .... kg (2)

    The total mass of the six puppies is 2 kg.

    (iii) Calculate the mass of puppy **F**.

    Answer: .... g (3)

    (iv) Complete the bar chart by drawing in the bar for puppy **F**. (2)

36. Five friends have been looking for conkers.

name	Alan	Bea	Cassie	Dick	Eva
number of conkers	4	9	3	6	3

(i) Arrange these numbers in order of increasing size.

Answer: .... (2)

(ii) (a) What is the difference between the largest and smallest numbers of conkers found?

Answer: .... (1)

(b) What word is used for this difference?

Answer: ...R... .... (1)

(iii) (a) What is the middle number when the numbers of conkers are arranged in order?

Answer: .... (1)

(b) What word is used for this middle number?

Answer: ...M.. ....A.. .... (1)

(iv) (a) What is the most common number of conkers found?

Answer: .... (1)

(b) What word is used for this most common number?

Answer: ....D.. .... (1)

(v) (a) What is the total number of conkers found by all five friends?

Answer: .... (2)

The five friends decide to share out the conkers equally.

(b) How many conkers will each friend then have?

Answer: .... (1)

(c) What word is used to describe this number?

Answer: ....N.. (1)

37. Here are the numbers of books read in a week by six children:

Ray	Sonya	Tim	Uri	Vivienne	Will
2	3	4	6	6	9

For these numbers, what is

(i) the range   Answer: .... (1)

(ii) the median   Answer: .... (2)

(iii) the mode   Answer: .... (1)

(iv) the mean?

Answer: .... (3)

38. Jonty counted the number of spectators at the under-ten netball matches.
He made this list:

1 October	34
8 October	21
15 October	18
5 November	9
12 November	25
19 November	13
26 November	26

(i) Arrange the numbers of spectators in order of increasing size.

.... (2)

(ii) What was the range of numbers of spectators?

Answer: .... (1)

(iii) What was the median number of spectators?

Answer: .... (2)

November 97 Q13

39. The bar chart shows the number of hours of sunshine, correct to the nearest half hour, on each of the days of a given week.

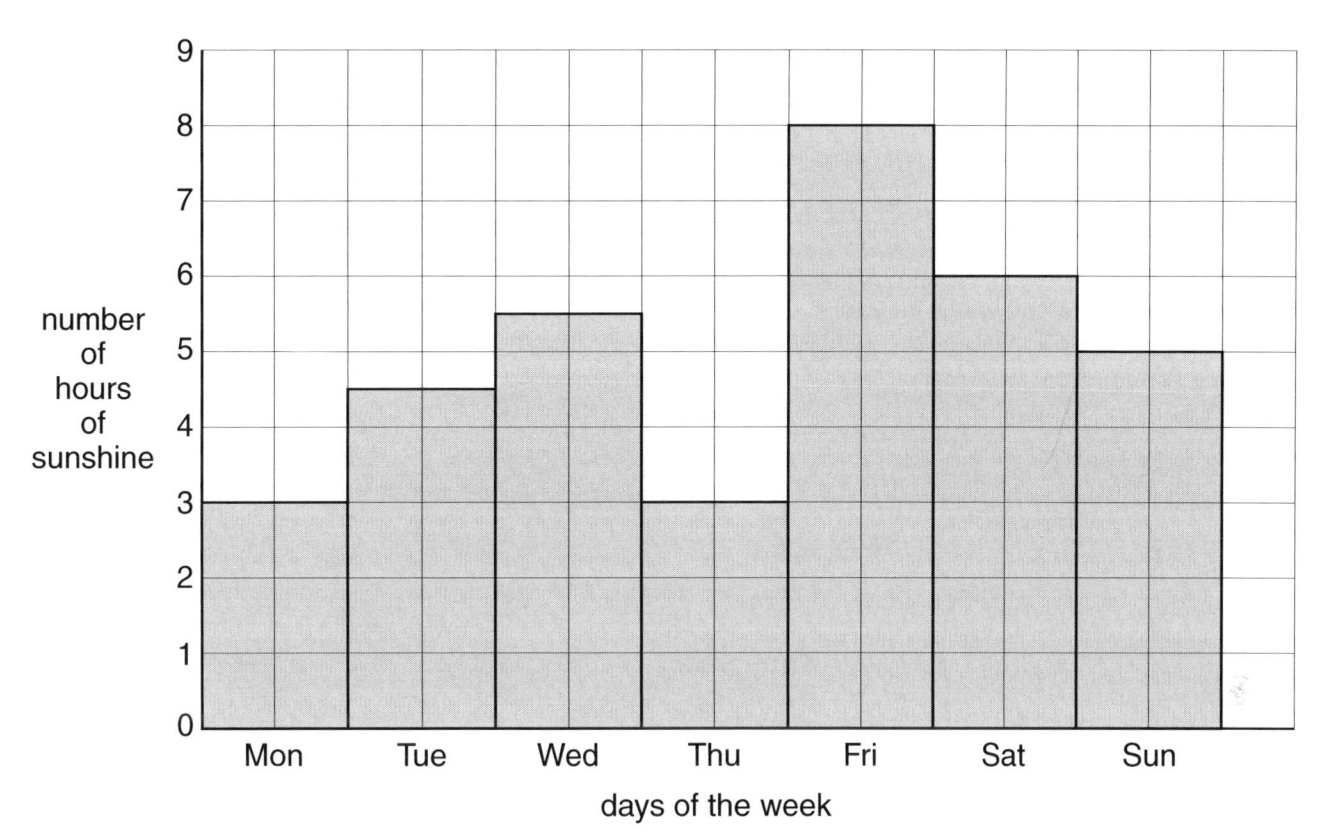

(i) How many hours of sunshine were there on Monday?

Answer: .... hours (1)

(ii) For how much longer was it sunny on Friday than on Wednesday?

Answer: .... hours (2)

(iii) What was the total number of hours of sunshine in the week?

Answer: .... hours (3)

(iv) What was the mean (average) number of hours of sunshine per day in the week?

Answer: .... hours (2)

November 94 Q15

40. The heights of five children are 160 cm, 169 cm, 156 cm, 159 cm and 166 cm. What is the mean (average) height of the children?

Answer: .... cm   (4)

November 95 Q15

41. The numbers of ice creams sold one weekend were

   Saturday: 45 ; Sunday: 63

What was the mean number of ice creams sold on the two days?

Answer: ....   (2)

42. The raw data recorded here was collected in a survey of test scores.

| 5 | 3 | 8 | 6 | 3 | 10 | 9 | 7 | 7 | 5 |
| 10 | 4 | 8 | 7 | 6 | 7 | 8 | 4 | 2 | 9 |

(i) Record this basic information as a tally.

score	0	1	2	3	4	5	6	7	8	9	10
tally											

(2)

(ii) Record the same basic information in a frequency table.

score	0	1	2	3	4	5	6	7	8	9	10
frequency											

(2)

43. This frequency table records the results of a survey into the ages of children in a club.

age of pupil	6	7	8	9	10	11	12	13
frequency	2	4	5	8	4	3	6	3

(i) How many children are in the club?   Answer: .... (1)

(ii) What is the range of ages of the children in the club?

Answer: .... (1)

This can also be written in the form   .... to .... (1)

(iii) How many children could swim in a competition for children aged ten and under?

Answer: .... (1)

(iv) What is the median age?   Answer: .... (2)

44. The ages, in years, of the 25 children in a gymnastics club are:

7	10	8	12	7	10	10	8	13
7	8	12	13	11	8	7	10	7
12	8	9	11	11	8	10		

(i) Complete the tally chart.

ages in years	tally	frequency
7		
8		
9		
10		
11		
12		
13		

(4)

(ii) What is the range of ages?

Answer: .... years (2)

(iii) What is the median age?

Answer: .... years (3)

(iv) What is the modal age?

Answer: .... years (1)

45. George asked some children how much pocket money they were given each week.

He drew this frequency diagram to show the results.

There were 50 children altogether.

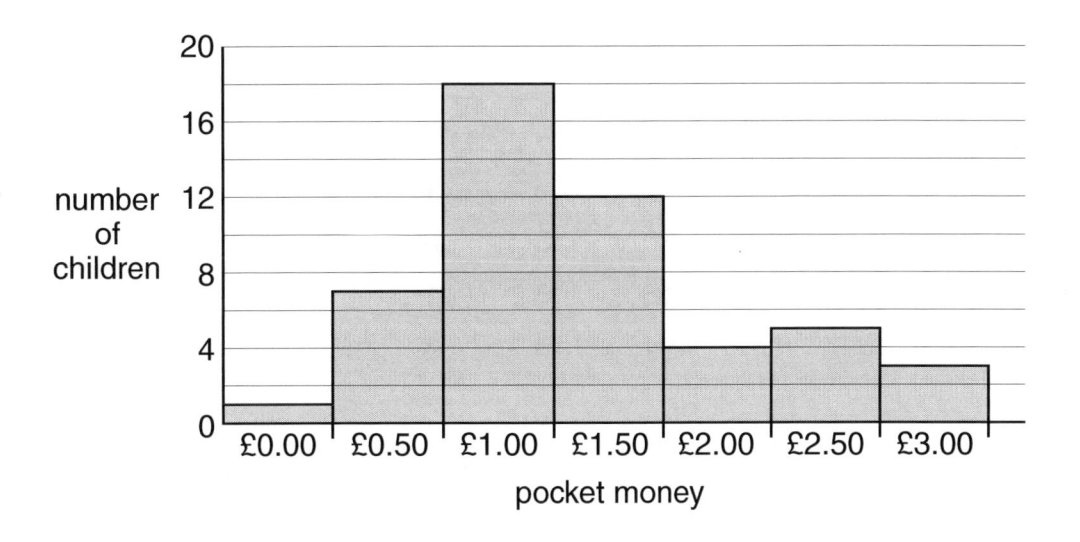

(i) From the diagram complete this table:

pocket money	£0.00	£0.50	£1.00	£1.50	£2.00	£2.50	£3.00
number of children	………	………	18	………	………	………	………

(4)

(ii) What is the modal amount of pocket money?

Answer: £ ………………………………… (2)

(iii) Complete the statement:

Three times as many children received ……………… as received £2.00

(2)

46. Tim and Ben play a game with a pair of dice.
    When the dice are thrown, the two numbers shown are multiplied together.
    The first to reach a total score of 300 wins.
    Tim wins the game.
    This is a record of Tim's scores:

    | 8 | 10 | 4 | 1 | 18 |
    | 24 | 2 | 36 | 1 | 5 |
    | 20 | 20 | 8 | 6 | 36 |
    | 25 | 16 | 6 | 1 | 9 |
    | 15 | 4 | 10 | 3 | 16 |

    (i) Explain why Tim could not possibly score 14

    Answer: ....

    .... (2)

    (ii) Complete the tally chart.

scores	tally	frequency
1–6		
7–12		
13–18		
19–24		
25–30		
31–36		
	total	

    (4)

    (iii) What is Tim's median score?   Answer: .... (2)

(iv) Use the information from the tally chart to complete the frequency diagram.

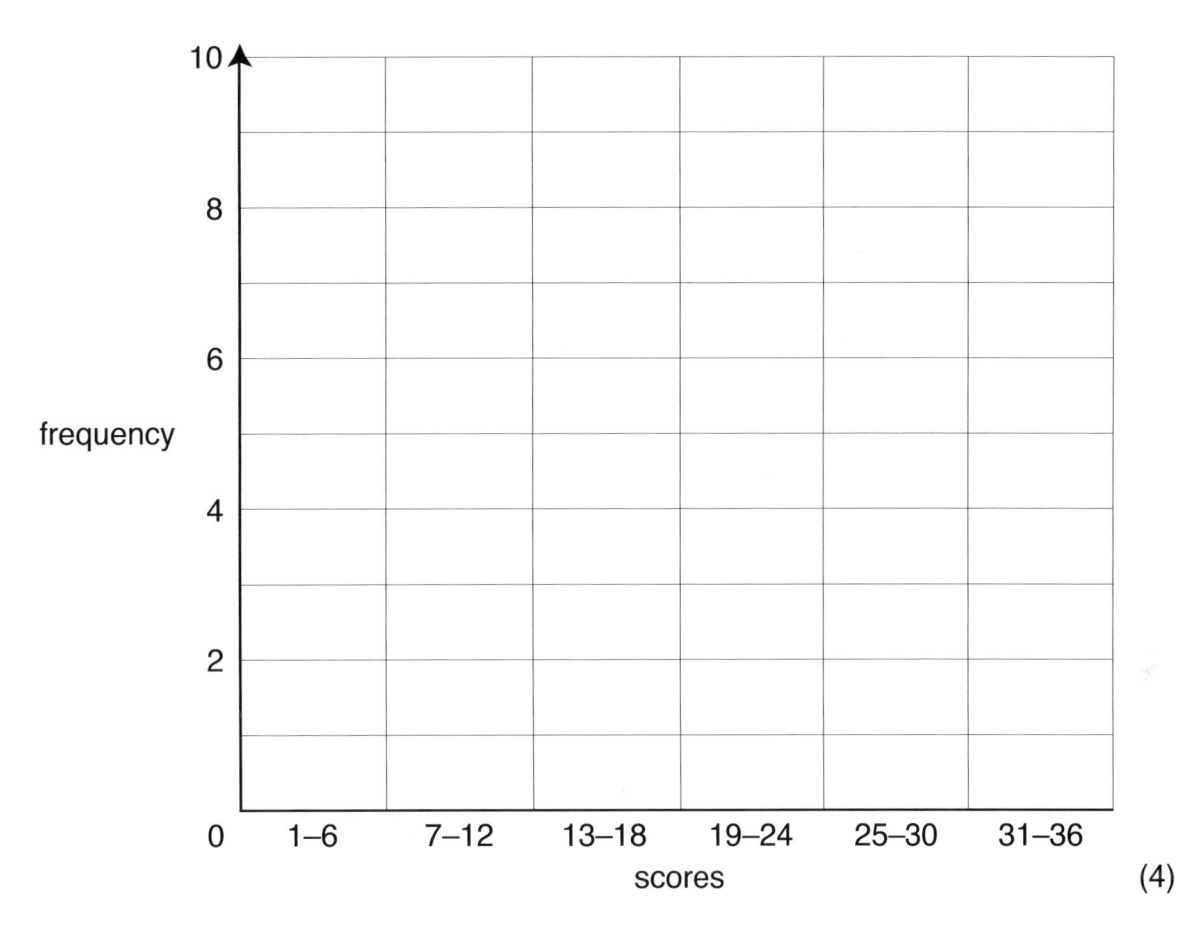

frequency (y-axis from 0 to 10)
scores (x-axis): 1–6, 7–12, 13–18, 19–24, 25–30, 31–36

(4)

(v) (a) Which is the modal class interval?

Answer: .... (1)

(b) Explain why you would expect this to be the modal class.

Answer: ....

....

.... (2)

January 99 Q14

205

47. The children in Miss Khan's class make this list of their heights in metres:

1.42	1.53	1.29	1.44	1.50
1.47	1.36	1.51	1.38	1.46
1.31	1.50	1.39	1.47	1.56
1.46	1.34	1.43	1.45	

(i) Using the list, complete this table of frequencies:

height (m)	tally marks	frequency
1.25 to 1.29		
1.30 to 1.34		
1.35 to 1.39		
1.40 to 1.44		
1.45 to 1.49		
1.50 to 1.54		
1.55 to 1.59		
	total	

(4)

(ii) Use this table to complete the frequency diagram:

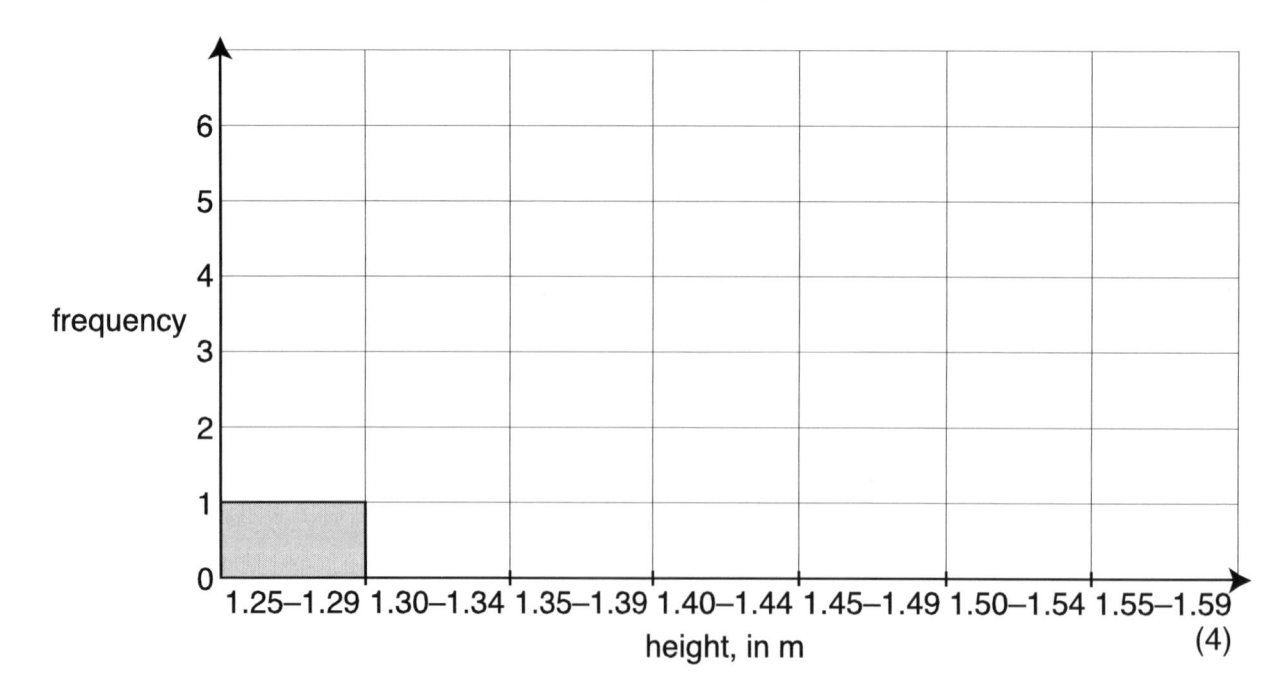

(4)

(iii) Which group of heights is the mode?

Answer: .... m to .... m (2)

48. Some teachers were asked how many tickets they usually bought for a raffle.
The results are shown in the table below.

number of tickets	number of teachers
0	2
1	7
2	5
3	2
4	0
5	3
6	1

(i) Which number of tickets is the mode?

Answer: .... (1)

(ii) Which number of tickets is the median?
Show clearly how you do this.

Answer: .... (2)

49. The children in the class tell Sarah how much pocket money they are given each week.

She shows the results in this table:

amount of pocket money	number of children
£0	1
£1	7
£2	6
£3	1
£4	4
£5	2
£6	1
£7	3

(i) Use these figures to complete the frequency diagram below.

(The first bar has been drawn for you.)

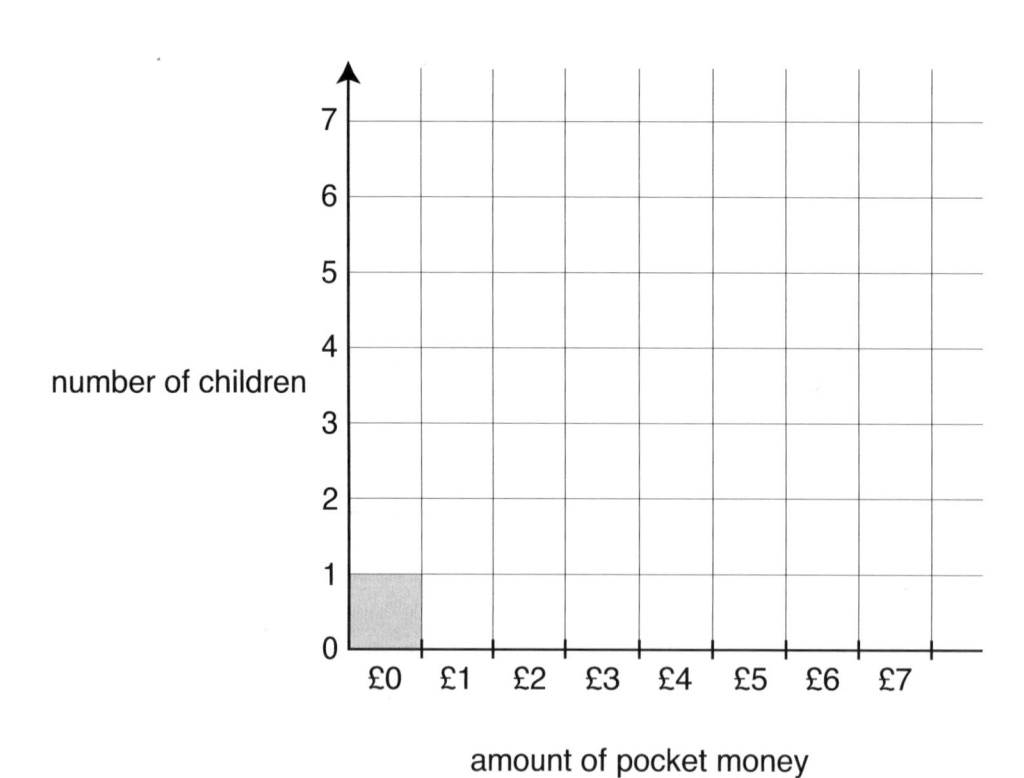

(5)

(ii) How many children are in Sarah's class?

Answer: .... (2)

(iii) What is the range of pocket money in the class?

Answer: £ .... (1)

(iv) What is the mode?

Answer: £ .... (1)

January 96 Q14

50. Here are Tom's spelling test marks arranged in order of increasing size:

2 3 3 4 5 5 5 6 6 7 7 7 7 8 8 9

(i) What is the range?

Answer: .... (1)

(ii) What is the mode?

Answer: .... (1)

(iii) What is the median?

Answer: .... (1)

51. This frequency diagram shows the results of a survey of the heights of pupils.

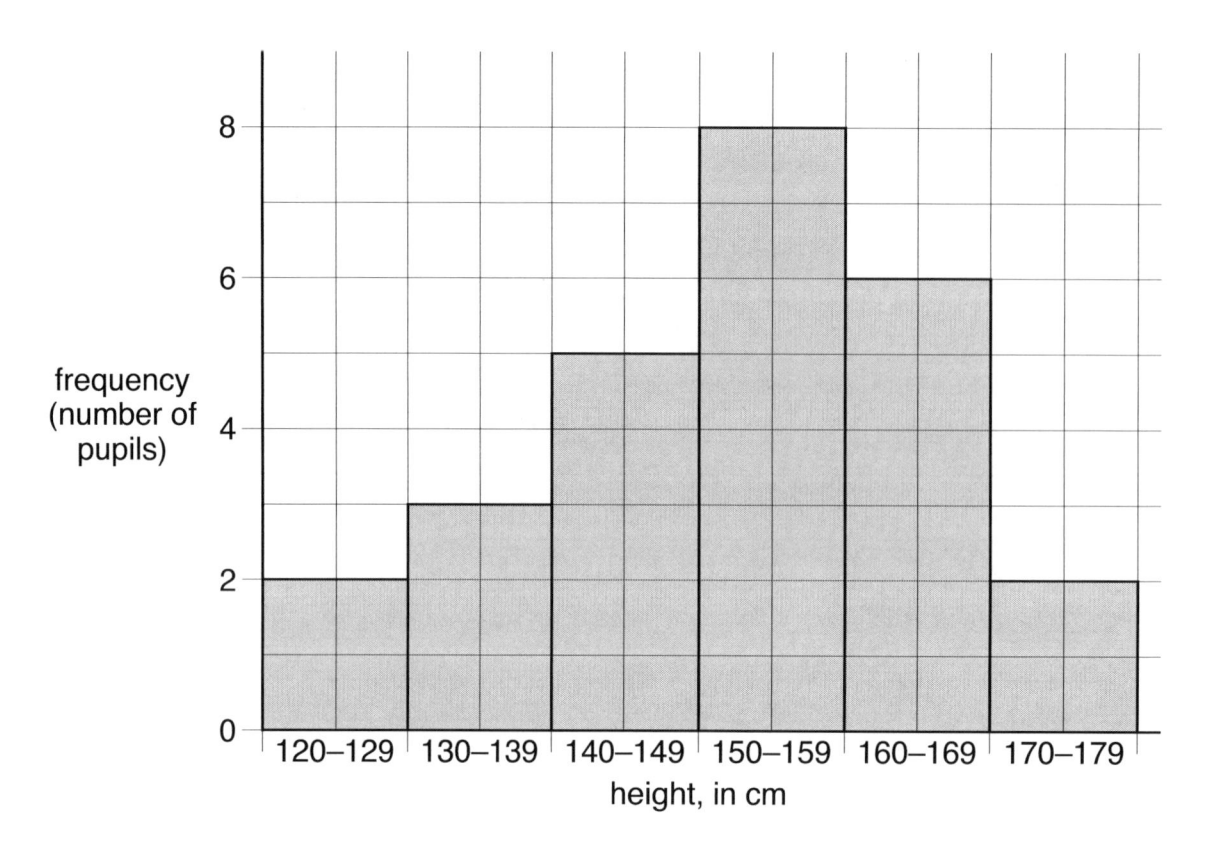

(i) How many pupils were included in the survey?

Answer: .... (2)

(ii) How many pupils had a height less than 1.5 m?

Answer: .... (2)

(iii) What can you say about the height of the shortest pupil?
Give as much information as possible.

Answer: ....

.... (2)

52. Here is a frequency table from a survey of the ages of pupils at a school:

age of pupil	6	7	8	9	10	11	12	13
frequency	4	6	6	13	18	26	27	8

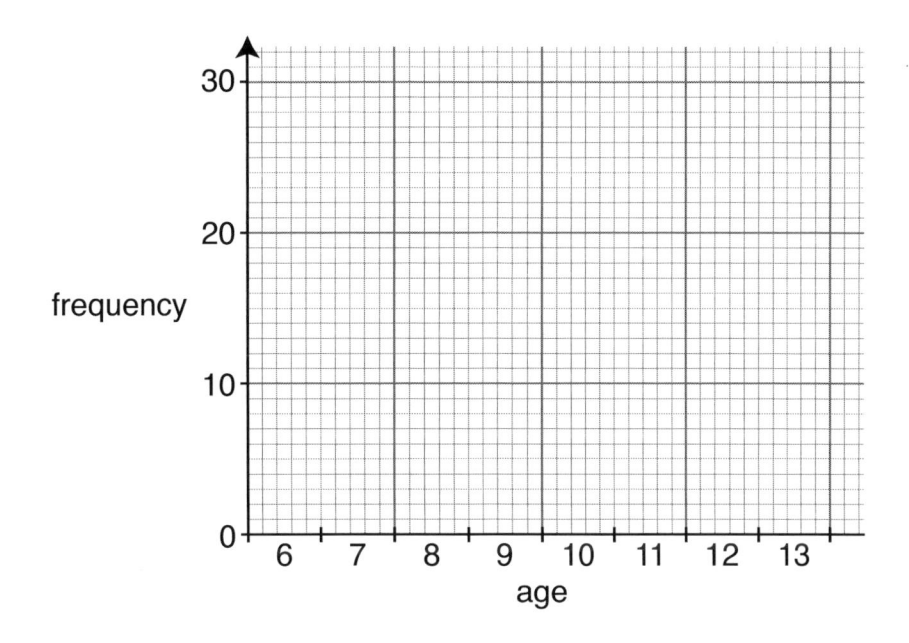

(i) On the grid above, represent the information as a frequency diagram. (4)

(ii) What age is the mode?

Answer: .... (1)

(iii) How many pupils are aged

(a) 10 and under   Answer: .... (1)

(b) 11 and over?   Answer: .... (1)

(iv) What is the median age?

Answer: .... (2)

53. The frequency diagram below shows the range of masses, correct to the nearest kilogramme, of some school children.

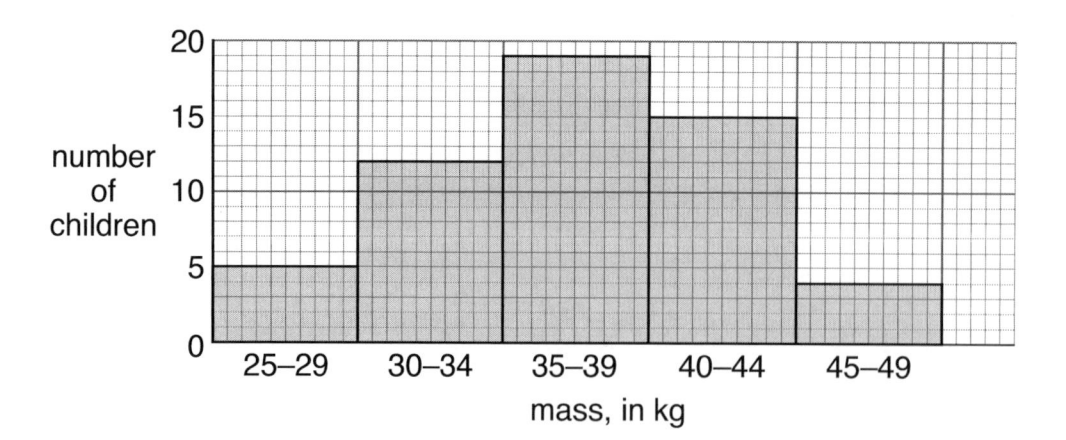

(i) How many children have masses between 30 and 34 kg?

Answer: .... (1)

(ii) What is the total number of children whose masses are shown in the diagram?

Answer: .... (2)

The children whose masses are 25–29 kg are: Fiona (25 kg), David (28 kg), Ian (29 kg), Ann (25 kg), Beth (28 kg).

(iii) What is the mean mass of these children?

Answer: .... kg (2)

January 95 Q15

54. In this frequency diagram, the data has been grouped into class intervals:

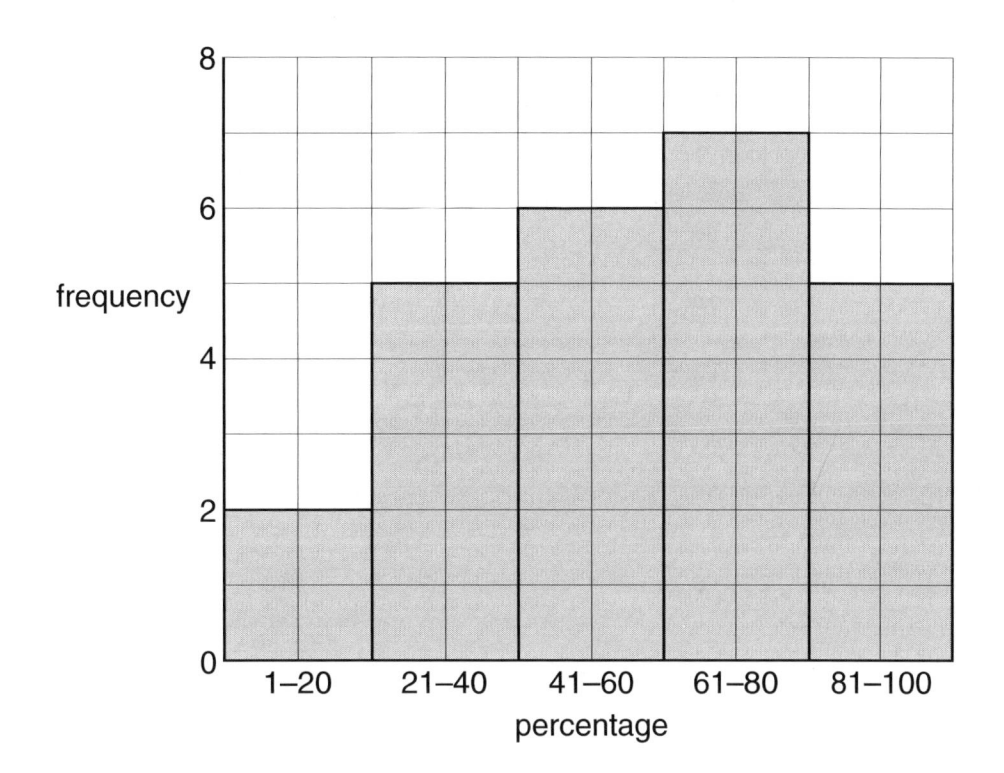

(i) What can you say about the highest mark?

Answer: ....

.... (2)

(ii) How many pupils were included in the survey?

Answer: .... (2)

(iii) What percentage of the pupils achieved 41% or more?

Answer: .... % (2)

55. Here are the scores of 25 children in a game:

6	16	5	21	14
7	21	13	11	7
36	29	4	22	15
20	43	10	38	11
14	24	48	16	3

(i) Complete the following statements.

(a) The highest score is .... (1)

(b) The lowest score is .... (1)

(c) The range of the scores is .... (1)

(ii) What is the median score?

Answer: .... (4)

(iii) Complete the table below.

score	tally marks	frequency
0–9		
10–19		
20–29		
30–39		
40–49		
	total	

(5)

(iv) Draw a frequency diagram on the grid below to show these results.

frequency

0–9   10–19   20–29   30–39   40–49
score

(4)

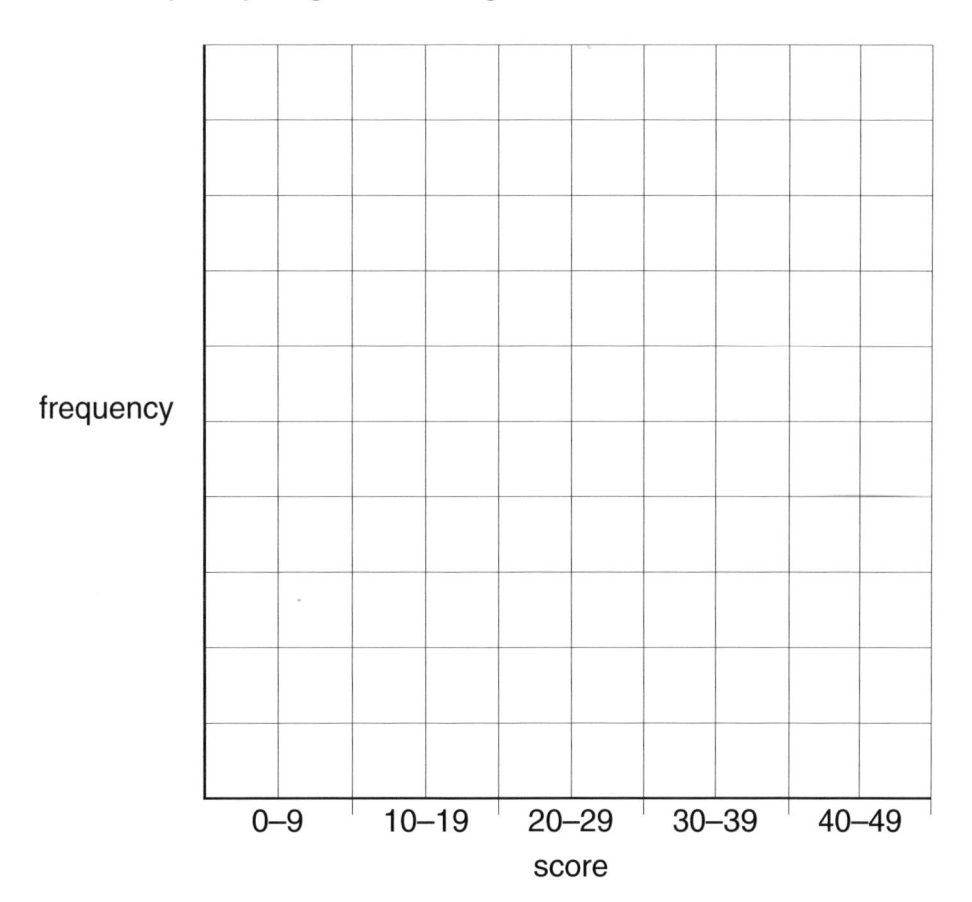

(v) How many scores are less than 20?

Answer: .... (2)

January 97 Q14

56. 30 pupils took a mathematics test.

    Their marks are given below.

    | 23 | 32 | 40 | 51 | 60 | 70 | 32 | 18 | 26 | 42 |
    | 27 | 34 | 39 | 48 | 47 | 62 | 35 | 18 | 19 | 17 |
    | 43 | 46 | 47 | 36 | 32 | 53 | 29 | 33 | 28 | 26 |

    (i) Complete the tally and frequency table.

mark	tally	frequency
10–19		
20–29		
30–39		
40–49		
50–59		
60–69		
70–79		
	total	

    (4)

    (ii) What is the range of these marks?

    Answer: .... (2)

(iii) Complete the frequency diagram for the table in part (i).

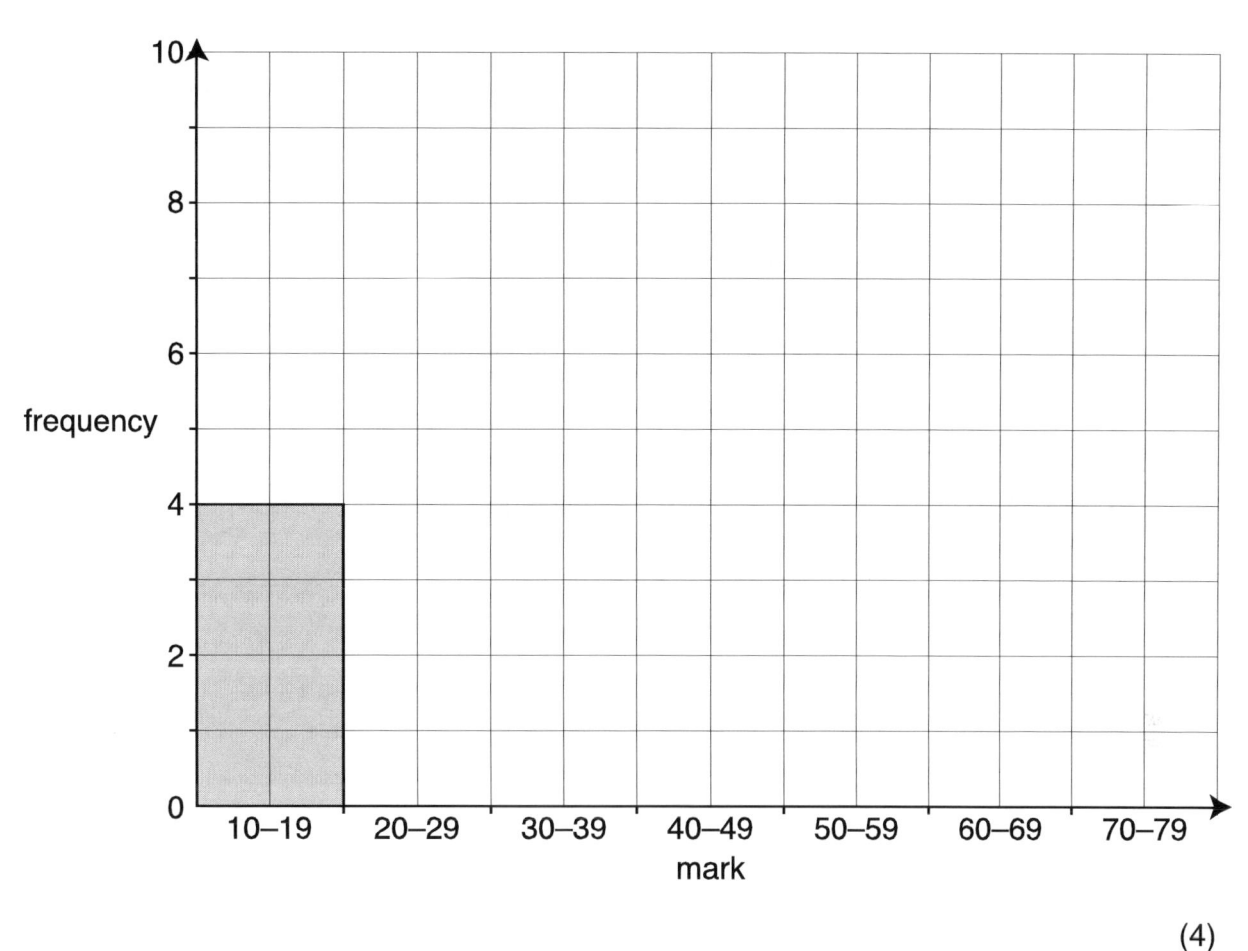

(4)

57. Peter has five stones with these masses (in grams):

150 g   200 g   220 g   300 g   330 g

(i) What is the range of these masses?

Answer: .... g   (2)

(ii) What is the mean mass?

Answer: .... g   (4)

217

58. The midday outside temperatures, one week in January, were recorded.

day	Sun	Mon	Tue	Wed	Thu	Fri	Sat
temperature (°C)	2	3	0	1	⁻1	2	1

What is the range of these temperatures?

Answer: .... degrees (2)

59. During one season, St Mary's 'A' netball team scored the following numbers of goals:

7	8	3	12	10
4	5	6	10	13
6	9	11	9	14
3	10	7	5	7
8	9	6	3	5

(i) Complete the tally chart for these results.

number of goals scored	tally	frequency
1–3		
4–6		
7–9		
10–12		
13–15		
	total	

(4)

218

(ii) On the grid below, draw a frequency diagram to show this information.

frequency

1–3

number of goals scored

(4)

(iii) From your frequency diagram, state which group is the mode.

Answer: .... (1)

(iv) What is the median score?

Answer: .... (2)

(v) In how many games were more than nine goals scored?

Answer: .... (1)

January 98 Q14

60. The line graph below shows the midday temperatures recorded during one week in summer.

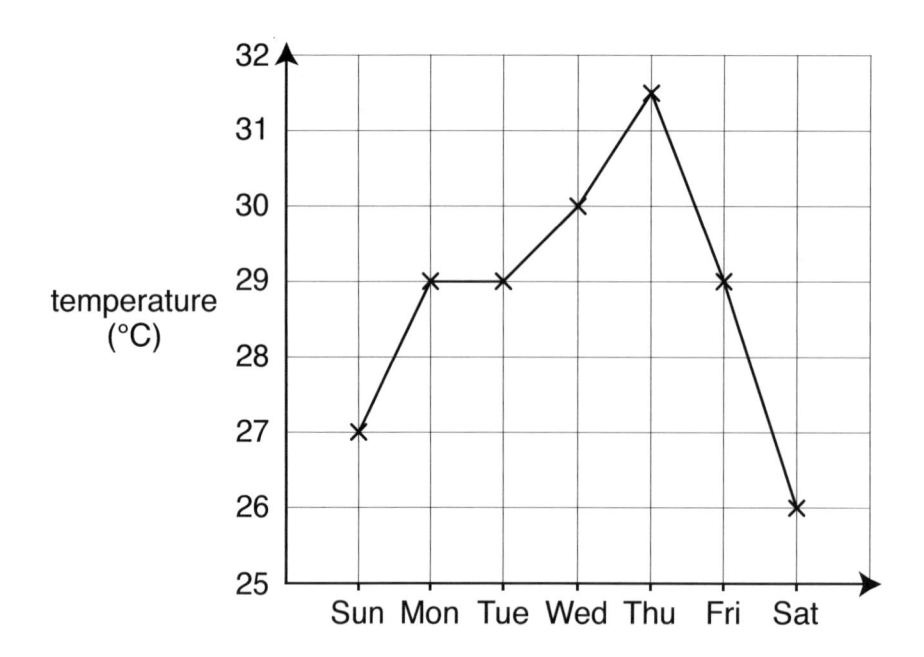

(i) What was the highest midday temperature recorded that week?

Answer: ....°C (1)

(ii) What was the range of midday temperatures recorded that week?

Answer: .... degrees (1)

(iii) Which midday temperature was the mode?

Answer: ....°C (1)

(iv) From the line graph, can you say what the temperature was at midnight on Tuesday?

Answer: .... (yes / no) because ....

.... (2)

61. This line graph shows William's cycle ride to visit his aunt who lives 30 km away from William's home.

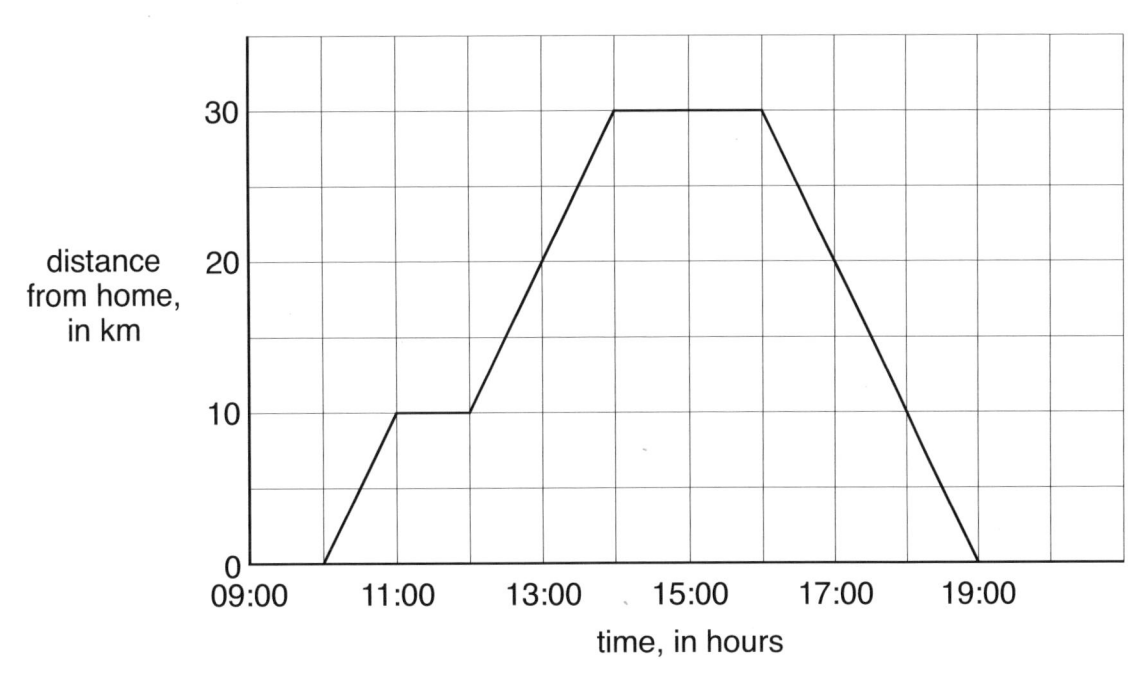

(i) At what time did William leave home?

Answer: .... (1)

William stopped for a rest at 11:00

(ii) For how long did he rest?

Answer: .... (1)

(iii) At what time did William leave his aunt's house for his return journey?

Answer: .... (1)

(iv) How far had William cycled altogether?

Answer: .... km (1)

(v) For how long had William been away from home?

Answer: .... hours (1)

62. The line graph below shows the amount of fuel in the fuel tank of Dr Foster's car.

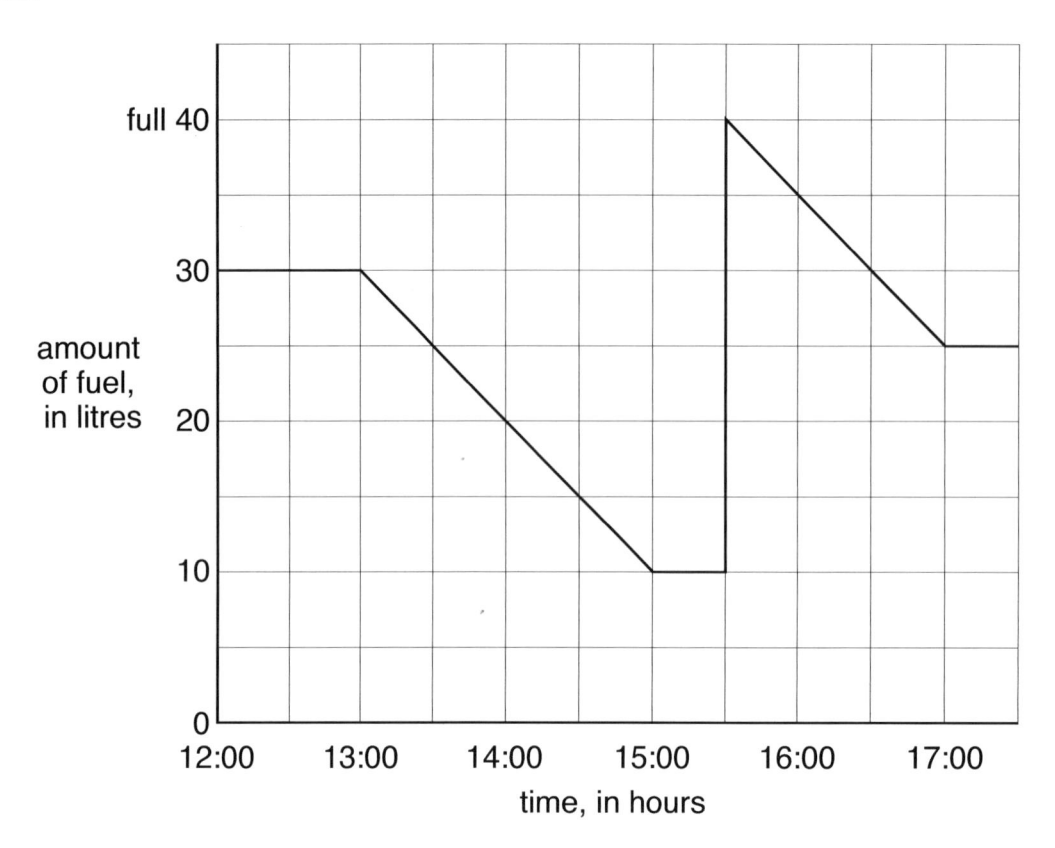

(i) At what time did Dr Foster begin his journey?

Answer: .... (1)

(ii) How many litres of fuel had he used when he stopped at a service station?

Answer: .... litres (1)

(iii) At what time did he fill his fuel tank?

Answer: .... (1)

(iv) How many litres of fuel did Dr Foster use on his journey?

Answer: .... litres (2)

63. The line graph below shows the midday temperatures at Aley during Simon's holiday.

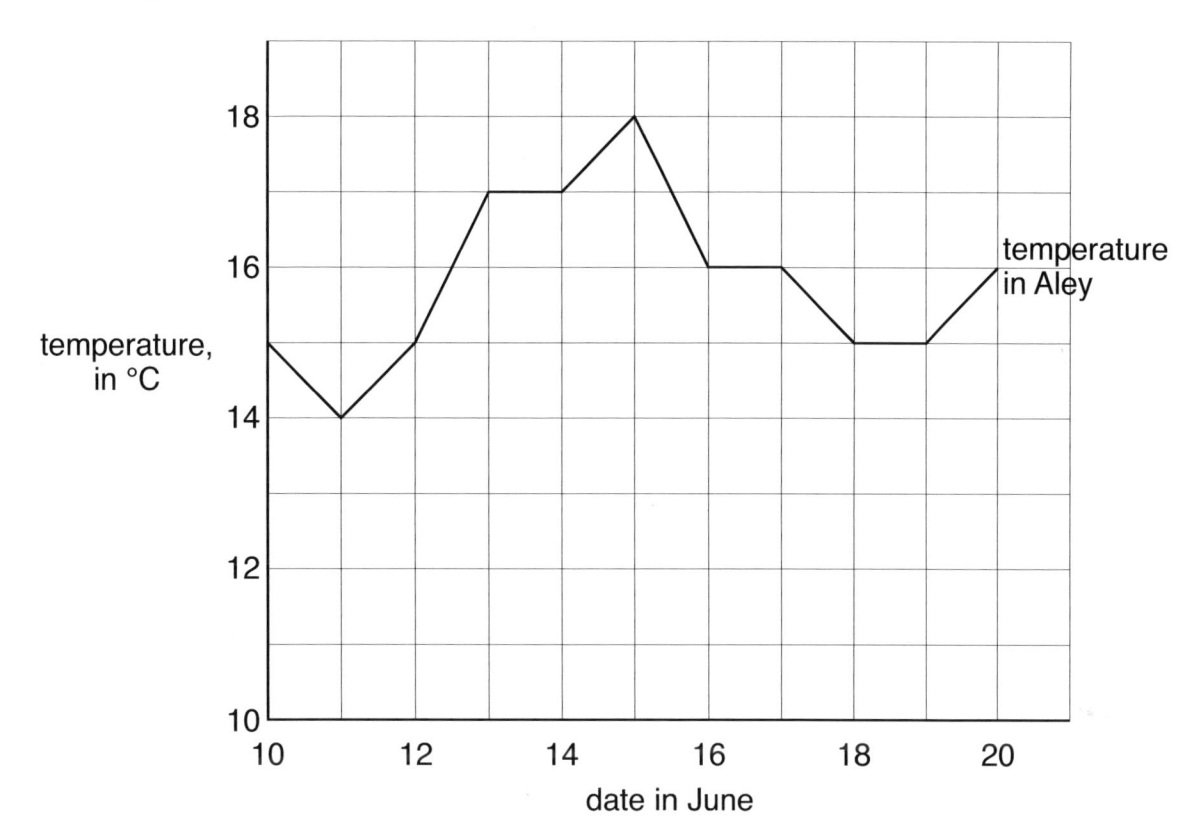

The midday temperatures on the same dates at Beeton are shown in this table:

date in June	10	11	12	13	14	15	16	17	18	19	20
temperature (°C)	13	12	12	13	12	14	15	16	17	17	15

(i) Draw a line graph to show the midday temperatures in Beeton. (3)

(ii) Which town had the greater range of midday temperatures between 10 and 20 June inclusive?

Answer: town .... (1)

range .... degrees (1)

64. The line graphs below show the temperature just inside (•) and just outside (x) a window one day in January.

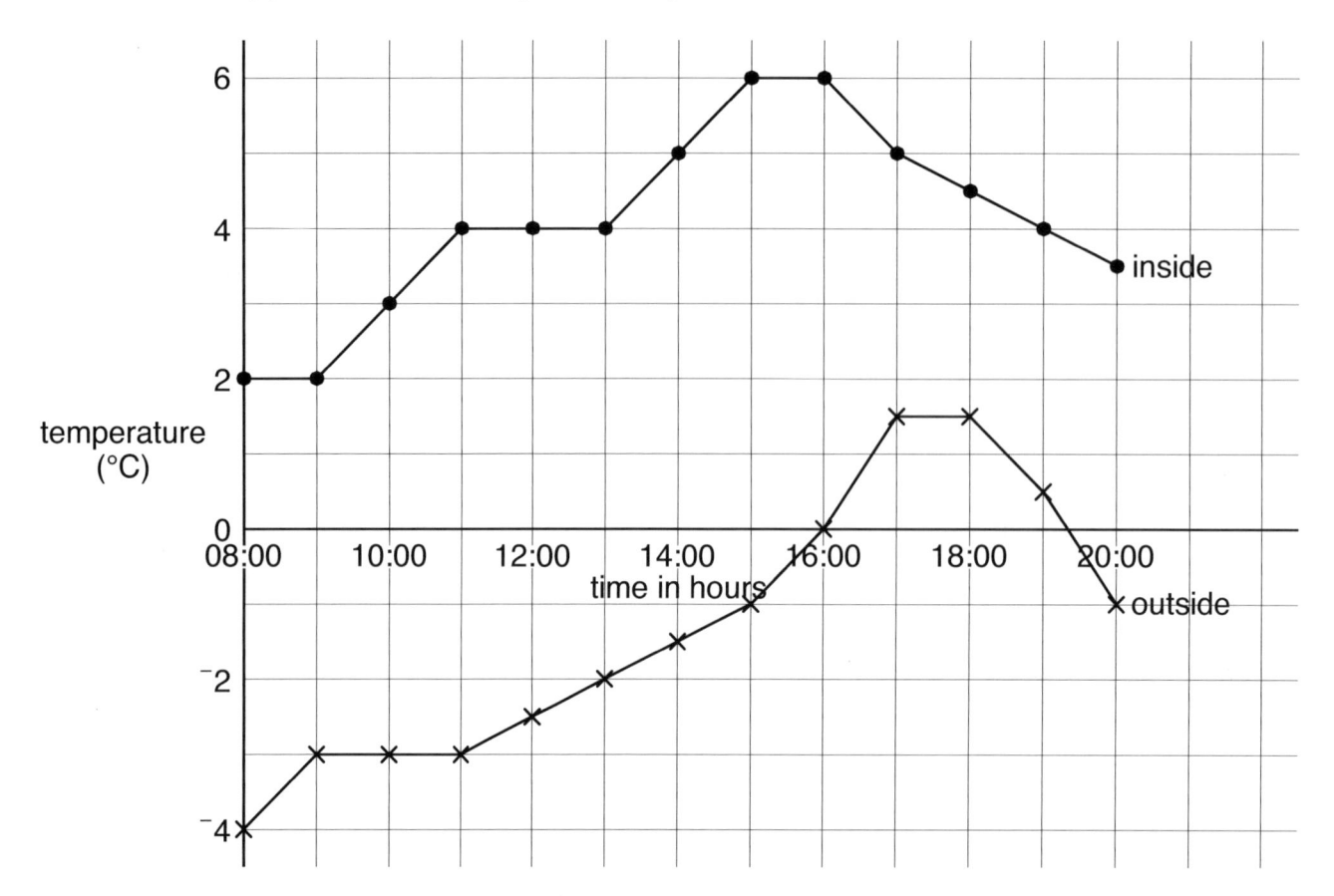

(i) (a) At which times was the temperature difference greatest?

Answer: .... and .... (1)

(b) What was this difference?

Answer: .... degrees (1)

(ii) What was the outside temperature recorded at 14:00?

Answer: ....°C (2)

(iii) What was the maximum recorded outside temperature?

Answer: ....°C (1)

B Probability: understanding basic ideas of probability

1. (i) Yasmin and Zac have made a spinner.

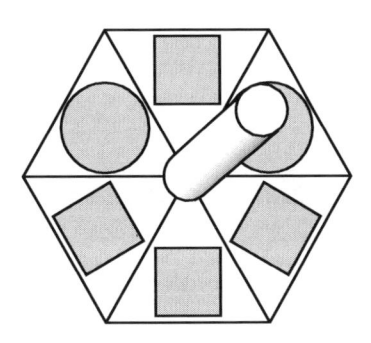

   Yasmin says

   'If it lands on a square, then you give me a sweet.
   If it lands on a circle, then I give you a sweet.'

   Is that fair?

   Answer: .... (yes / no) because ....

   .... (2)

   (ii) Mary has a Russian coin.
   She asks Tom to toss it in the air.

   She says

   'If it lands 'head' up, then I win.
   If it lands 'tail' up, then you win.'

   Is that fair?

   Answer: .... (yes / no) because ....

   .... (2)

2. When an ordinary coin is tossed, there are two possible outcomes.

heads   tails

(i) List all the possible outcomes when this spinner is used.

Answer: ....

....

....

....

....

.... (2)

(ii) (a) List all the possible outcomes when an ordinary die is rolled.

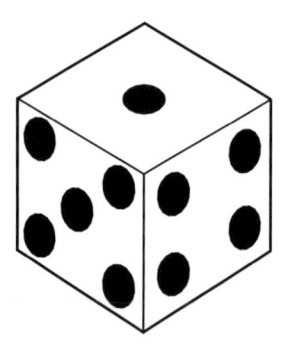

Answer: .... (2)

(b) What fraction of these outcomes are even numbers?

Answer: .... (1)

226

3. Two ordinary dice are thrown (one red and one blue).

   The scores are added.

   List all the possible ways of getting a total of six.

   (The first has been done for you.)

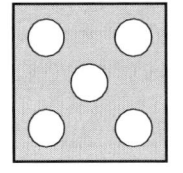

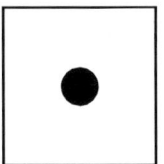

Answer: red	blue
5	1

   (4)

   November 94 Q13

4. Jane has two ordinary dice; one yellow and one green.

   (i) Describe all the ways it is possible for her to score (a) 4 and (b) 7

4	
yellow	green
3	1

7	
yellow	green

   (3)

   To start a game, Jane has to throw 2 sixes.

   Her brother says it would be easier to throw 2 twos.

   (ii) Do you think it is easier to throw 2 sixes or 2 twos or are the chances equal?

   Answer: .... (1)

   January 95 Q10

227

5. Mr Smith buys only black, navy and grey socks.

   One evening during a power cut, he takes two socks from the drawer.

   List the possible colour combinations of the two socks.

   Answer: ....

   ....

   .... (6)

   November 91 Q16

6. When we consider the likelihood of an event, an outcome could be **certain**, or it could be **uncertain**, or it could be **impossible**.

   Write **certain**, **uncertain** or **impossible** for these events.

   (i) The sun will shine tomorrow.

   Answer: .... (1)

   (ii) If you toss an ordinary coin, it will fall either heads or tails.

   Answer: .... (1)

   (iii) If you let go of a cricket ball held above your head, it will fall.

   Answer: .... (1)

   (iv) If you spin this spinner, it will land on number 5

   Answer: .... (1)

7. Here are some sentences. Some of them are more likely to be true than others.

   A Ben cleans his teeth before going to bed.
   B Grass is blue.
   C John likes washing up.
   D Christmas Day is on 25 December.
   E Susie tosses a coin and gets 'heads'.

   Beside each of these likelihoods write the letter for the sentence which you think fits it best.

   Answer: certain: ....

   very likely: ....

   even chance: ....

   not likely: ....

   cannot happen: .... (5)

November 96 Q10

8. Choose from the words:

   impossible, very unlikely, unlikely, even chance, likely, very likely, certain

   to describe the chance of these events happening.

   (i) throwing a three when an ordinary die is rolled

   Answer: .... (1)

   (ii) getting heads when a two-headed coin is tossed

   Answer: .... (1)

   (iii) choosing a red card (heart or diamond) from a pack

   Answer: .... (1)

   (iv) a snowfall on 21 July in Rome

   Answer: .... (1)

9. Tom tosses a fair coin five times.

   He gets

         heads   tails   heads   heads   heads

   He tosses the coin again.
   This time is he
   - **A** more likely to get heads
   - **B** more likely to get tails
   - **C** equally likely to get heads or tails?

   Write **A**, **B** or **C**.

   Answer: .... (2)

   November 97 Q9

10. Jane and Mark are throwing two fair dice in a game.
    In the first round, Jane throws 6 and Mark throws 2

    In the second round, Jane throws another 6 and Mark throws 5

    Mark says that he is now more likely than Jane to get a 6 with the next throw.

    (i) Is he correct?

    Answer: .... (1)

    (ii) Explain your answer.

    Answer: ....

    .... (2)

    November 93 Q6

11.

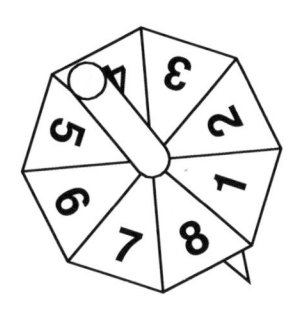

John is using this spinner in a game. Look at the following statements which John makes.

    A   I will get a number smaller than nine.

    B   I will get a three.

    C   I will get an even number.

    D   I will get a nine.

Place John's statements, using **A**, **B**, **C** and **D**, on this probability line.

impossible   certain

(4)

January 98 Q5

12. Mark with a cross the probabilities of the following events on the probability scales.

(i) When a fair die is rolled the score will be 3

impossible   certain

(1)

(ii) When a fair coin is tossed it will land showing tails.

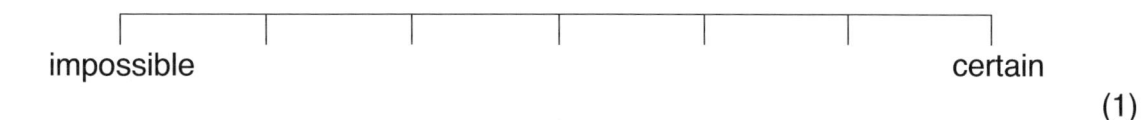

impossible   certain

(1)

(iii) There will be 30 days in June next year.

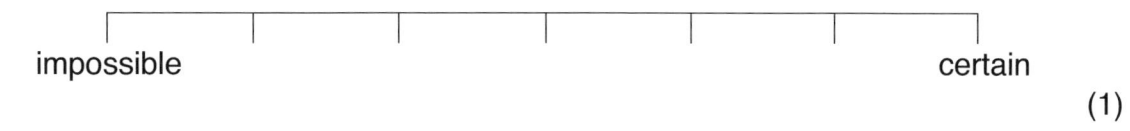

impossible   certain

(1)

November 98 Q12

13. Joe is throwing a fair die.

Using the probability scale, how likely is each of the following statements?

|———————|———————|———————|———————|
no chance   poor chance   even chance   good chance   certain

(i) He will throw a 6

Answer: .... (2)

(ii) He will throw an odd number.

Answer: .... (2)

(iii) He will not throw an even number.

Answer: .... (1)

(iv) He will not throw a 7

Answer: .... (2)

Specimen 94 Q9

14. Sandra rolled an ordinary die 30 times.

She scored 6 three times.

How many times might she have been expected to score 6?

Answer: .... times (2)

232

15. (i) This line represents the probability of an event happening.

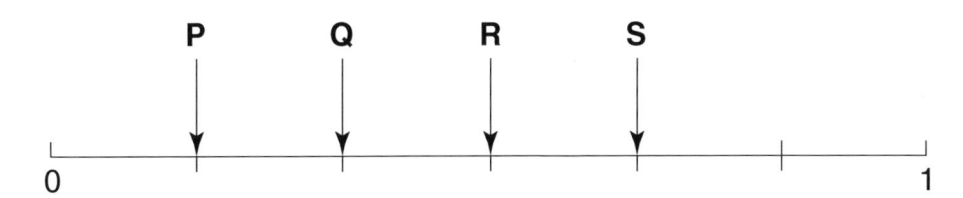

Which of the points, **P**, **Q**, **R** or **S** represents

(a) the probability of getting a head when a coin is tossed

Answer: .... (1)

(b) the probability of scoring a six when an ordinary die is thrown?

Answer: .... (1)

(ii) Philip has four 1p coins, five 2p coins and three 20p coins in his pocket.

(a) What fraction of the coins are 20p coins?

Answer: .... (2)

He takes out one coin at random.

(b) On the diagram, mark with a cross the point which represents the probability of Philip getting a bronze coin.

Label the point T. (2)

November 94 Q16

16. Joanne has rolled a die 60 times.

    She has recorded her scores as a tally.

score	tally	frequency
1	II	2
2	HHT HHT I	....
3	HHT IIII	....
4	HHT HHT II	....
5	HHT III	....
6	HHT HHT HHT III	....

    (i) Complete the table of frequencies above. (3)

    (ii) How many times might Joanne have expected to score each number 1 to 6?

    Answer: .... (2)

    (iii) Suggest a reason why the results are not what Joanne might have expected.

    Answer: ....

    .... (2)

    (iv) If Joanne were to roll this die 6000 times, about how many sixes might she expect to score?

    Answer: .... (2)

17. In a game, two dice, one red and one blue, are thrown and the numbers are multiplied together.

   (i) On the table complete all the possible outcomes.

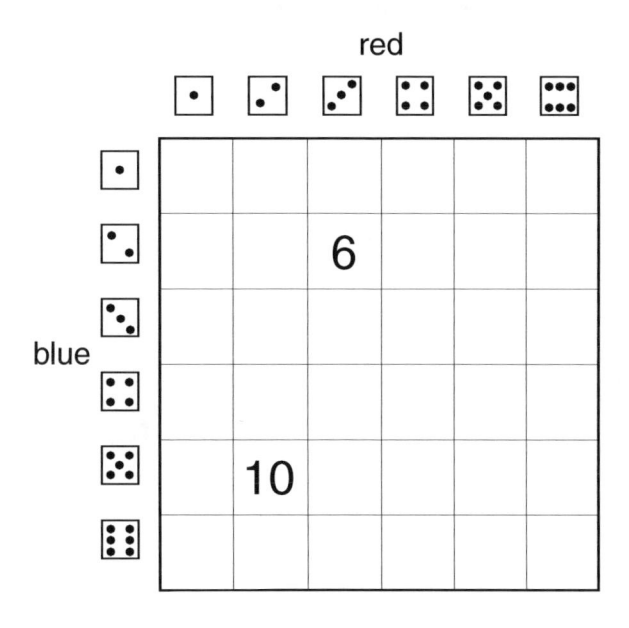

	1	2	3	4	5	6
1						
2		6				
3						
4						
5	10					
6						

   (red across top, blue down side)

   (4)

   Points are awarded depending on the outcome.

   1 point if the outcome is even.
   2 points if the outcome is divisible by 5
   3 points if the outcome is divisible by both 2 and 5

   blue × red = 12   1 point awarded.

   (ii) How many outcomes are awarded one point?

   Answer: .... (2)

   (iii) How many outcomes are awarded two points?

   Answer: .... (2)

   (iv) How many outcomes are awarded three points?

   Answer: .... (2)

   (v) What is the probability that a throw will result in the award of three points?

   Answer: .... (2)

February 94 Q18

Galore Park
ISEB REVISION GUIDES

- All titles endorsed by the Independent Schools Examinations Board
- Perfect for 11+, 13+ and scholarship entrance exam preparation
- Consolidates the key subject information into ONE resource making revision a breeze!
- Enables pupils to identify gaps in knowledge to focus their revision
- Worked examples show pupils how to gain the best possible marks
- Each guide includes practice material and answers to test understanding

For more information please visit our website:
www.galorepark.co.uk

Galore Park

So you really want to learn

- Many titles endorsed by the Independent Schools Examinations Board
- Perfect for 11+, 13+ and scholarship entrance exam preparation
- Contains explanations and exercises for a complete learning and revision resource
- Developed specifically for those in independent education
- Questions styled for Common Entrance exam preparation
- Suitable for the specialist or non specialist teacher or parent

For more information please visit our website:
www.galorepark.co.uk